THE
PERFECT
AMOUNT
OF WRONG

THE RISE OF ALT COMEDY ON CHICAGO'S NORTH SIDE

FOREWORD BY **PETE HOLMES**
MIKE BRIDENSTINE

THE
Hiſtory
PRESS

Published by The History Press
Charleston, SC
www.historypress.com

Copyright © 2023 by Mike Bridenstine
All rights reserved

Cover design contributed to by Jake Lloyd Bacon.

First published 2023

Manufactured in the United States

ISBN 9781540258342

Library of Congress Control Number: 2023934776

I often tell people there should be a statue of Mark Geary in the vicinity of the old Lincoln Lodge. Preferably depicted standing on a ladder with a scowl on his face. The last time I was in Chicago—at the new Lincoln Lodge, actually—I mentioned my statue idea to comedian Marty DeRosa. And he agreed, but he added that the actual Mark Geary should have to take the statue down every night, haul it into storage and then put back up again every morning.

This book is dedicated to Mark.

CONTENTS

CONTENTS

FOREWORD

Like you, I haven't read this book yet. But I did see it coming.

I vividly remember sitting in a shitty bar in 2001, which was normal for me at the time as I had just moved to Chicago from Boston and was trying my best to become a stand-up comedian. (It's a funny thing, trying to become a stand-up comedian. Really, the first time someone brings you up on stage to do stand-up comedy, you become a stand-up comedian. It's sort of instant and hard to quantify, but it happens. Somewhere between standing nervously at the bar looking at your notes—hands trembling, most likely—and walking up on stage when they say your name, you just sort of become one. You do comedy, so you become a comedian. Sort of like, I suppose, the first time you take scissors to someone's hair and remove their bangs. In that moment of the first *snip*, instantly—boom—you're a hairdresser. You just may be a terrible one. I'm not sure, I'd have to see the bangs.)

I remember looking at my notebook waiting to go on stage at a comedy open mic across from Wrigley Field with three other comics who were doing the same. We were nervous. We were sweaty. Each of us was less than a year into comedy, which is just a fancy way of saying we were bad. *Really* bad. I remember opening my set that night riffing about the neon sign across the street that said "ATM HERE." "Do you really need the 'here'?" I asked the crowd (and by "crowd" I mean the sub-dozen group of stragglers looking for a warm place to drink). "The 'HERE' is assumed," I Seinfeld-ed, then paused for a laugh that never came.

The rest of the set went just as poorly. Observations about how the "Robo" in *Robocop* is a silly abbreviation for "robot." ("By dropping that *t*, are you really saving any time?") And then my big closer about how vampires are afraid of crosses, but "do you think they're also afraid of lower case *t*'s?" Crickets. Whatever this crowd was looking for, I wasn't it.

You'd think after a set so quiet you could've easily taken the bar exam in the back of the room that I might've slumped back to my table, put my face in my hands and told my friends I was going back east to become a plumber. But no. There was something magic to this scene, even on the off nights. Which, frankly, were most of the nights. And that magic carried me back to the table, feeling high on the one or two chuckles that I *did* get, where I sat down, softened the blow of my bomb with several three-dollar Miller Lites and said to my friends, "You know, one day, they're going to write a book about this." And I *meant* it.

I had been reading a couple books that chronicled the humble beginnings of other comedy scenes—the obvious choices, New York and LA—and the scene in Chicago didn't seem that different. We weren't great *yet*. But I could see the seeds of something great. And I'm not the only one.

Thankfully, the very funny Mike Bridenstine agreed with me, and a lot of us, that this special time in Chicago deserved to be documented and has done the work the rest of us were too lazy or unskilled to undertake. Like me, he was there. And like me, he smelled something brewing in our scene that he thought might, one day, prove to be worth remembering. And it did. And he remembers it. So here we are.

I'm sure this book is filled with moments and stories that will undoubtedly jog my memory of that raw and exciting time in my life. I'm excited to look back with you. A lot of the stories, in fact, lead to some pretty interesting places. For one, the other comic I was talking to in the open mic bomb story was Kumail Nanjiani, who is now a bona fide movie star and part of the MCU for crying out loud. And it started in those shitty bars where, back then, he was a nervous open mic-er with a unibrow who chain-smoked Parliaments.

It's fun to see how things change. It's fun to see how things begin. So I'm glad this book exists. I know Mike to be a good dude and a very funny comic, so I trust we're in good hands. But if I'm being completely honest, I have no idea how this book turned out.

Let's find out together.

PETE HOLMES, 2022

ACKNOWLEDGEMENTS

Thank you to all the people who took the time to do an interview with me. They say that history is written by the victors, but it's also written by people who respond to e-mails.

Thank you to my parents for their love and support.

Thank you to Philip Hollingsworth, Jake Lloyd Bacon and especially Robert Buscemi and Janet T Planet, for all the help.

Thank you to Ben Gibson and everyone at The History Press.

Thank you to Dave Odd for suggesting I submit to The History Press. *Of course* it was you.

Thank you to Pete Holmes for the foreword.

Thank you to Kristy Mangel, Erin Nekervis, Krystle Gemnich, Mark Geary, Forest Casey, Cayne Collier, Jeff Klinger, Josh Cheney, Matt Dwyer and Chris Pagnozzi from The Second City for the photos.

Thank you to Kumail Nanjiani, Rob Delaney, Kyle Kinane, Kelly Leonard and Dana Gould for the nice quotes. And to Kumail for the encouraging texts.

And thank you to Victoria and Taker. For being my "why."

PROLOGUE

C hicago was an improv town and everybody knew it. The Second City arrived in the late '50s and had consistently produced some of the biggest names in comedy ever since. It had basically become a feeding system to *Saturday Night Live* since the show's debut in 1975. And if anyone had memories of Lenny Bruce at the Gate of Horn, Mort Sahl at Mister Kelly's or Dick Gregory at the Playboy Club, they had faded decades prior. When people thought of comedy in Chicago, or when people in Chicago thought of comedy, they inevitably thought of Dan Aykroyd, John Belushi, Chris Farley, Tina Fey, Bill Murray and Gilda Radner. Chicago was Second City. Chicago was improv. And that's the way it was. Period.

Then something weird happened. In just over a decade, from 1996 to 2008, a tiny do-it-yourself stand-up scene on the North Side of Chicago produced some of the most successful and influential stand-up comedians of their generation. They did it without much industry attention, without a home club and—if we're being completely honest—mostly performing to drunks in the backs of dingy bars on their off nights. None of it was glamorous. None of it should have worked at all. But somehow, some way, the comedians from this scene have managed to etch their own names into the vaunted Chicago comedy pantheon.

Hannibal Buress has performed stand-up on practically every late night show on television. He's also appeared on *30 Rock*, *The Eric Andre Show*, *Broad City* and in the Marvel *Spider-Man* franchise. He's written for *Saturday Night Live*. He's had multiple specials on Comedy Central. And in 2014, a leaked

Hannibal Buress. *Erin Nekervis.*

Kumail Nanjiani. *Krystle Gemnich.*

clip of one of Buress's performances made national news and effectively ended the career of Bill Cosby.

T.J. Miller has starred in several movies and TV shows, including *Silicon Valley*, *Cloverfield*, *How to Train Your Dragon* and the *Deadpool* franchise. He's also appeared on *Conan, Jimmy Kimmel Live!* and *The Late Show with Stephen Colbert* and has released stand-up specials with Comedy Central and HBO.

Kyle Kinane has multiple stand-up specials on Comedy Central, where he also served as the on-air announcer. He has also performed stand-up sets on Netflix, *The Tonight Show Starring Jimmy Fallon, Last Call with Carson Daly* and *Conan*.

Cameron Esposito has appeared on *The Late, Late Show with Craig Ferguson* (where Jay Leno called her "the future of comedy"), *Conan* and *Last Call with Carson Daly* and starred in *Take My Wife* on Seeso with her then-partner River Butcher.

Pete Holmes has appeared on Comedy Central, *VH1's Best Week Ever, Late Night with Jimmy Fallon* and *Conan*. He hosted the popular podcast *You Made It Weird*, which led to his own talk show on TBS. He starred in a semi-autobiographical HBO series, *Crashing*. He has put out multiple stand-up specials on HBO. And he was the star of *How We Roll* on CBS.

Beth Stelling has performed on *Jimmy Kimmel Live!, Last Call with Carson Daly* and multiple shows on Comedy Central. She wrote for *Crashing* on HBO and has her own HBOMax special, *Girl Daddy*.

Matt Braunger has stand-up specials on Comedy Central, Netflix and Amazon Prime. He has appeared on *Late Show with David Letterman* and *Conan*. And his acting credits include *MADtv* and *Agent Carter*.

Kumail Nanjiani has starred on HBO's *Silicon Valley* and *The Meltdown with Jonah and Kumail* on Comedy Central. In 2017, he co-wrote and starred in *The Big Sick*. That movie, which was co-written by Nanjiani's wife, Emily V. Gordon, covers Nanjiani and Gordon's life in and around the Chicago stand-up scene in 2007. The screenplay got the couple nominated for an Oscar. In 2018, TIME magazine named Nanjiani one of the one hundred most influential people in the world. And in 2021, he became a superhero in the Marvel Cinematic Universe, playing Kingo in *Eternals*. I own two of his action figures.

This is just a partial list of names from a tiny Chicago alt scene that would be recognizable to any real comedy fan around the United States. There are also well-known comedians who made brief appearances in the scene before they got known (like W. Kamau Bell, Tommy Johnagin and Nate Bargatze) and well-respected comics' comics who should probably be more famous than they currently are (like Dwayne Kennedy and Nick Vatterott). There are a lot of names of comics still on their way up (like Liza Treyger, Megan Gailey and Drew Michael), and there are beloved locals who never left Chicago or are mostly legends within the scene (including Pat Brice, RIP).

Not all their timelines in Chicago overlap, but these comics were all there, around the same time, on the same lineups, performing for the same drink tickets. All these people performed on makeshift stages in the backs of pancake houses, in poorly lit corners of dive bars, sometimes pausing mid-sentence so an L train could roar past. It was all part of an alt scene that arose out of necessity when clubs like the Improv and the Funny Firm closed and when Zanies, the last club standing, showed little to no interest in nurturing a local scene. It also came at a historic downtime in stand-up on a national level, when the genre felt more like a passing fad than a ticket to stardom. It began years before social media, when the only sign these performers had that they were on the right track was the vague notion that alt scenes like theirs also existed in New York and Los Angeles. And yes, it happened when Chicago was an improv town and everyone knew it.

For four years, I did the same shows and drank the same cheap beers and downed the same Jamo shots in all the same smoke-filled bars. And I just thought the history of the scene should be documented. So I've appointed myself to play the part of John and Alan Lomax recording old American folk songs or of Lawrence Ritter talking to the deadball-era baseball players in *The Glory of Their Times*. And since I'll be playing the role of your trusted narrator, I thought it might be worthwhile to introduce you to the North Side Chicago scene the same way it was introduced to me.

INTRO

My first encounter with the Den was a total fluke. It was late summer 2003. And as a recent graduate from the University of Iowa, I was looking for a full-time job somewhere close to the city. But with a communications degree and no real employable skills or life experience to speak of, the only job offers I received were from a suburban Chevy dealership managed by my friend's dad and a shady pyramid scheme masquerading as an advertising company. I went with the "advertising company," at least for my first month in Chicago, since I didn't know anything about cars—or pyramid schemes.

On the night of my first job interview with the "advertising company," where the only question I was asked was whether I considered myself a leader or a follower (I went with "leader," thank you very much), I had to rush down the Kennedy Expressway from the northern suburb of Niles to the Irving Park exit, glancing frantically at directions I'd written down on a napkin, because I was running late to sign up for an open mic.

When I spotted the bar, I parked on a side street and started running toward it, still in my interview suit. When I finally arrived, I was almost positive I'd also gone to the wrong place. Through the front windows, this sure didn't look like the "big open mic" I'd been promised. It looked more like a dive bar on a slow night. But as I entered the bar, I was greeted by the person who had told me about this place, Mike Holmes.

"The show already started," Holmes told me. "And there are already thirty-five comics on the list."

"Where's the show?" I asked, feeling more confused than disappointed. And did he say *thirty-fucking-five* comics?

"Back there," he pointed, "there's a big room with a stage."

Unbeknownst to me, back there in the big room with the stage would also be lifelong friends, future roommates, the best man and officiant at my wedding and the first place I'd ever truly fit in anywhere in my life. Back there would also be future movie stars and people who would get their own TV shows and release comedy specials on HBO, Comedy Central and Netflix. And in four years' time, a huge group of us would move, seemingly in one large mass, to Los Angeles, all at the same time.

The reason I was at this Chicago open mic in the first place was because I'd met Mike Holmes the previous summer in Iowa City, where I became the host of "Comedy Night" at a University of Iowa campus bar called the Summit. Another comedian you may have heard of named Brooks Wheelan also got his start at the Summit three years after Holmes and I left. But if there was a comedy scene in Iowa City to speak of when I was there, it consisted of me and Holmes and, like, two other dudes. We all loved Mitch Hedberg, we'd all seen the Jerry Seinfeld documentary *Comedian* a thousand times and we would all make monthly treks to Penguin's Comedy Club in Cedar Rapids to do its open mic. Where we would crush, I'd like to add—at least in our own minds.

Holmes and I decided to move to Chicago together to keep pursuing careers in comedy. And even though Holmes had heard good things about this particular open mic, I had no reason to assume it would be any different than Penguin's. Boy was I wrong.

As I settled into my seat in the back room of the Lyon's Den, where this open mic was held, a thirtysomething host named Robert Buscemi was on stage wearing a plain white T-shirt, dress pants and dark-rimmed glasses. His voice had a hint of a southern twang, but on that night he might as well have been from an alien planet.

"I'm aware most of you are here tonight because you follow my blog," he started, laying the absurdist irony on thick. "And I appreciate that. For those who don't know, my blog fans divide themselves into two warring factions. One faction believes firmly that my best feature is my gossamer-soft body hair. Their rivals in the other camp argue with equal vigor that my best quality is my vestigial tail."

This crowd was loving every second of it. This shit was *killing*, and at the time, I had no idea why. After a year of mostly seeing hack road comics doing the same dated acts at Comedy Night in Iowa City, this Buscemi guy was talking about *vestigial tails* and *gossamer-soft body hair*? It just didn't make any sense.

"Now I personally believe that my best quality is my world-class Hamburglar drinking glass collection," Buscemi continued. "But what do I know? I'm only the most innovative comedian that you'll ever see."

A little later in the night, a young, unibrowed Pakistani guy went up and absolutely destroyed with a joke about a bassoon. I remember thinking, "He could have picked any musical instrument and the joke still would have worked. But he picked a bassoon because it has the funniest name. This guy is good."

Since I'd missed the beginning of the show, I asked Holmes if that guy, who had only been introduced as "Kumail," was the best comic of the night so far. "Him or that guy over there," he said pointing to a tall blond guy who also seemed to be around our age. "His name is Holmes too. Pete Holmes."

Not long after Kumail performed, a large and intimidating guy named Steve O. Harvey was introduced, accompanied by Darth Vader's theme song. And once he was on stage, he challenged everyone in the audience to a thumb wrestling contest. There were a handful of takers, and one by one, he defeated them all, laughing maniacally the whole time. That was the entirety of his act.

I also had experienced no thumb wrestling villains in my year of comedy in Iowa. But just like Robert Buscemi, Kumail Somebody and apparently Pete Holmes, the crowd also loved Steve O. Harvey. "We had no idea," Mike Holmes told me, when I talked to him about that night seventeen years after the fact. "*No* idea."

By the time he went up twenty-sixth on the list, Holmes was convinced that he needed to have an intro song picked out for his performance. And when he requested "No Rain" by Blind Melon, Josh Cheney, the way-too-skinny kid in the suit working the sound booth, greeted him with a dirty look before he begrudgingly agreed to play it.

The song didn't help. After he was introduced by Buscemi, Holmes launched into a pretty straightforward bit about driving with his mother in the passenger seat. It had worked the handful of times he'd told it in Iowa in front of friends. But it died a slow, painful death that night in Chicago. The next joke suffered a similar fate. And by the time Holmes got to his closer about Indiana Jones, which had been absolutely bulletproof in Iowa, most of the audience had already tuned him out.

"I bombed," Holmes remembered. "We were coming off a couple Iowa shows. With loaded crowds, I was doing well. Crushing enough that we were like, 'Yep, let's go to Chicago.' And I'd been to a few open mics to know that 'Yeah, some people bomb, some people crush. But the people that are bombing *suck*. And I've got good bits.' And then I went up and it was a soft set."

After the open mic, we went back to Holmes's sister's apartment, where we were staying. Holmes was demoralized, and I remember sitting with him on the front stoop and having to talk him out of staying in Iowa and bailing on our Chicago plans (I told you I was a leader). And now that I think about it, it's probably a good thing that I didn't also perform that first night. Because I definitely would have bombed, and we might have aborted everything. Luckily, from the safety of my non-bomb, I got to give a pep talk and remind Holmes that Chicago was huge, and there was still sketch and improv comedy for us to try. And most importantly, there were probably a thousand other stand-up shows and open mics just like that one, scattered all throughout the city—but without the eccentric weirdos talking about the Hamburglar.

We didn't show up at the Lyon's Den again for five months. And it pains me to think of what I almost missed. Around the same time, some of the people who would go on to become the best comedians of their generation would pass through that stage. The names bear repeating: Pete Holmes, Kumail Nanjiani, Hannibal Buress, T.J. Miller, Tommy Johnagin, Nate Bargatze, Nick Vatterott, Pat Brice and Kyle Kinane all performed at the Lyon's Den open mic on a regular basis. At some point, George Carlin dropped in just to watch. And when John Roy won *Star Search* earlier in 2003, he shouted out the Lyon's Den in his victory interview with Arsenio Hall. It's entirely possible that the Lyon's Den could go down as the greatest open mic in the history of comedy. If the scene had a center, that was definitely it. And unbeknownst to me, I'd just entered into it one night wearing my interview suit.

Well, now you've entered into it with me. So pull up a stool and order a drink. What you're about to read is the culmination of hundreds of hours of interviews with veterans of the scene. This is the story they told me, as well as the story as I remember it.

Our starting point for this story is in the mid-'90s, roughly a decade before my arrival, in a desolate period known as the Comedy Bust. At that time, there was no thriving North Side scene to speak of. There were no emerging comedy stars. There was essentially nothing. In our beginning—if I'm allowed to paraphrase the beginning of another popular book—there was darkness.

Chapter 1

GENESIS

Before the North Side Chicago stand-up scene could spawn a generation of comedic talent, it first had to crawl out from under the rubble of the Comedy Bust of the mid-'90s. That was when a number of comedy clubs that had opened in the Boom times of the '80s were closing their doors for good due to a drop in popularity. And the decline and fall of stand-up seems to have hit Chicago especially hard.

The most telling quote from this period comes from a late '90s *Chicago Tribune* article[1] written by its comedy critic, Allan Johnson, which opened with a list of shuttered comedy clubs in the Chicagoland area: "The Comedy Cottage. The Comedy Womb. The Last Laff. Who's on First. The Funny Firm. The Improv. All Jokes Aside. Double Exposure. The Laugh Factory. Catch a Rising Star. Wacko's Comedy Shop. TNT Comedy Hook....The above list, unfortunately, is a scroll of the dead."

By the mid-'90s, only three "white" clubs remained, and the number was dwindling fast. "It was the Improv,[2] the Funny Firm[3] and Zanies,[4] which you had to fight to get into," comedian Cayne Collier said. "Then there were a handful of open mics. And not even that many." Due to the segregated nature of Chicago at the time, clubs like All Jokes Aside were created to specifically target the city's "long-underserved Black market," as owner Raymond Lambert put it in his book.[5] But even that club closed its doors in 1998.

Johnson's article cited "too many mediocre rooms, too much comedy on television, too many hack comics, a devaluation of the craft, a disrespect by the audience and plain, old-fashioned greed" as the culprits for the Bust. But Zanies became the last club standing. And the perception among comics was that Zanies showed little, if any, interest in a local scene.

"I don't want to shit-talk it too much—it is an institution," said Kyle Kinane, one of the scene's success stories. "There's so many examples of a club nurturing a local scene—Comedy Works in Denver, the Punchline and Cobb's in San Francisco, the Heliums....If you nurture these local acts, if you want to bring loyalty out of respect and admiration, that's how you get it...they come back and are happy to play their home club. How many big-time headliners left Chicago and came back and play Zanies?"

Zanies, which is still open after forty-plus years in operation, obviously did something right as a business to earn that longevity. But comedy clubs tend to produce club comics. And in the post-Bust era, that often meant comedians who were safe and pandered to tourists. It also meant there was zero incentive for comics to be original. And I don't think any of the things I'm going to discuss in this book would have happened if Zanies had been hospitable to new talent. So there was a symbiotic relationship of sorts, where Zanies got to stay in business and the local comedians got to go become their own thing.

"All the gates were closing," said Mick Betancourt, another veteran of the scene, of the Bust period. "Bert Haas at Zanies had the one sinking ship that he was trying to keep afloat, and he had to protect that business model. But all of that, unbeknownst to him probably, was what inspired the alt scene in Chicago—*not* putting comics up."

It wasn't just happening in Chicago. With comedy clubs closing across the country during the Bust, a new generation of comics was rejecting the remaining clubs, as well as the type of comedy performed in them. Suddenly, a brick wall backdrop and an observational premise became shorthand for the hackneyed clichés of Baby Boomers and squares. On the other hand, alternative comedy, or "alt comedy" as it became known, was emerging from nontraditional places like UnCabaret at LunaPark in Los Angeles, as well as Eating It at Luna Lounge in New York City. And it was also about to emerge in Chicago. All it took was the ingenuity of a recent clown school graduate from Wisconsin.

Chapter 2

THE COMEDY ASYLUM

Tom Tenney hitched a ride to Chicago from Baraboo, Wisconsin, in 1993. He had just graduated from Ringling Bros. Clown College and had forty-three cents in his pocket to show for it—this kind of reads like a Mad Libs version of my own story. But after paying his dues and getting a few lucky breaks, Tenney became the main booker at the Chicago Improv.

"You had your national headliners come through," Tenney remembered. "You had Rosie O'Donnell, Roseanne Barr, Bill Maher, Larry Miller, Rita Rudner, all those sort of '80s comics. But those were maybe every couple months."

The rest of the time, Tenney was booking Chicago locals, some of whom went on to become pretty famous in their own right (like Jeff Garlin and W. Kamau Bell), and in the process, Tenney got a reputation for working with and developing new talent. "It wasn't entirely from the goodness of my heart," Tenney admitted. "I was also trying to start a comedy management business. And so I wanted to find those people."

After the Improv closed in 1995, Tenney became increasingly interested in producing alternative and performance comedy. "I wanted to make it sort of more outrageous, more dirty," he said. "I wanted it to go to a place where you couldn't necessarily go as a part of a big, mainstream comedy club." And thus, the Comedy Asylum, on Thursday nights at the newly opened Subterranean in Wicker Park, was born. It was one of the first fully booked alt comedy shows in Chicago.

As a side note, picking the actual first alt show in Chicago might prove difficult, especially in a sea of one-nighters sprinkled throughout the city before anybody used the term "alt." But a decent candidate might be The Riff at the Cue Club in Lake View on Monday nights, which was put on by regulars from the Chicago Improv on the club's off night. And *Chicago Tribune* listings for that show go all the way back to July 29, 1994.

"We didn't call it [alternative comedy] yet," comedian and Riff producer Rob Paravonian said. "I think maybe around '95 or '96 we started hearing the term. When we started The Riff, the motivation was just to try different things and have a workshop vibe....In the '80s, stand-up became so popular. But it also became a very specific thing. It was one guy or one woman with a mic doing observational material. [The Riff] came from a need of these performers wanting to try things other than observational type monologues."

So while The Riff was an alt show put on by club comics before alt comedy was a thing, Tom Tenney might have been the first person to start a show in Chicago with the explicit intent of being alternative. The original mission statement for the show spelled it out pretty clearly: "The Comedy Asylum is a laboratory for the creation and development of new and alternative comedic forms. An atmosphere of danger and excitement exists. We feature acts which test and challenge the boundaries of traditional comedy....We are committed to the development of new talent in Chicago, and to giving new ideas a forum of expression. The Comedy Asylum drives to make comedy theatrical once again, to discover where it might be going and to help it on its way."

In other words, "This ain't Zanies." In May 1996, the *New York Times* printed an article[6] titled "Take the New Comedy. Please," by Neil Strauss. He described alternative comedy as a thinking person's brand of stand-up and stated that it has more in common with performance art and poetry than with its Comedy Boom predecessor, which was still being performed in clubs.

The article mainly discusses the Eating It show at Luna Lounge on New York's Lower East Side, along with performers like Sarah Silverman, Janeane Garofalo and Marc Maron, all of whom were in their late twenties or early thirties at the time. But it also name-checks other pioneering alt-rooms like LunaPark in Los Angeles and the Velveeta Room in Austin. And listed right alongside them was Tom Tenney's show at the Subterranean Cabaret in Chicago. At that point, it had been around for all of two months.

Recognition from the newspaper of record was nice, but what Tenney and co-producer Chuck Bowi wanted more than anything was to buy or lease a bar of their own. And according to Bowi, they looked at several places around the North Center intersection of Lincoln Avenue, Damen Avenue and Irving Park Road. But back in the mid-'90s, Tenney and Bowi weren't sure if anyone would want to venture "that far" north to see a comedy show. "Little did we know that the area would soon become the hotbed of the future alt comedy scene in Chicago," Bowi said, alluding to two of Chicago's most iconic stand-up rooms, the Lyon's Den and the original Lincoln Lodge, which we will be discussing later. In the meantime, Tenney and Bowi figured that the next logical step was to add a second show.

Chapter 3

THE ELEVATED (BEGINNINGS)

In the post-Bust era of the mid-'90s, the North Side scene may have been pretty dead, but luckily for Chicago, the stand-up scene in New Orleans—where Cayne Collier had been kicking around for a few years—was even deader. "It's like, 'What do you want to go to the French Quarter for? Well, there's jazz. There's amazing food. There's Bourbon Street. No, let's go hear stand-up comedy,'" Collier joked. "It just didn't work."

The comedy clubs in the French Quarter, as well as the suburbs of New Orleans, had flopped. But for Collier, hustling to find other performance venues for independent stand-up and improv shows was part of a skillset he took with him when he decided to drop out of the University of New Orleans and move to Chicago in 1994. Sure, that same New Orleans scene was about to see the arrival of comics like Ken Jeong of the *The Hangover* fame and Chicago native Mike O'Connell, who would become *Rolling Stone*'s "Hot Comic" in 2003 and one of *Variety*'s 10 Comics to Watch in 2007. But older guys in the scene were telling Collier that he had to move to a bigger market if he wanted to make it.

"I couldn't really afford New York," Collier said. "I wasn't too keen on LA. And Chicago offered improvisation." Sure enough, upon arrival, like so many aspiring funny people before him, Collier began training at Second City while also testing the waters in the city's sparse open mic scene. "Say what you will about open mics," Collier said, "If you wanna say, 'Where is the next thing gonna come from?' It's gonna be from an open mic. That's the heart of stand-up comedy."

Elevated negative sheet featuring, *from left*, Rob Paravonian, Cayne Collier, Mike Olson and Mike O'Connell. *Cayne Collier.*

In this case, the Next Thing was about to come out of open mics like Hitchcock's in Lincoln Park. "That one really took hold," Collier said of Hitchcock's, which was managed by Jim Maahs. "Jimmy loved comedy. He loved the comics and he really supported it. And it was a tiny place. But he packed it with as many people as you could get in there. A hundred people sometimes."

Cayne Collier. *Cayne Collier.*

"Hitchcock's was insane," Carl Kozlowski, a journalist and veteran comic, told me. "Everybody would go there." When I asked Kozlowski who he got the most excited to see perform at Hitchcock's, without hesitation he answered, "Cayne. I totally had a man crush on Cayne. And I don't think I hid it very well at all. He was just so talented. I don't know how to even compare him to anybody. He was such positive energy. Such innovative ideas. Such great writing. He would act out the stuff. He could do anything."

Not long into his Chicago stand-up career, Collier began getting booked at one-nighters in places like the Laugh Factory in Aurora, KJ Riddles in Orland Park and the Comedy Womb in Lyons—not really the most likely places for a performer to have a creative epiphany. But suburban rooms like these, which Collier told me felt extremely distant from the city and paid next to nothing, did provide a moment of clarity for him. "I sat there looking around like, 'Wait, we're in *Chicago*. And we're driving forty minutes to make ten dollars? Something doesn't equate.'"

Collier, who wasn't getting booked at Zanies, figured he would rely on the skills he'd learned in New Orleans—hustling for venues by approaching bar owners and begging them to let him produce shows on their off nights. And that's when an opportunity fell into his lap. Just as Collier began looking to start a show, Tom Tenney and Chuck Bowi were looking to get rid of one.

After running Comedy Asylum for six months, Tenney and Bowi started a second comedy show at the Cue Club in Lake View and then immediately regretted it. "Tom and I realized it would be too much to do two rooms each week on top of looking to buy a building of our own," Bowi said. "Cayne was hungry and had the chops to succeed in that space."

When Collier was offered the show, he gladly accepted. But as things turn out, Bowi and Tenney had chosen the wrong venue. Their relationship with the Subterranean soured shortly after they gave the Cue Club to Collier, and they were back to having nothing.

The show they gave away, which Collier named The Elevated, would run for the next ten years. During that decade, the Cue Club would become Philosofur's, and then Philosofur's would become Cherry Red. Only the site itself remained consistent—right next to one of the city's famous L tracks. So the location of the room, combined with Collier's mission of taking comedy to a higher level, led to Collier giving The Elevated its perfect name.

Where some comics might have looked at that landscape and seen stand-up as a dead end or a dying fad, Collier only saw opportunity. So what, the clubs had closed? He wasn't a fan of club comedy anyway. So the shuttering of those clubs, along with the dead local scene, gave Collier a chance to, I suppose, be the change he wanted to see in the world.

"I'm looking at it like, 'Okay, it's only gonna come up from the ashes,'" Collier said. "I was like, 'We're gonna go stake our claim.' Meaning the people who I felt were doing stuff that was interesting and wasn't hacky. 'Let's go get our thing.'"

Their "thing" caught on. And so did Collier's comedy ethos. "He's just such a great guy," Mike O'Connell said of Collier. "Sweet and also fostered the community. He kind of brought together disparate people. It was a great, warm environment to start in."

"Someone said to me, 'You need to go to this show because this is the shit. This is the high bar,'" Lincoln Lodge producer Mark Geary said. "And I went to The Elevated for the first time and basically walked out and threw away all of the jokes that I'd written for a year. I was like, 'What the hell am I doing?' And then I started going to Elevated every week. Like, 'Okay, this is how I should aim to be.'"

"Cayne Collier ran it so well," another comedian, who asked to remain anonymous, told me. "That is my first experience with a show that could be called 'curated,' not 'booked.' And as a performer, his stage presence was just amazing. He was really a force to watch."

Bridget Smith, Mike O'Connell, Bang Balutanski, Adam Kroshus, Cayne Collier and Ian Belknap. *Cayne Collier.*

"You gotta see it in its heyday," Geary told me, referring to the 1997 to 2000 period. "It was like, 'Okay, everyone's in the gutter. These are the stars. This is where I need to be.'"

One star of the early Elevated was the multitalented Greg Mills. "Greg Mills was probably the Elevated hero for me," John Roy told me. "That's the guy I laughed at the hardest."

"Greg Mills would destroy," Kyle Kinane added. "We all loved him."

Mills, who straddled the worlds of improv and stand-up, began his comedy career by faking his way into becoming a piano player for Second City and then faking his way into becoming *the* piano player for ImprovOlympic, another of the city's famed improv theaters and training centers. "That's where I was like, 'Holy shit. I'm playing piano for Tina [Fey] and Amy [Poehler],'" Mills told me. But it was doing stand-up where Mills was able to fuse all his performance chops into one act. And he could be an absolute force on stage.

Mills could begin with an observational joke about his confusion over seeing "Columbus Day" and "Columbus Day Observed" in his calendar and have it escalate into a show-stopping song-and-dance number, complete with spot-on impressions of Frank Sinatra and Sammy Davis Jr. Or he could portray

Greg Mills. *Cayne Collier.*

characters like the World's Worst Ragtime Piano Player, where he skillfully butchered songs like "The Entertainer" and "Sweet Georgia Brown" with the hysterical confidence and facial expressions of a silent film star.

About that character, Mills told me that he's just good enough at piano to know where the melody intervals and chord shapes should go and that he can mirror the tempo and syncopated style of the original songs while still banging on the wrong keys. So the results allow the audience to "hear" the songs the character *believes* he's playing while he noisily clangs away and mugs at them self-assuredly. And with the right crowd, the results could be explosive. "I lost my mind laughing at that," comedian Josh Cheney told me of the first time he saw the bit.

By 1998, the *Chicago Tribune* had taken notice of The Elevated, saying that the show was "generating a crowd of appreciative fans who don't feel stimulated by the standard 'where are you from?' material."[7]

In 2000, Allan Johnson of the *Tribune* did a feature on Collier and The Elevated for their four-year anniversary weekend. The article[8] also listed some of the show's highlights to that point. One of those highlights, the previous year's anniversary, is still frequently mentioned in Elevated lore and was said to include three stages and sixteen comedians. But with every successful comedy venture, it's only a matter of time before jealousy and resentment come from those who feel excluded from that success.

According to Geary, that three-year Elevated anniversary, with its three nights of shows, actually caused a lot of unintentional ill will in the scene. "Instead of doing three different lineups," he said, "they did the same people three nights in a row."

"That's not what Woodstock did," comedian Eric Acosta deadpanned when I brought the scenario up to him.

31

Eventually, the comedians who felt excluded from The Elevated started to get impatient. And when I was discussing this period with Geary, he pointed out a pattern that has consistently repeated itself throughout his time in Chicago. The pattern started when the clubs closed in 1995, when Zanies became the last club standing and when enterprising people like Tom Tenney and Cayne Collier still felt compelled to put on shows even though they'd been cast aside or rejected by the traditional routes. And the pattern inevitably repeated itself again when The Elevated became the most established alternative room in the city.

"There's a group of people who have the ball, and they're not letting the fucker go," Geary explained. "And then there's the up-and-comers who are like, 'Screw it. We'll do our own game.'"

In this case, Geary is speaking for himself and his peers. And just like Collier had predicted earlier, the Next Thing in comedy, at least on the North Side of Chicago, would come from an open mic.

Chapter 4

THE RED LION (BEGINNINGS)

would start the modern Chicago comedy scene at the Red Lion," comedian John Roy told me. "Because before that, you just don't have the main characters yet. The people that are gonna get famous aren't doing it yet."

The alt scene in Chicago may have gotten a running start with Cayne Collier and The Elevated. But the person who would have the biggest impact on the scene over the next few decades was unquestionably Mark Geary. Even though in 1996, when Geary arrived in Chicago from the Midlands of England to work an IT job, you'd be hard-pressed to find a less likely candidate to fill that role.

"Believe it or not," Geary laughed, "I didn't know where Chicago actually was when I came here. Once I landed the job, I looked on the map and it shocked the shit out of me that Chicago was in the middle of the country."

At first, Geary's only real American pleasure was the food court at the Old Orchard Mall in suburban Skokie. "I thought it was the greatest thing ever," he said. "Understand, I come from England. I had never seen a food court in my life. So I was like, 'This is the best! This is everything! And if I'm feeling posh, I'll just go to Corner Bakery instead.'"

Besides having a food court, Old Orchard Mall also had a Barnes & Noble bookstore. And one fateful day in the store, Geary picked up a copy of *Stand-Up Comedy: The Book* by Judy Carter. "I read it and I was like, 'Okay. I need to find open mics.'"

Eventually, Geary moved from Skokie to the North Side of the city, even though unbeknownst to him, and probably to Judy Carter, who wrote her stand-up book prior to the Comedy Bust, Chicago had only two comedy open mics at the time. And that left Geary craving more. "I started an open mic just so I would have another open mic to go to," he said.

Geary had been frequenting a pub called the Red Lion in Lincoln Park: an "oasis in the middle of a whole lot of douche baggery," as he put it to me. The owner's father had been a flight lieutenant in the British Royal Air Force in World War II, was shot down over Belgium and had served three years in a German POW camp.[9]

"His dad was one of the guys who was actually in the Great Escape. Like, not in the film. But in the goddamn thing," Geary said. "And he moved to America and was an architect, and he was one of the people who designed the Blue Line going up the middle of the mobile way. That was his idea. That was the sort of pub it was. It was not full of Michigan State graduates whipping each other's dicks."

"Loud conversation and blaring music are found elsewhere in the area," is how a review on the Chicago Bar Project website put it.[10] But "[if] you're alone and want someone to talk to, head to the Red Lion and you'll be discussing literature, history, politics and sport before you know it."

On multiple occasions, Geary begged the owner to let him use the upstairs room for an open mic, but he wasn't making any headway. That's when one of his friends had an idea. "She had a little bit of personal dirt on him," Geary said. "So she goes, 'Let me talk to him. I'll see what I can do.' Ten minutes later, she called me back. She's like, 'Your open mic's on Thursday.'"

Once Geary, a self-described control freak, took the reins of his mic, he was determined to run it as if it were a top-quality showcase. His biggest production innovation, at least if you ask him, was the implementation of guest spots—a simple but often overlooked fix to a lot of problems inherent to open mics. As Geary explained it, "If I can get eight or nine real people in the room watching, I'm not gonna have the worst comedians be the first four to go up. Because [the audience is] just gonna finish their beer and leave. So we're gonna apply a bit of intelligence to the anarchy."

Geary encouraged the more bizarre and innovative comics on the scene to really go for it while also rigging the sign-up sheet to make sure those weirdo acts were balanced out by the more traditional stand-ups on the lineup. And the formula worked, both for the Red Lion and for the Lyon's Den, the legendary open mic that comes later in our story. "I was inventing the blueprint that the Lyon's Den then cashed in on," Geary joked, even though I can tell he totally meant it.

"Mark Geary ran a great show," Kinane said. "Even if it was an open mic, he still would get in there and put up a stage with a curtain and lights. He produced the show. And that mattered so much."

"From the minute it started it was full," Roy said. "The room was really tightly packed. It was a great location. Lincoln Park was the cool place to be at that point for yuppie people. So all of a sudden you had a show in Chicago that was actually where the people were already going. And also Kyle Kinane and Matt Braunger started right then. And you had Dwayne Kennedy coming around all the time. So the comedy was good. People stuck around. They wanted to see it."

Of the many things the Red Lion open mic is said to have inspired—including the Midnight Bible School, the Lincoln Lodge and possibly the Lyon's Den open mic—there was also the fact that it launched the early career of Kyle Kinane. And even so, he had to take an odd detour to find it.

"I started because I saw an ad in the newspaper," Kinane told me. "The HBO Comedy Festival was like, 'We're doing open auditions for stand-ups at Zanies.' I knew nothing about stand-up other than I'd watch it on TV and I thought it was cool, but I didn't know where it happened. We didn't have that shit in the suburbs. And so I saw the open casting call for that, and everybody got three minutes. I'm like, 'I can probably pull three minutes out of my ass.'"

This particular HBO open call at Zanies from 1999 remains pretty infamous among the comics who auditioned. "There were hundreds of us lined up down the street from six in the morning waiting for it to open," comedian Mike Olson remembered. "Sonya White did an impression of a horse and won the whole thing." But the funniest gag of all seems to be that Bert Haas, the manager of Zanies, had to say "Thank you" into the sound booth mic (or "God mic") after every comic's allotted time, no matter how terribly their act had gone. This led to a few unintentionally hilarious moments.

On the positive side of the "Thank you" spectrum was Mike Olson himself. At 6:00 a.m., Olson had lugged a full drum set into Zanies with the help of his coworker, who then curled himself up among the drums, hidden from view by a dust cover, and then waited for hours until he was revealed during Olson's set. "That was his idea," Olson said. "So he blew people's minds when I went up there and told a couple terrible jokes, and then I peel off this thing and there's a guy back there."

After the shock and disbelief of Olson's coworker being revealed, the main gag of Olson's act was essentially that the drummer would deliver rim shots where no rim shots belonged. But it got a tad bit more complicated from there. "By the end, he's just doing the rim shots and I'm doing the 'thank you's' like he's dancing me on a string," Olson explained. "It ended up being so perfect because Bert was saying 'Thank you' at the end of everybody's thing. And then Bert did the last 'thank you,' and he got the last rim shot on that. So it caused such a reaction. I got attention, and people like The Elevated invited me to perform there despite the fact that I didn't do much else at the time."

The Zanies experience left Kinane wanting more. Luckily, he was a student at Columbia College at the time, and he recognized one of his classmates, Johnny Berger, from the Zanies audition. "I was like, 'Where do you do comedy?'" Kinane remembered. "And he's like, 'Oh, you gotta go to open mics. You go to the *Chicago Reader* and check the listings.'"

Kinane followed Berger's instructions, but at first, he just went to shows to watch. "I would see people that sucked come back week after week," Kinane said. "So I'm like, 'Well, I gotta be better than that guy. I'm not gonna be good. But if this guy can keep coming back without encouragement, I can at least try this.'"

"Kyle Kinane did something I'd never seen anybody do," comedian Jeff Klinger said. "He would go in the showroom from comic one and watch it all the way to comic fifty-two and really study what they did. Not just once or twice. Almost all the time. And a lot of comics respected that. And I respected it. But there's just no way I could do that. I couldn't sit through that many comics."

Eventually, Kinane made his way to the stage at Red Lion. But his set didn't really go the way he'd hoped. "I did see Kyle Kinane the first time he did stand-up," comedian Monte said. "He was like, a punk. Like, that greaser look. His hair was slicked. I think he had a denim jacket. And he had tight pants. He was one of *those* guys. He wore the creepers, maybe Cons. And I thought he was hilarious. He was really good. And we were standing outside, and he walked out and was bummed. I was with Dwayne Kennedy. And I was like, 'Dude, you did really good. You should come back.' And Dwayne backed me up on it. And he didn't think he did well."

"I go, 'It wasn't great,'" Kinane said. "'I had a couple bits that got laughs.' And they were both like, 'You should come back and keep doing this. That was funny.' So it was their encouragement that kept me going....If anybody dislikes my comedy, I've said it before, blame Dwayne Kennedy and Monte."

"This is how much of a dipshit a twenty-seven/twenty-eight-year-old Geary is," Mark Geary said. "When I first met Kinane, I didn't like him. He had the wallet on a chain, he still had hair in a little quiff and he had this rockabilly look going. And I just looked at him like, 'What a dick.' And then he was a really good comedian, so I hated him even more. And then, when I went to The Elevated one night, Monte was meant to do a set, and he went up to the mic and goes, 'I'm meant to do six minutes now. But there's a comedian in this crowd that is way better than me. And deserves to be on this stage. And he should go up. So Kyle Kinane, come up on this stage.'"

"I think I was booked for fifteen minutes," Monte remembered. "I say [to Collier], 'This kid Kyle Kinane is here. You should put him up sometime, and maybe even tonight. He's really funny, man. You're gonna like him a lot.' And he's like, 'He's only been around for three months. I'm not gonna put him up.' And I'm an idiot. This is ignorant on my part, but I was like, 'What does that guy know? That's ridiculous. This guy's good. Who cares how long he's been in the game for?' And then, when I was up there doing my time, I think I had a beeper then, I checked the time and saw that I had six minutes left. And I did what I called my closing bit. And I was like, 'All right, everybody. I want to bring up to the stage a friend of mine. I think he's really funny. He's new, but he's one of the best. Believe me, you're gonna see his name in lights one day. Please give it up for Kyle Kinane.' And Kyle didn't even know I was gonna do it."

"I was like, 'Oh, wow. *What?*'" Kinane remembered.

When I asked Geary if Kyle's set went okay, he reacted like it was the dumbest question he'd ever been asked. "Name the set where Kyle Kinane did not do okay," Geary said. And...point taken.

"He killed," Monte said. "He killed."

"I had my few one-liners," Kinane said modestly. "It was fun. But I didn't realize that Cayne, who ran The Elevated, had, let's say, 'an affinity for control.' And that really upset him."

"Cayne controlled his show like a good producer," Geary said. "So Monte calls someone who hasn't been booked, has never been viewed, up on the stage. I was *fuming*. Because everyone else had worked their ass off to get up there. And this little suburban fucking punk-ass Cramps wannabe gets to go up."

Geary seems completely aware of how ridiculous it all sounds now. "We are such assholes," Geary laughed. But just for the record, when I asked Kinane to describe his look at the time, it sounds pretty similar to what Geary described.

"I'm sure I was just a fucking asshole," Kinane said. "I thought I was a real cool guy. I was like, 'I'm coming from the music world. Let me show these nerds what's up. Let me show these dorks how it's done.' I [had] a mild rockabilly/garage rock look I was trying to pull off, but not with skill. Just real stupid hair. Like that's changed. I really wanted to be confused for someone in Social Distortion. I really wanted people to know that like, 'Hey, man, I'm not really about this stand-up thing. I'm gonna drive by, but this guy [points to himself with this thumbs], he's actually pretty cool. Anyway, I'm gotta get out of here because I gotta get back home. Otherwise dinner's gonna get cold that my mom made.'"

Now that you're picturing *that* version of Kyle Kinane, we can continue with the story of his Elevated debut. "Cayne totally scolded me," Monte said. "Which I deserved. I wasn't allowed back there for months. He let me come back, but he never booked me again. I did what I did, and he did what he did, and I got what I deserved."

Collier, I should mention, has no memory of any of this. He agrees that he probably would have been upset with Monte, but he doesn't think of himself as very "scoldy." And he also doesn't recall ever banning anyone from the room. Except for maybe the woman who stalked one of the other comedians. But I'll tell you about that later.

"I think some of that from Monte might be self-imposed," Collier said. "Geary seems more upset about it than me." And if Collier seems annoyed by anything, it's that after all these years, Monte still doesn't understand The Elevated's booking policy. "I wouldn't have just 'put someone up,'" Collier insisted. "If a night was booked, it was booked."

The Elevated was still the top show in the scene. And if a night at The Elevated was booked, it usually wasn't booked with new stars from the Red Lion—at least not yet. "I'm trying to tell [Collier], 'We got some guys, dude. They're definitely your caliber,'" Geary said. "But obviously it's hard. You've already establish a room. You want to stay loyal to the folks that got it there. And it becomes really hard. Enter Matt Dwyer."

Chapter 5

MIDNIGHT BIBLE SCHOOL

Comics have been put on notice by Matt Dwyer: Don't bring those weak jokes about airline food to *his* stage."

That's the opening line of another Allan Johnson piece[11] in the *Tribune*, this time from February 26, 1999. In it, Dwyer declares, "I will not let up anything that seems standup-y and has that patter and that delivery." And in 2021, the article made Dwyer cringe. Except it's not his own words that bothered him.

"Okay, 'put on notice' is a strong term," he said. "That implies that I have some kind of power I clearly didn't have. That's bad writing is what that is."

But what about the rest of it? "Yeah. I said *that*," Dwyer admitted. "I think I was trying to say, 'We're trying to do something different, and we're trying not to do typical stand-up,' which is what a lot of people were talking about in those days. The way that guy words it makes it sound like I should be wearing a beret."

There is not much you could call "typical" about Matt Dwyer. In fact, of all the comics to frequent the Red Lion open mic, with the possible exception of Dwayne Kennedy (who we'll discuss in detail in a few chapters), Dwyer might have had the most impressive comedy pedigree of them all. He grew up the youngest of five boys in the working-class Northwest suburb of Streamwood, and he started taking improv classes at Second City when he was only fifteen.

Once he got his driver's license, Dwyer went to the improv theater so often that the staff started letting him in free. "I started giving them rides

Matt Dwyer. *The Second City*.

home and hanging out with them at diners afterwards," Dwyer said. "So I was this young kid, and I was hanging out at parties. And they would let me drink and do drugs. They didn't treat me like a kid."

This would lead to a fifteen-year run of Dwyer being around some of the most famous and celebrated sketch and improv talent of all time. He was there the night Tracey Ullman hired Dan Castellaneta to be on her show, which led to him voicing Homer Simpson. Dwyer would regularly hang out at Chris Farley's Old Town apartment, often bringing him acid. And if you ask Dwyer about Second City alumni like Bob Odenkirk, Amy Sedaris, Stephen Colbert, Rachel Dratch, Adam McKay or Tina Fey, he'll have plenty of stories because he knew, or was at least around, all of them at Second City. Hell, he and McKay have worked together on projects as recently as 2022.

Oh, and I almost forgot: Dwyer was also a performer. In his twenties, Dwyer joined Second City's Touring Company. And things went well enough for Dwyer that he was flown to New York to audition for *Saturday Night Live*. It was the same season, by the way, that David Koechner, Jim Breuer, Will Ferrell, Darrell Hammond, Cheri Oteri and Nancy Walls were hired by the show. And it was actually the same day of auditions (as retold in the 2017 Hulu documentary *Too Funny to Fail*) where improviser Bill Chott did his impression of a defecating Jackie Gleason that got him rejected by *SNL* but then immediately hired by Robert Smigel to be on the cast of *The Dana Carvey Show*. Dwyer was present for all of it.

After his brush with *SNL*, Dwyer made it to the Second City e.t.c. stage in 1997. There's even a picture of him in Sheldon Patinkin's *Second City* book[12] in that e.t.c. cast alongside future *SNL* cast members Jerry Minor and Horatio Sanz and Chicago comedy legend Mick Napier. The book's accompanying CD set of the theater's all-time greatest hits features a sketch with Dwyer entitled "Dirty Doctor." So Dwyer's Second City ties run pretty deep.

But then Second City fired him in 1998. "They didn't renew my contract," Dwyer said. "Which is a nice way of saying they fired me." Dwyer's life was kind of spiraling at the time. His girlfriend kicked him out a month later, and he wound up sleeping on a couch in a seedy basement apartment. "I was so miserable," Dwyer said. "But I was like, 'All right, I'll focus on stand-up.'"

Second City e.t.c. cast. *Top row*: Rich Talarico, Jerry Minor, Rachel Hamilton, Aaron Carney, Rebecca Sohn, Jeff Richardson and Mick Napier. *Bottom row*: Horatio Sanz, Laura Kraft and Matt Dwyer. *The Second City*.

Once he started in the stand-up scene, Dwyer quickly realized that there weren't enough opportunities to perform in front of real audiences. Luckily, he had that long relationship with Second City, and he asked if he could use its upstairs space at Donny's Skybox Theater to put on a show.

The Midnight Bible School debuted on February 19, 1999—just days before Dwyer officially put his fellow comedians on notice in the *Tribune*— and as advertised, the show was held at midnight for the first few weeks. "Then I was like, 'This is a fucking terrible idea,'" Dwyer said.

"Dwyer's been given Donny's Skybox for Saturday nights," Geary remembered. "He's got access to some really good improv people like Jerry Minor and Fred Armisen and Stephnie Weir. They're all Second City people who were doing Mainstage and e.t.c. But what the lucky bastards got is, they could literally do their show, run upstairs, do a set, run back down. Because it's all on-site."

"Because there was such a separation between stand-up and improv," Dwyer said, "I wanted to bring those worlds together. Stand-ups would do character pieces, improv people would try stand-up and people would do sketches. It was really exciting," Dwyer said.

Or as Geary put it, "So Dwyer marries this great improv talent and great stand-up talent into a show that, out of the gate, is the biggest pile of shit you've ever seen."

On April 4, 1999, Allan Johnson of the *Tribune* wrote an article[13] titled "Where's the Punchline?" where he skewered alt comedy as a genre that "isn't even funny." And what Johnson seemed to have especially disliked was the Midnight Bible School, with its anti-club-comedy attitude.

But if the show did start as the Biggest Pile of Shit You've Ever Seen, it certainly didn't stay that way for long. Eventually, the Midnight Bible School became the hottest alt room in the city. And its meteoric rise spawned a number of theories as to how it happened.

Geary seems to think that the show turned around as a result of Second City's intervention after the bad review in the *Tribune*. Dwyer, however, doesn't seem to remember much about that review and says

JESUS HATES YOU!!!

alternative comedy

THE SHOW....

THE MIDNIGHT BIBLE SCHOOL

Fridays at midnight
$5.00
DONNY'S SKYBOX STUDIO THEATER
312-337-3992
1608 N. WELLS... 4th floor
"THIS SHOW GOES TOO FAR..."THE CHICAGO TRIBUNE

Midnight Bible School flier. *Matt Dwyer.*

Second City didn't intervene at all. "It's probably better that I didn't go up there a lot," was how Second City producer Kelly Leonard put it. But no press is bad press, and some people actually saw that article as a good thing. "That made an impression upon me," comedian and Lincoln Lodge co-creator Tom Lawler said. "I'd heard about these kinds of shows on the coasts. That was making me think that there's something starting to develop in Chicago for stand-up."

I think my favorite of the Bible School success theories comes from comedian "Chet Lactacious," who told me, "I'm not being egotistical when I say this, but I am definitely 100% one of the reasons the Bible School took off and everything like that." And then he proceeded to tell me a seemingly made-up-on-the-spot story about sending the *Tribune* a press release promising "complimentary [Chet Lactacious] Action Sticks" at the next show. I decided to look into his story, despite not believing it, and sure enough, it was right there in the paper in October 1999.

"Come to comic [Chet Lactacious's] performance and get a complimentary pair of '[Chet Lactacious] Action Sticks,'" it read. "They're available only Saturday at the alternative-comedy extravaganza Midnight Bible School, which is now on Saturdays at 10 pm."[14]

"[Lactacious] is high," Dwyer said.

Another theory of why the Bible School got popular is because of a particularly good review in the *Chicago Reader*. "Early on, the show wasn't that good, and then it got a Critic's Choice in the *Reader*," comedian Adam Kroshus told me. "And then it just took off. That show was sold out for several years, really."

When I found the *Chicago Reader* blurb[15] from January 6, 2000, it doesn't seem like that spectacular of a review. It quotes Dwyer saying, "I don't know what you're going to see tonight…it could be lame bullshit. But I've got your money so I don't care." So if this review is the reason the Bible School took off, it might have something to do with the part where one of the female performers "stripped off her shirt, bared her breasts, and launched into a wonderfully bittersweet story about stalking her first love," before adding, "That's something you don't see every night at your typical comedy club."

Oddly enough, another reason the Midnight Bible School took off might have to do with Lewis Black and the Y2K panic. On December 31, 1999, for the low price of seventy-five dollars per ticket, any drinking-age comedy fan in Chicago could have braved the elements, as well as the infamous millennium computer bug, and headed out to see comedian Lewis Black at Zanies. But almost no one did.

"It was empty because of Y2K," John Roy remembered. "[Lewis Black was] in a tux. He's miserable. And I'm the opener. And the middle was Skip Griparis. He was a guitar act. And he goes up to Lewis before the show and goes, 'Lewis, when we're done doing the countdown, can I do a singalong?' And Lewis Black goes, 'You can do whatever the *fuck* you want.'"

On New Year's Day, Black was apparently still looking to do a show somewhere. And Second City happens to be about 350 feet away from Zanies on Wells Street. "[Comedian] Mike Lukas called me and was like, 'Lewis wants to do your show,'" Dwyer said. "And I was like, 'I don't have one scheduled, but I could try to pull it together.' And word got out, and it was just fucking jam-packed. Lewis said to me, 'I was really worried because this weekend was terrible. This was a real blast.'" And then Dwyer added, "That guy can drink a lot of vodka."

"[Midnight Bible School] suffered up until the Lewis Black thing," Dwyer said, in a pretty good summation of all the various theories. "We would do okay, but we were also at midnight at first. Once we switched to ten, it became more accessible. And between Lewis Black and Critic's Choice, we were sold out for, like, forty shows. It was crazy. Packed, turning people away. After that, people would be in town and want to do the show. Sarah Silverman did it. Jeff Garlin did it a bunch."

"That's where I met Rachel Dratch and Tina Fey and Jordan Peele," Kroshus added. "They all introduced themselves to *me*! They were like, 'You're funny.' I'm like, 'Well, thanks! I appreciate that.'"

By January 28, 2000, the *Daily Herald*[16] was calling the Midnight Bible School "a late night phenomenon." No mention, however, of the Action Sticks.

Since the show was at Second City, it might make sense to take a brief detour to discuss the famous improv theater itself. It was, after all, the main reason Chicago had become a destination city for comedy in the first place. Even though the only thing most tourists or suburbanites or even the aspiring funny people knew back in the late '90s was that Second City had been an institution in Chicago for decades, that it had been a feeding system for *Saturday Night Live* and that the list of alumni included Chris Farley, who had just passed away in December 1997. But much like the stand-up scene in Chicago, the world of '90s improv was undergoing some big artistic changes of its own.

Chapter 6

PIÑATA FULL OF BEES

To put it bluntly, by the late '80s, Second City had become pretty stale. Even the *Second City* book the theater sold to tourists in the gift shop has admitted that its formula had become predictable. Second City was artistically dead and essentially just a tourist trap at that point. Not that the tourists seemed to mind. "Your aunt was just as likely to say, 'Second City—we went with my office,'" comedian John Roy said. "It was just ingrained into Chicago, like hot dogs with no ketchup."

"We were sold out every single night, months in advance," longtime Second City producer Kelly Leonard told me. "There was not necessarily an impetus to be different."

Luckily for everyone besides the tourists and your aunt, Second City and the improv community at large were going through an artistic transformation of their own. Long-form improvisation and the structure known as "The Harold" were inspiring performers to shake things up and to push some artistic boundaries. Once again, comedian Matt Dwyer saw it all happen in real time.

"There were people who were breaking out of the mold," Dwyer said.

There was Jazz Freddy, which was David Koechner, Brian Stack, Kevin Dorff and Rachel Dratch. That was a big long-form improvisational show that really fucked things up. And then there was The Armando Diaz Experience, Theatrical Movement and Hootenanny, which was another that broke the mold. Armando, for the longest time, would do

Piñata Full of Bees cast: Scott Adsit, Jon Glaser, Adam McKay, Jenna Jolovitz and Rachel Dratch, 1995. *The Second City.*

monologues, and people would improvise around them, which later became ASSSSCAT *at* [Upright Citizens Brigade Theatre]. *There was also the Family, which was a Harold team at* [ImprovOlympic] *which also spun out to* [the hugely influential Upright Citizens Brigade team]. *So a lot of those people ended up at Second City. And that sort of influence is why, specifically, Adam McKay started people wanting to fuck with the form of what was happening at Second City, because it was very stale.*

"Second City was not interrogating improvisation," Leonard said. "It just did what it did and stayed there. And there was really seminal work being done outside these walls. What was happening all over the city of Chicago was really inventive, creative work, whether it was at ImprovOlympic or the Annoyance [Theatre] and there was a group of sort of young artists that I fell in with—people like Adam McKay [and] Matt Dwyer....We liked punk music, and we were reading Noam Chomsky...and we liked going and seeing that alternative stuff....We all wanted to do something big and different....And then when I got the producing gig, I started hiring all my friends and people who I thought were doing cutting-edge art."

"I met McKay when I was in the Touring Company and Second City hired him," Dwyer said. "And I remember the first time he did a rehearsal with us, and we had to improvise together, and I was like, 'I'm fucked.' It was like how the hair metals probably felt when Nirvana showed up. He changed the entire chemistry of Second City."

The show that made the most artistic impact, at least on the stand-ups in the scene, was *Piñata Full of Bees* from 1995, which was produced by Leonard and directed by Tom Gianas. It also starred a hybrid team of Scott Allman, Scott Adsit and Jenna Jolovitz, all of whom had been Second City trained, along with McKay, Rachel Dratch and Jon Glaser, who had been ImprovOlympic/long-form trained. And that combination of "craft and mess," as Leonard put it, was said to have changed the way Second City did everything going forward.

"It was phenomenal," comedian Rob Paravonian said of *Piñata Full of Bees*. "I liked the way they transitioned from scene to scene without blackouts. It wasn't like, 'Lights up, we're doing the scene. Lights down. Now lights up, we're doing another scene.' They kind of flowed together. The back wall was open, and all the costumes were kind of up on the back wall. So they'd just grab shit and start a new scene. Instead of two acts, it was one seventy-minute rollercoaster ride. The crowd would get so riled up. They'd almost want to just carry the cast off the stage. It was a really amazing show."

"Tony Adler, who reviewed for the *Reader*, had asked if he could come be a fly on the wall," Leonard said. "And after the show, he's like, 'That's the most brilliant thing I've ever seen at Second City, Kelly. Are you worried for your job?'"

"*Piñata Full of Bees* was the *Sgt. Pepper's*," Dwyer said. "Where everyone is like, 'They fucking did it.' And then after that, it was *Magical Mystery Tour* and *Revolver*. Then it went back to being Hanson."

After the success of *Piñata Full of Bees*, McKay and Gianas were immediately hired by *Saturday Night Live*. So the next big, influential show, or the *Magical Mystery Tour* in this comedy equation, was *Paradigm Lost*. It starred Adsit, Dratch and Jolovitz from the *Piñata Full of Bees* cast, as well as Tina Fey, Kevin Dorff and Jim Zulevic. And it was directed by Mick Napier, who had founded the Annoyance Theatre, which was the more absurdist cousin to Second City and ImprovOlympic.

Napier also seems to have had a massive impact on the improvisers turned stand-ups of the era. "Mick Napier is a huge influence. Oh my God," comedian Chet Lactacious exclaimed. "He was a goddamn fucking comedy genius. I don't know if you had the benefit of seeing the Annoyance Theatre in the '90s, but it was amazing. It was incredible, and they were doing very edgy, groundbreaking stuff. That was my inspiration."

"I know him as a chain-smoking, vulgar, bisexual madman with an incredible heart of gold," Leonard said. "And he's one of the best teachers and revue directors that I've ever worked with."

"When I took the classes at Annoyance," T.J. Miller said, "and when I finally got to [study under] Mick Napier, that's how I learned to improvise. When you were in his class, he was collaborating with you to help you get better. The people in Second City classes weren't that good, and they didn't get much better. The people in the Annoyance classes weren't that great [either]. But they got *good*."

"He was able to do a show that both young people and a traditional Second City audience could come in and appreciate," Leonard said. "We wouldn't have gotten to *Paradigm* if we hadn't done *Piñata*. But we also couldn't survive on *Piñata* shows. We needed to rediscover what a contemporary Second City would look like with craft....It wasn't gonna work if it was punk rock all the time."

"People rave about [legendary Second City guru and ImprovOlympic cofounder] Del Close," Dwyer said. "I would put Mick above Del, and I will get in trouble for that but I don't care." And that's coming from someone who shot a TV pilot with Close and Amy Poehler called *RVTV* in the mid-'90s.

Leonard agrees. "I was here when Del directed his last show," he said. "And it was *terrible*. I think Del had a spotty record as a Second City director. So I'd put Mick above Del....What I appreciate mostly about Mick is that he wasn't trying to direct Annoyance at Second City. He directed Annoyance at Annoyance. He tried to direct the best Second City show he could do. And those early shows—*Citizen Gates* and *Paradigm Lost*—were amazing. It was beautiful, beautiful work."

"I took all the improv lessons," Roy said. "I finished Second City Conservatory. I took ImprovOlympic right up until I couldn't take any more classes because I had to be on the road. And I took all of Annoyance. I went hard in improv. We all did. Well not all of us, but a lot of us did. There were people like Greg Mills...who did both. And so you could see the value of it. And we were at a time when *Piñata Full of Bees* and *Paradigm Lost* were like, these big groundbreaking things. Second City was like, groundbreaking again. And edgy. Because Mick Napier was there. I mean, all of this means nothing now."

Perhaps not. But with all the intermingling of stand-ups and improvisers within the city in the late '90s and early 2000s, it's impossible that these types of attitudes and philosophies didn't intermingle as well. Especially since the stars of *Piñata Full of Bees* and *Paradigm Lost* all did Midnight Bible School around the same time. And apparently, in the case of Tina Fey, fairly regularly.

In the summer of 2000, Matt Dwyer moved to New York, and the Midnight Bible School was effectively no more. But there are two subjects that comics from this era inevitably bring up whenever they talk about their time at Midnight Bible School. The first is naming a future *SNL* cast member with whom they shared a bill. And the second thing, which occurs with just as much reverence, is the retelling of something specifically outrageous they saw done on stage by either Chet Lactacious or Bill O'Donnell.

I think by now you're ready for some specifics about the envelope-pushing that occurred. But consider yourself warned.

Chapter 7

ANTI-COMEDY

O n December 22, 1999, the Andy Kaufman biopic *Man on the Moon* was released in theaters across the United States. It starred Jim Carrey as Kaufman. And if it didn't directly influence the comics in the Chicago scene, it at least put the life and career of the boundary-pushing comedian back into their consciousness.

"Those of us who were drawn to Kaufman, like [Chet Lactacious] and I, were definitely exploring the boundaries in the shadow of that movie being out," Bill O'Donnell told me. "Kaufman was getting his second act during that time, and we were gobbling up everything we could about him."

The movie might have been one of the rare chances at the time for comics in Chicago to see actual alternative comedy in action. "Everybody was trying to figure out what alternative comedy was," comedian John Roy said. "Because we'd read about it in *Rolling Stone* in the Hot Issue. They name-dropped [the Los Angeles nightclub] Largo and told us all that Patton Oswalt and Janeane Garofalo were doing these things. And you could see the Janeane special on HBO if you had recorded it. Because you can't get video off the Internet at this point. Patton had a half hour on Comedy Central. But you're trying to reverse engineer this idea of alternative comedy from a couple articles in *Rolling Stone* and one special. So you don't really know what it is. But you subsequently get a lot of real creativity because people start going, 'Well, I gotta be weird. But I don't know what that is. So I'm just gonna try to be weird.'"

"I think as a whole, Chicago comedy was trying to find its identity," comedian Monte said, "and trying to become something. And there were some guys that were taking it to the next level, and they were doing things other people didn't do. There was one time we were at a show, and Bill O'Donnell went up on stage with a bucket and he just started gagging himself. Just to make himself throw up on stage. There was a part of me that was like, 'What am I watching right now?' And there was a part of me that was like, 'This guy's a genius!'"

In *Man on the Moon*, Danny DeVito's George Shapiro character tells Carrey's Andy Kaufman, "You're insane, but you might also be brilliant." So the influence of the movie, and the renewed interest in Kaufman's career, might have given people the vocabulary to process and evaluate the weird-as-fuck comedy they were seeing, however reverse-engineered it might have been. It also gave those people the belief that something super weird must also involve comedic brilliance. And the two comedians in Chicago from that time who evoked the greatest sense of antagonistic danger, of fearless boundary pushing and possibly even comedic genius, were Chet Lactacious and Bill O'Donnell.

"Chet Lactacious," you might have noticed, is an obviously fake name, in the place of another obviously fake name. But this very real guy with a very fake name specifically asked me not to mention his real name, or his former stage name, in the book, and I agreed to his terms. "Dude, we're living in cancel culture," he told me in 2021. "I'm not a comedian anymore. I have a nice little life. I don't want to lose my job over something I did over twenty years ago."

The most well-known of all the Lactacious bits, at least among the comics in the scene, is a performance piece he refers to as "Super Fans." "In all the times I did it, it always worked," Lactacious insisted, knowing full well how the joke can come across on paper. "There was never anything negative to come out of it, and, if anything, nothing but positivity….It's just the times that we live in. I'd be an idiot if I wasn't defensive."

The bit itself was as simple as it was shocking. Lactacious got the idea from watching MTV's hit show *Total Request Live* (or *TRL*), where the live crowd that gathered outside the Times Square studio often held up signs in praise of whichever boy band or pop star was being featured on that day's show. So when Lactacious did the "Super Fans" bit at places like Midnight Bible School, he told the audience that it was his birthday and then asked them for a favor. When they inevitably agreed, he would pass out poster boards that said things like, "We Love You," "Marry Me" and "You're the Best," just like the ones held up by the Times Square teens on *TRL*.

"So the audience has the signs," Lactacious explained. "The next part, I'm like, 'I'm gonna go backstage. The host is gonna come back out and reintroduce me. And just go ape shit. Pretend like you love me. Go crazy. And then I promise I'll tell some really funny jokes.' So then I would go backstage. The emcee would come back on stage. He'd say, 'All right folks, this is the guy you've been waiting for all night. You know him. You love him. Welcome to the stage, So-and-So.'"

And with the crowd going wild, Lactacious would reemerge wearing a full Ku Klux Klan costume.

"You could hear the jaws hitting the floor," Lactacious said of the initial reaction to the sight gag. And the crowd, who had been enthusiastic about participating in a playful birthday favor, immediately had this mortifying realization that they were standing and *cheering* for one of the worst things imaginable. Then there's a tug of war in their minds between knowing it's totally wrong but also acknowledging and, dare I say, appreciating how good someone just got them.

"It's a good prank," comedian CJ Sullivan said. "Then he starts doing his set, and you're like, 'Okay, take the outfit off. Now we're getting uncomfortable.'"

When I saw "Super Fans" performed live in 2006 or 2007, there were almost waves or layers of reactions coming from the crowd, within seconds of his outfit being revealed, almost like the audience was going through all the stages of grief in fast forward. The denial, anger and bargaining happened within the first few seconds of his reemergence. And then one of the rarest reactions in comedy occurred, when the audience was actually mad at *themselves* for laughing (Stage 4: Depression).

When one comic discussed the bit in 2021, they started off remembering it in a negative light and then paused to reflect for a second before admitting, "The Ku Klux Klan thing's pretty funny. He was pretty cringeworthy. But he took risks." In other words, you definitely don't have to love it. But you almost have to respect it (Stage 5: Acceptance).

"Oh, dude. He would walk the *line*," comedian Darren Bodeker said of Lactacious. "That was comedy. That's why these times are so dangerous for comedy. Because just being a comedian, you have to go across that line into the devil's territory. And the devil ain't got no ideology but the devil, bro."

"You have to be shocking to pull it off," comedian David Angelo said. "And that's what it takes."

Nonetheless, in 2021 Lactacious was still concerned with how you, the reader, might react to the bit. "You just have to hear 'a white man in a Ku Klux Klan outfit' and, right away, people are gonna condemn me," he said, before clarifying further. "It was never mean-spirited. There was never any agenda behind it. Twenty-plus years ago, I did not think these bits all the way through. Even though I honestly don't regret 'Super Fans.' It's just that we live in a time where someone reads that and, right away, they don't care. They just want to make the person pay for this perceived wrong that they committed."

The first time Lactacious did the bit, there was no Klan costume to speak of—or anything to speak of, really. In the first draft, Lactacious reemerged from the back completely naked, with his hands covering his genitals. But the logistics of doing a set, and retrieving the poster boards afterward without the use of his hands, were a little too complicated. So Lactacious needed a different method of shocking the audience when he was reintroduced.

"Let me explain how I got the Klan outfit," Lactacious said, which is never how you want someone to start a sentence. "There's a celebrated theater in Chicago, and there was a time when I had access to their prop closet. And so I borrowed their Ku Klux Klan outfit....But the thing is, I don't know what the statute of limitations is on borrowing a Ku Klux Klan outfit from a celebrated theater in Chicago."

To be clear, Lactacious would love for me to stress that (1) it's not a *real* Klan outfit, and (2) for all he knows, the celebrated theater company in Chicago has several of these costumes and doesn't miss the one he borrowed. He also admitted that (3) his provocative style of comedy might not have been for everyone. Because believe it or not, Lactacious would take things a little too far—both on stage and off. And sometimes the exact wrong person, at the exact wrong time, was the one being provoked.

"[Chet Lactacious's] sister was one of my students when I was teaching improv at Lincoln Park High School," Monte said. "She knew my real last name. And she did not know that, back then, I would keep it hidden."

"I know what his last name is, but I'm not gonna say it," comedian Adam Kroshus told me. "I'm a friend."

Chet Lactacious was also a friend of Monte's. Except, to Lactacious, revealing private information about someone that he knew would infuriate them, no matter who it was, proved too tempting to pass up. "If I knew what to do to piss somebody off, there's a good chance I would do it," Lactacious admitted. "I love Monte. I think he's very talented. But I do have an issue with comedians who can't take jokes. And I'm not saying that Monte is one of those comedians. But he was so protective of his brand that he wanted to be known as just 'Monte,' and I knew this."

The irony of the fact that Chet Lactacious, which isn't his real name, was also using an invented stage name at the time wasn't lost on Kyle Kinane.

And when I asked if he remembered an incident between Lactacious and Monte, he said, "Yeah, I remember. Two guys with unspoken last names getting upset about showbiz-deadnaming each other."

"So, one night, I'm hanging out," Monte said, "I was dating this girl… and we were driving. We were just a few blocks from Coyle's Tippling House [a bar and performance venue in Lake View]. It was late at night. And I get a phone call on my cellphone. So I look at it, I don't recognize the number."

"It was after the show," Lactacious said. "We were all hanging out. I called him up and I just keep repeating his last name over and over again. Like, 'I'm gonna get ya. I know your last name.' And I don't know if he wants me to say his last name now, so I'm not saying it."

For the record, Monte absolutely does *not* want his last name revealed, so I will also not be sharing it. You'll understand my reasoning shortly. "I pick up the phone," Monte said, "and someone goes, 'Is this Monte?' And I go, 'Yeah.' And he goes, 'We know your last name, and you know what? I'm gonna kill you. Your ass is grass.' And he says my last name and hangs up on me. And I'm like, 'What the fuck?'"

"I'm pretty sure I didn't say I was gonna kill him," Lactacious objected. "But in my mind, I was trying to be some 1930s gangster. Because I'm kind of talking in that voice."

"My girl goes, 'What just happened?'" Monte said. "I go, 'I just got this crazy phone call from someone trying to kill me.' And here's the thing, a little bit of backstory: In high school, someone had threatened to kill me. And it was a serious thing. And they actually brought a shotgun to school. So threatening to kill me was something I did not take lightly. And so when this happened, I completely panicked. And I called that number back. The guy answered and goes, 'Monte?' And it was [comedian] Tommy Mayo. And I'm like, 'Tommy?' and he goes, 'Yeah. What's up?' I go, 'Who just called me?' He goes, 'That was [Chet Lactacious].' I go, 'Where are you?' He goes, 'Coyle's Tippling House.'"

"[Lactacious] used my cellphone," comedian Emily Dorezas said. "I was so shocked [he called back that] I handed my phone to Mayo. Because at the time, no one knew Monte's last name. So for [Lactacious] to call him and say that so aggressively, it was like saying Voldemort three times. I was stunned."

"I do not recall that, sir," Tommy Mayo laughed. "My twenties: there's probably a lot of shit that went down, I just don't remember most of it." And in case you were wondering, no, "Tommy Mayo" is not *his* real name either.

"I drove there like a maniac," Monte said. "I pulled up right in front. I left the car running. And I said, 'I'll be back in less than five minutes. Don't touch anything.' And I went inside."

"We're all hanging out drinking," Lactacious said. "And in walks Monte, and everyone's like, 'Hey Monte.' And he just keeps walking, making a beeline for me. And he sits down next to me. And I'm like, 'How's it going?' Not thinking anything of it."

"[Lactacious was] laughing," Dorezas said. "Then I was like, 'Oh, this is gonna go bad.'"

"I go, '[Lactacious], did you just prank me?'" Monte recalled. "And he goes, 'No, I didn't.' I go, 'Fucking liar,' and I grab him by the face and then I...*oh boy*."

Monte paused like he didn't want to complete the sentence before appearing to will himself through it anyway. "And then I...*yeah*, I feel real bad about this," he continued before finally forcing it all out in one burst. "And then I smashed his head into the back of the thing and then I stuck my thumb in his eye."

"I don't know if you've ever had anybody dig their thumb into your eye socket, but it's not pleasant," Lactacious assured me. "It's not comfortable and everything like that."

"I was *screaming*," Dorezas recalled. "And Monte and I made eye contact. And then he stopped because I think he could see true terror."

"Emily had this weird power over Monte," Lactacious remembered. "He really respected her and wanted her to think well of him. It was amazing."

"I think Monte had seen some shit [in his life]. And I really haven't," Dorezas said. "So I think Monte could see, 'A real person is terrified right now.' I don't know how that happened. Maybe I just reminded him of his mom. I have no idea."

"It was fucked up," Monte admitted. "I shouldn't have done that. I'm glad that [Lactacious] has forgiven me."

"The fact that he didn't gouge my eyes out, I automatically forgave him," Lactacious said. "But I have to take responsibility. If I didn't apologize that night, I definitely apologized as soon as it dawned on me that I almost lost an eye over something incredibly stupid. But I knew he had a temper. And if I knew what buttons to push, I would push them. Because to me, it was funny to see people get all worked up."

"I like [Chet Lactacious]," Kinane said, "But Andy Kaufman had a lot more success than you, and people wanted to punch him in the face all the time.'"

"In Monte's defense," comedian Shawn Cole said, "he probably tried to murder everyone at least one time."

"I'd never been in a fight," Lactacious said. "One time I insulted somebody in the audience and they threw a beer bottle at me, but he didn't hit me though. Up until that point, I had suffered no consequences."

"This is the problem with me," Monte explained, in stark biographical contrast to Lactacious. "When I came into stand-up, I came from the West Side of Chicago. I was a drug dealer. A lot of my friends were gang members. And I would sometimes fight with some of the gangs. And when I stepped into a comedy world, people were clever and witty and sarcastic. I didn't have that. I just had this personality, and I was gruff. That's where my comedy came from. But I was still this neighborhood guy. And growing up, I had been in fights with almost everybody I was friends with. So I didn't understand that you shouldn't put your hands on people. Ignorance isn't a good excuse. But I was ignorant. And I put my hands on a few people. And I think it really hurt—well, I don't think, I *know* it really hurt my [comedy] career. I choked a few people at ImprovOlympic. I literally put my hand on some people's throats. At parties, in front of people, not thinking about it. Like, that shit will fuck you up. That'll take you out of the game really quick."

It's hard to know exactly how much his violent, street-tough reputation hurt Monte's career. But I can say that I was warned very early on that if I ever learned Monte's last name, I should definitely never say it out loud. Even though whoever told me that probably also whispered it to me in the very next breath.

There is a happy ending of sorts for Monte. "The best thing that ever happened to him was Anne, his wife," Dorezas said. "He has become totally even-Steven now. But man, he was very volatile."

Another person who seems to have mellowed with time is Bill O'Donnell, the second half of our dynamic duo of anti-comedy. "O'Donnell was certainly a fucking lunatic," Kroshus told me. "The man has four children now. Regularly goes to Catholic church. *Regularly* goes. I think that he goes to services in the week."

"The great thing about [Lactacious is]," Monte said, trying to differentiate between the two antiheroes, "he would say something that would almost turn the crowd. Then he'd win them right back. He was good with that. But Bill O'Donnell wasn't really good at winning the crowd over too much. And if he lost the crowd, Bill definitely was not getting the crowd back. It was over."

"O'Donnell was great," Lactacious said. "He didn't give a shit, and he was just there on stage to say the most outrageous things you could imagine. And we were all along for the ride. It was wonderful."

With no YouTube or Instagram around to capture and share most of these moments, O'Donnell was kind of a mythical figure by the time I entered the scene in 2004. There were tall tales of him having sex with his wife on stage through a sheet. Or of him changing her soiled diaper. There were stories of semi-nudity and other various genital-based performances. But out of all the wild and boundary-obliterating shit he allegedly did in the name of comedy, the thing that seems to have retained the most infamy among the other comics is that Bill O'Donnell would intentionally make himself vomit on stage.

As I waited to interview O'Donnell in 2021, I found myself a little nervous. I had no idea what to expect. Surprisingly, he was one of the most mild-mannered, unassuming comedians I've ever met, especially considering his reputation as a boundary-smashing performance artist. He's not GG Allin. He's just a dude.

"The appeal with Bill O'Donnell is that he's so normal looking," producer Tom Lawler said. "And he's got that shit-eating smile when he's doing it. It's this cognitive dissonance between how outrageous and profane his material is and what he looks like and the way he's delivering it."

"I always wanted to be just like Jerry Seinfeld," O'Donnell said. "But once I got on stage, I could not do it. Whatever I might have planned—the lights would hit and it would go in a whole other direction."

As a result, O'Donnell wound up completely rejecting traditional comedy. "The guys that did well, it's just not my type of act," he told me. "It's all subjective. They would say the same about me, I'm sure. But John Roy was starting to do really well right about that time….And you'd see him every night doing the same act. And I get that's what it is, but there was a handful of us that were always trying to do a different act every night."

"I thought Bill O'Donnell was a clown back then, to be honest," Roy said. "I appreciated the transgression, but anyone can shock me. Be funny. But there were guys that worshipped him. And I'm like, 'Well, all right. If that's what you want…Enjoy.'"

Chapter 8

THE END OF THE RED LION

Y2K didn't wreak havoc on society the way the American public had been warned it might. But New Year's Eve 1999 did begin two seismic shifts in the alt comedy scene in Chicago. First, Lewis Black's poorly attended show at Zanies may have given the necessary bump to the Midnight Bible School to set off its run of sold-out shows. And secondly, a New Year's party held at the home of Chet Lactacious created an opportunity for an open mic comic named Tom Lawler to tell Red Lion producer Mark Geary about a back room he found at the Lincoln Restaurant on the corner of Lincoln Avenue, Damen Avenue and Irving Park Road, as well as his idea for a potential show there.

"He said, 'If you can build the show, I can promote the show, and it'll win,'" Geary said. "At that point, I realized it would be big. And I said, 'All right, but I have to get rid of the open mic first.'"

That seems easier said than done, since handing off the open mic would take Geary months to complete. On August 17, 2000, Geary put together a special "Hall of Fame" night at the Red Lion, perhaps as a coda of sorts for his own time there. "I was an IT nerd, so I had an access database," Geary said. "I logged every single name of everybody who went up, how many minutes they did, and after about a year and a half, I went through the database and said, 'Who's done the most sets? That's our Hall of Fame.'"

Comics have shown me programs they saved from the event, which read "Legends of Red Lion Comedy" and featured the insanely young and mostly amateurish headshots of all the regulars. And on the back, it featured a large picture of Bill O'Donnell, all by himself, with the inscription, "We Salute your 50th Appearance and 400 stage minutes."

I think my favorite story to come out of the Hall of Fame night is one that no access database could have predicted. "That was the only week the Red Lion wasn't an open mic," Geary said. "There were twenty people booked. I told the comedians, 'All we have to do is get one person each here, one neutral person who has never seen our act, and we've got a great crowd to really have a nice celebration.' So guess how many comedians actually got someone to come. *None.* But someone who did arrive that week was Pat Brice."

Brice would go on to become one of the most beloved comedians in the scene's history. "He's got all his mates with him," Geary said. "Prepared to do his first ever comedy set. And I go to him, 'You can't go up tonight.' And he's like, 'But I've been working up to this for three weeks, and I've got all my mates here, and they just want to see me do five minutes,' and I'm like, 'Nope. Not fucking happening. Sling your hook.' Because we were doing that bullshit Hall of Fame. Pat probably had fifty people waiting downstairs. He told me about that five or six years later. 'Yeah, Geary. You fucked me doing my first ever set.'"

"He brought all these people," comedian and Brice's close friend CJ Sullivan said. "And then Kroshus got heckled by Brice's buddies, and he faked a heart attack. And he was on the floor for, like, five minutes doing a seizure. Because it was such a devastating blow of a roast to [Kroshus]. And Brice is going, 'What the fuck am I doing with my life? This is what I want to be a part of?'"

With the Lincoln Lodge beginning in 2000, Geary decided to move on from the open mic. And he decided to hand off the Red Lion to the King of the Red Lion himself. "I was like, 'Hey, so you gonna let me have the Red Lion?'" O'Donnell remembered. "And he was reluctant. And I was like, 'I'll do right by it. I'll do a good job.' And I ran it into the ground."

"Within, like, four weeks he'd killed it," Geary confirmed. "But at that point I didn't really care."

"God bless Bill O'Donnell, but giving him the keys to your car is not something I would want to do in those days," Midnight Bible School's Matt Dwyer said.

"He was like the Joker," Sullivan said. "He liked to see the world burn."

In the Chicago Bar Project review of the Red Lion, the blogger was decidedly *not* impressed with the bar's comedy night. "It was in the beer garden one Thursday night that I experienced some of the worst comedy I have ever heard," the blogger wrote. "I wish I could have that part of my life back, as I would have gladly paid a cover to *not* have heard these 'comedians.'

What I heard was not even remotely funny, but instead was full of swearing to get cheap laughs. In addition, the comedians were encouraged by an audience that seemed to be comprised only of other comedians."

This basically sounds like a description of an open mic, which would make sense, since that's what it was. But it's especially funny to me because what the joyless writer could have been hearing was a set by a brilliant comic like Dwayne Kennedy or Kyle Kinane or the John Roy set that won *Star Search* or even the first jokes told in the city by future movie star Kumail Nanjiani. But sure, I get his point.

"The owner of the Red Lion, Colin, told me mid-show he'd had enough," O'Donnell said of the show's ending. "So we went into funeral mode right then and there. That night we had turned the stage around to face the outdoor deck, through the windows, trying to entertain the people outside. Got a bunch of complaints. One of many disasters. In this case, the last one. And I felt horrible."

"They had a beautiful back porch for people who did not want to see an awful open microphone," Sullivan said. "Of course, that's gonna cause a conflict. Someone who's trying to enjoy their Thursday night, and we are twenty-five and hate ourselves. The bartender hated O'Donnell and all the comics. Because who's gonna like open mic comics at their bar on a Thursday night? They're not gonna tip. They're gonna be terrible. They're gonna bum out normal people who are out for the night with jobs and attractiveness."

I've seen grainy footage of the last night of the Red Lion open mic, and I immediately recognized the insanely young and mostly amateurish faces of comedians like T.J. Miller, Pat Brice, Nate Craig and CJ Sullivan, both in the crowd and on stage.

"We didn't know when we showed up it'd be the last show," O'Donnell told the mostly comedian audience. "But over the course of the evening, some things happened. It made this the last show ever. More specifically, it was my yelling," and he gestured toward the people in the beer garden. "And calling them pieces of shit."

At this point, a microphone was passed around, and the comics gave impromptu but uncharacteristically sincere and respectful (seeming)[17] eulogies to commemorate the times they had in the room together. It's hard to catch everything. But since comedian Mike Olson was so close to the camera's microphone, he can clearly be heard saying, "This is a bummer. What else can you say? Much like Radiohead didn't become Radiohead until they released *OK Computer*, Red Lion didn't become the Red Lion, I don't think, until Bill…took it over."

"Did I say that in that video?" Olson said, sounding slightly embarrassed in 2021. "I don't listen to Radiohead. I don't know what I was talking about. Making analogies was a big thing for me then. I really wanted to make one thing analogous to another thing. That was how I talked about stuff. I mean, they were good analogies. I worked on some of these analogies. And that was a good one, probably."

But then he added, "I didn't say it was *better* in that clip, did I?" before further clarifying. "I had a group that I was a part of, or that I felt like I was a part of, that came every week to top ourselves, top each other, surprise each other, do something 'out there,' and maybe that's what I meant by how it didn't become that until Bill took it over. I mean, that was already an aspect of it, but he gave it free flight. 'Let's set it on fire and dance around while it's burning and it'll be awesome. And you come here every week and pour gas on the flames.'" Olson knows he let the metaphor get away from him. "This doesn't sound like a lot of fun, what I'm saying."

Not necessarily, but the comics of the Red Lion era know what he means, and they apparently still think highly of the dance Olson performed around those flames. "He's one of the most experimental of us all," T.J. Miller said. "He was doing stuff where all of us were like, 'That is so fucking hysterical and I have no idea why.'"

"Mike Olson was probably the person that, on that stage, I learned from the most," Nate Craig said. "Mike would have ideas, and he would just kind of dig and dig and dig until there was nothing left to mine, or until he made it the most beautiful piece of comedy that was never to be performed again."

There seems to be a sweetness, or an almost dorky innocence, about everything in the video. Sure, one minute these comics were calling the audience members "pieces of shit," but the next minute those same iconoclastic twentysomethings were bonding together over the loss of their clubhouse and spiritual home. They had no way of knowing that the Red Lion's demise left an opening both for a new clubhouse for the scene, as well as a new place for Geary to truly spread his wings. But that was all right around the corner.

"There's clarity now," Geary said. "Like every idiot that comes onto the scene, you get into it. It means something. You sit in the backs of bars talking about, 'The revolution's coming.' Now I've looked back twenty years later, I'm wincing with embarrassment. [Zanies manager] Bert Haas must have been sitting in his office laughing his ass off."

Long before anyone had any clarity about anything, however, there was the Chicago Comedy Festival.

Chapter 9

THE FESTIVAL

When the entertainment industry came to Chicago in the late '90s and early 2000s, the scene wasn't quite ready for its close-up. But the first iteration of the Chicago Comedy Festival, which was started by a former comedian named Dan Carlson, lasted in the city from 1998 to 2002.

Carlson began his career in stand-up in the late '80s as the house emcee for Ron Bennington's club in Clearwater, Florida. From there, he toured alongside Carl LaBove and Jimmy Schubert as part of Bennington's "Disciples of Comedy." And in 1997, Carlson was invited to perform at the Florida Comedy Festival in Jacksonville. It was at this festival that Carlson started thinking of creating a festival of his own.

He'd already been to the Just for Laughs festival in Montreal, and he noticed that most of the comics in these festivals already had industry representation. So when he landed in Chicago later in the year, Carlson decided to attempt his festival there, with the specific goal of getting deals for the best un-repped comedians.

"I was trying to make this about the funniest people and have them seen by agents," Carlson said. "That was the whole thing—getting a deal. They were giving away six-figure deals for all kinds of stuff [at festivals]. That's where stuff would happen."

According to Geary, the first year of the festival passed without anyone really noticing. And if that was the case, it might be because Carlson was just a little ahead of his time with his bookings. When Geary showed me the program from that first festival in 1998, he read aloud from one of the listings. "Comedy Central presents the Upright Citizens Brigade, Louis CK, and Mitch Hedberg," Geary deadpanned. "There's your ten o'clock show."

"I was there," comedian John Roy told me of that lineup. "Maybe ten people there, max. They weren't famous yet. Only comedy dorks knew who they were."

The *Chicago Tribune* comedy critic, Allan Johnson, seemed to agree,[18] saying that the "lack of big-name talent" was noticeable at the 1998 festival, before conceding that the Upright Citizens Brigade (Matt Besser, Amy Poehler, Ian Roberts and Matt Walsh) were getting a series on Comedy Central later in the year.

I thoroughly enjoyed looking through Geary's 1998 program and seeing the old headshots of people like CK, Hedberg and Doug Stanhope, all of whom were in their early thirties at the time. And the "Fresh Mugs" lineup (new talent showcases for entertainment industry types) also included a twenty-six-year-old Deon Cole and a twenty-three-year-old Daniel Tosh, who was apparently going by "DT Tosh" at the time.

The 1999 Fresh Mugs shows were hosted by Marc Maron and Patton Oswalt. "That was the year my good friend David Stebbins got a quarter of a million development contract and tooted it all up his nose on Colombian marching powder," Geary said. "Him and Maron holed up in a hotel room for the entire festival coked out of their heads."

Like Carlson, Stebbins also began his stand-up career in Florida, where he frequently worked with, and apparently befriended, comedy legend Bill Hicks. After working the road for a few years, Stebbins came to Chicago, with his self-described "novelty-character act" in 1996.

It's when Stebbins finally switched up his act and found his authentic voice that things really started to take off in his career. "Dave Stebbins was the first guy I ever saw that would perform as if he was in front of a thousand people if there were only two people in the audience," comedian Monte said. "You got the same show with two people in the crowd, with fifty, or with hundreds."

"David Stebbins was a North Side room *wrecker*," comedian Aaron Foster raved.

When Stebbins got his chance to perform in front of industry at the festival, he knocked it out of the park. "I killed so hard," Stebbins recalled. "I was *the* hot comic. Instantly. I walked off stage and everyone was handing me their cards, explaining why I should sign with them. Dave Becky [from 3 Arts Entertainment] was calling me, imploring me to not sign with anyone but him."

A six-figure development deal from NBC came shortly after. It was essentially everything Carlson had envisioned when he started the festival. "We made the *Hollywood Reporter*," Carlson said. "And [Stebbins] was described as 'the next Michael J. Fox' in that article, after he had got the deal. And I remember I was proud of the headline that said, 'Who Needs the Montreal Comedy Festival When You Got Chicago?' For me, it was like, '*Wow*.'"[19]

"Stebbins was just given opportunities when he had like, maybe twenty minutes of material, because he looked like Michael J. Fox," Roy said. "But he was the guy who showed that Chicago people could get deals. So for a while, we thought he was a genius. But his closing bit was a lions fucking bit. That was his closer. *Lions fucking*."

"While I was exploding all over the festival," Stebbins said, "I ended up going on a very respectable coke binge with Marc Maron."

"Respectable if you're trying to break a world record!" Carlson replied. "Yeah, he made a respectable effort. Holy shit!"

"Stebbins had just gotten a big development deal and was going nuts," comedian Adam Kroshus said. "He and Maron were blowing coke in the hotel room the festival provided to Maron. I was there with Mike Olson, who was brand new to the scene. He had never seen coke, and Maron singled him out and was being a total sarcastic prick to him."

"[Maron] was just so angry," Olson said. "He was so coked up and angry at these upstarts. And I was one of those anti-comedy people at the time. He hosted the showcase I was in earlier in the night. I don't even know how we got to come to his room—maybe Stebbins invited us. And Kroshus and I drove down to the Drake [Hotel], and we went inside. I was pretty green at that time about everything. And here's this guy yelling at me about, 'You and your anti-comedy. I've got an hour I can take anywhere in this country!' I didn't know what I was getting attacked for."

"We fucking held court, barricaded in his hotel room, coked out of our heads," Stebbins said. "[Maron] laughs about it because I knew all these young Chicago comics I'd get into the room with us hoping to hear comedy secrets."

Olson must not have taken kindly to the comedy secrets he received from Maron that night. "Olson was big buds with Stebbins and rarely drank himself," Geary said, "but I think he was upset that Marc Maron had 'led Stebbins astray' with a forty-eight-hour cocaine binge. And Maron comes up to us, so Olson says, 'Hey, you should have my autograph for when I'm famous,' whips out a Sharpie and scrawls his name across Maron's T-shirt while Maron just looks at me and takes it. Now that was funny."

"[Years later] Maron was back in town to talk about his ex-wife," Olson said. "He had a theater show. And I thought, 'I'm gonna get a ticket to this and talk to him afterwards and see if he remembers that night.' So I sat through him talking about his ex-wife, and I went up to his table afterwards and said, 'Hey man, I was at the Chicago Comedy Festival in 1999 with you and David Stebbins.' And he goes, 'I was talking about Stebbins in my act.' And I go, 'Yeah. I figured. I was in that room that night.' He gave me this look. He's like, 'How did I look? Was I sweaty?' I go, 'Oh yeah. You were *really* sweaty.' He was like, 'I was right in the middle of my last bender. After that, I was done with everything.'"

Maron also came back to Chicago and performed at Geary's Lincoln Lodge in 2012. "I told him the story," Geary smiled. "He said to me, 'That was the last weekend I ever did cocaine.' And I went, 'Are we sure about that, Marc?'"

While Marc Maron's last bender gave a handful of comics in Chicago a set of stories they're still telling over two decades later, Stebbins's road to sobriety was a little bit bumpier. "I'd get these weird phone calls in the middle of the night," Olson said. "I'd go answer the call in the kitchen in my underpants. And there'd be David Stebbins just talking some shit about I-don't-know-what. He seemed fucked up, and he was telling me stuff that was going on out there. I just knew that he had got a bunch of money, and he was off in another town and it was pretty fucking crazy."

According to Stebbins, he shot, snorted and drank away all the money he received from NBC and burned every bridge in town along the way. "By the time I returned to the Chicago Comedy Festival the following year," Stebbins said, "to kinda peacock for the festival like, 'Look what can happen to you,' I had a two-8-ball-a-day-mixed-with-heroin habit. I was the *worst* emissary you could've sent....All you have to say to Dan Carlson is, 'Stebbins wants to know if you've seen any peanut butter' and he will die."

"He wants this story told too, huh? *Okay*," Carlson laughed. "So [Stebbins] wants to get more 'candy.' And his connection is in LA, but he doesn't have a place to send it. So Stebbins [had him] send it to the host hotel in the festival's name. This guy would pack the stuff into the peanut butter. And then off it would go. So it arrives at the host hotel. And [festival organizer] Stu Golfman is at the check-in desk. So this thing arrives and he opens it, and he puts it on the table with the crackers for all of the industry to dip their cracker into the peanut butter as a little welcome."

"I was like, 'Maybe someone knows we don't get a chance to eat much and sent us something to snack on,'" Golfman said. "So I left it on the table the entire festival, just sitting there. About the last day of the festival, Stebbins comes up, literally itching himself, and is like, 'Uh, did somebody send a package to the comedy festival?'"

"I was like, 'Where the fuck did you get this peanut butter?'" Stebbins said. "And he said, 'Some joker sent it to the comedy festival as a prank, I guess.' I immediately grabbed it and went running up to my room, and sure enough, inside of it was four 8 balls, a bunch of heroin and tons of pills. It was all uphill from there."

"The first year, he had been this golden boy," Chet Lactacious said of Stebbins. "The second year, he'd done that thing where he was partying too much and he lost focus. And so he takes the stage at Zanies and he's super bombing. And he's doing everything in his power to turn it around, but it just isn't happening. And he overstays his welcome on the stage. People are beginning to hate him at this point. So [former Zanies employee and current club owner Andrew Dorfman] walks up on stage, lifts Stebbins onto his shoulder and carries him off stage. And the crowd just goes crazy. They love it. It's like this awesome moment. That was sort of the end of Dave Stebbins."

Brian McKim from *SHECKY!* magazine was kind enough to direct me to his review[20] of that evening at Zanies, which he wrote was standing room only and included Stebbins, Daniel Tosh, Doug Stanhope, Zach Galifianakis and no female comedians. "Then it happened," the post reads. "Stebbins came highly recommended. He mounted the stage at what might be considered the sweetest spot in the program and proceeded to MELT DOWN. Quite simply, he wouldn't get off the stage. I lost track of how many minutes....I looked over and saw a Zanies operative waggling TWO flashlights at Stebbins from the back of the house. This was a tipoff that things weren't going well. Shortly after that, Stebbins dropped his pants and mooned the audience, challenging the club to physically remove him from stage. That got a laugh. Then it became clear that he was serious. Eventually, someone larger than Stebbins appeared, bear-hugged the delinquent comic and dragged him from the stage. That got one of the biggest responses of the evening. I say *one of* because the biggest response was for the tension-relieving, night-saving set delivered by Daniel Tosh. He scrambled onto the stage without an intro and immediately re-tracked the show. Tosh was the hero of the evening."

The *SHECKY!* post also refers to "mild ballbusting" that Stebbins took in the greenroom after his set. But from the sound of it, things were much, *much* worse for Stebbins than the article reported. "It all kept unraveling from there," Stebbins told me in 2021. "It was my own little *Permanent Midnight* without the notoriety....I wouldn't change a thing. I just got eighteen years of sobriety, and I look back fondly."

For the rest of the scene that *wasn't* David Stebbins, the festival was somehow even more contentious.

Chapter 10

THE ANTI-FESTIVAL

Besides Dan Carlson, the other main people involved in the festival were Stu Golfman (the innocent party in the cocaine peanut butter story) and then Mark Geary, who basically represented the alt scene on their behalf.

"In '99, Zanies participates in [the festival], and the scene first takes notice of it," Geary said. "[The Chicago alternative scene comics said,] 'What the fuck is this? If I'm not involved in it, it's some sort of bullshit appropriation of Chicago comedy that is illegal.' So I come into [the festival] and I start pushing harder to get the local scene more involved, but of course, being comedians, it's like, 'If it's not on my terms and I don't get exactly what I want, then there's no point in being involved in this.'"

"It seemed like there wasn't a lot of Chicago comedy being represented," The Elevated's Cayne Collier said. "It felt like we were fighting hard to be part of it. The 'bigger shows' were not necessarily people we knew. Very few and far between."

"So they've been doing this for a couple years," comedian Andy Lurie said. "It never really took off the way it should. Partly because, this is just my opinion, but for what was supposed to be the Chicago Comedy Fest, they relied too much on bringing in outside celebrities to help sell the festival. You would think, 'Hey, let's focus on the Chicago comics,' as opposed to, 'Let's have a comedy festival and throw out a few crumbs to the local comics. But let's bring in Michael Palin.' I love Michael Palin, but when I think Chicago comedy, I don't come up with Michael Palin."

He means Eric Idle, but his point works (and is wrong) for either Python. I guess I was surprised by the number of comics who still seem to agree with that "locals only" sentiment all these years later. Even though, intellectually, I'm guessing that they understand that the Woodstock music festival didn't consist of musicians from the towns of Woodstock or Bethel, New York. And the Coachella festival isn't a bunch of bands from Coachella Valley, California. That's not how festivals work. But Carlson reminded me, "When you label something 'the Chicago Comedy Festival,' every comic in Chicago thinks, 'I'm gonna be showcased.' No matter what level of comic they were."

"Daniel Tosh was one of the people they put on our show," Collier said. "And they were gonna send all these industry people. Well, then they didn't. The feeling was, 'Wait a minute. This whole thing was supposed to celebrate this thing we've all been a part of, but it feels like it's more about celebrating people who have not been around here this whole time.'"

"I get what Cayne is saying," Elevated regular Mike O'Connell said. "When somebody comes on your turf, [you get] a little defensive and these were fucking Hollywood guys. You get a little jealous, or there's an element of 'This is *our* scene.'"

In 2001, Collier's argument seemed to be slightly different. According to the *Chicago Reader*,[21] "Collier's main complaint: they raided some of his best performers to showcase elsewhere in the festival, leaving him with only part of a lineup." "[W]hy not just let us do our show and highlight us?" Collier asked the *Reader*. "The show that's been around all these years?…If none of these rooms existed, where would the performers go?"

"Cayne took real fucking umbrage to [the festival]," Geary said in 2021. "And I was like, 'I take your point. Absolutely I do. But this is a comedy festival. There are protocols. And things that are done.' And of course the comedians that were in Fresh Mugs were ecstatic and the comedians that weren't in Fresh Mugs were going, 'This is fucking bullshit.' And [I'm] stuck in the middle trying to broker a peace between a festival management crew that thinks these are a bunch of whining ingrates who think they own this city, and a local scene that's going, 'These people are just carpetbaggers. Fuck them.'"

The final straw for Collier seems to be when Carlson once again tried to book a bigger-name outsider for his show at The Elevated. "Cayne wouldn't trust me to book who was going in his room," Carlson said. "I booked Lewis Black, and he wanted to have tape of him."

You almost have to admire how stubbornly Collier stuck to his "locals only" guns. "At that point, we had a full show and they were coming up to me like, 'Will you put this other person, who is not a Chicagoan [on the show?],'" Collier explained. "And it was for no other reason than to give them more stage time. And I said, 'No.' And I think that ruffled some people a little and they thought I was crazy, but I felt like, 'No, this was supposed to be about Chicago comedy. And what I know that to be is these [local comics]. And I'm not gonna bump that person so I can put up Lewis Black.'"

The animosity between the scene and the festival only grew from there. "Let me give you the *Gossip Girl* story you want," Geary said. "A bunch of comedians that decided they didn't like what the Chicago Comedy Festival stood for said, 'Fuck you. We're gonna do a festival the exact same week, and it'll be on our terms.' To which I said, 'But it's not on your terms, is it? Because you're doing it to try to get festival industry to go to your shows instead of the shows that we've worked our bullocks off to get people to. *Disingenuous*. You want to do another festival? Great. Do it six months later and let's see what the fucking point of that is.'"

It all seems to have stemmed from a misunderstanding over Eric Idle (not Michael Palin!) tickets in 2000. "I had helped with the Chicago Comedy Festival for two years," comedian Carl Kozlowski explained. "Then the third year, they had this epic show where Eric Idle was doing a variation of *Spamalot*, the Monty Python musical. And I had this date. And I was like, 'I busted my ass doing all sorts of things—hosted shows, driven tons of comics, wrote articles, etc.' And I was acting entitled, but they had tons of tickets [available]. They sent me to the hotel room of the organizers one time to grab a bunch of tickets that they were giving away or putting on sale. I saw tons of them laying around for shows. So I said, 'I want to go to that. Make that a priority for me, please. And really good seats.'"

The only problem was that the show, *Eric Idle Exploits Monty Python*, wasn't officially part of the festival. It was put on by Jam Productions, which then let the festival list the show in its programs to beef up its roster. "I wasn't involved with paying Eric Idle or the financials of anything," Carlson explained before turning his focus to Kozlowski. "Carl volunteered with a load of other people. And they got badges—credentials that would allow them to go to any show. But we specifically said, 'Not this show. Because we have no control over it.' Plus, I think it was sold out in advance. I couldn't get *anybody* tickets."

"I was supposed to have really good seats for that," Kozlowski insisted. "And they're not answering me the day of the show. And I'm like, 'Oh my God, what am I gonna do? I have this hot date and I don't know how I can possibly miss this.' And so I call the Chicago Theatre and they're like,

'There's no will call for this. This is gonna sell out on its own.' And they laughed at me. And so I was irate."

"I call up the organizer," Kozlowski continued, "And I was like, 'How dare you? This is totally embarrassing. I worked my ass off. And I'll be damned if I'm gonna miss this show.' And I thought that was that. I ran onto the street and scalped tickets and paid $120, got second row seats and everything seemed okay. And then I come home and my roommate goes, 'You need to listen to the answering machine.'"

"I get a call from Dan," Golfman said, "[saying] that Carl has left an angry voicemail about not getting a ticket to the show, and to call Carl and tell him to go fuck himself. I vaguely remember [placing] the call, sharing Dan's feelings happily and then waiting for Carl to respond. I don't know if he was in shock or what, but he didn't respond, so I hung up the phone. Was it my proudest moment? No."

According to Kozlowski, Golfman's voicemail was something to the effect of, "Hey Carl, what are you, a fucking retard? Do you know who you're messing with? Your career is over. Over!"

And Kozlowski, who worked as a reporter, was friendly with the *Chicago Tribune*'s comedy critic, Allan Johnson. "I said [to Johnson], 'Hey, get a load of this.'" Kozlowski said. "And so he listens and his eyes pop out of his head. And he was like, 'Oh my God. Well, you got two options here. Either I can write a story about how shitty they treated people, because I've heard some other complaints of volunteers who were stepped on. Or how about you lay low and create your own festival? Because I know you can do it. And next year I'll write about your festival and not give them any ink.' I was like, 'Wow. Game on.' And so I went to Cayne."

Both Geary and Carlson seemed dumbfounded by Kozlowski's claim about Allan Johnson. And I can't really confirm it with Johnson since he passed away in 2006. But Kozlowski did take his grievance, as well as a recording of the voicemail, to Cayne Collier. "Carl played me a voice recording, and I felt like Stu acted in a way that I did not think was kind," Collier said. "At that point, I was already a little bit put out."

Then Kozlowski allegedly went to the press with the Eric Idle story anyway. "He does one of these letters to the editor of [weekly arts rag] *New City* magazine," Carlson said. "They made it matter-of-factly that this is what happened. It's like, 'Wait a second. Nobody called me. You didn't get anybody's perspective other than one person's.' And so I just lost my shit on them, hardcore, and asked for a retraction. And then they investigated it and found out that yeah, everybody knew that that was the policy. He just made it sound like I fucked him over. And that wasn't the case at all. So I have just not been a fan of his."

And still, after all that, the admittedly cleverly named Year-Round Chi-Town Comedy Celebration took place from May 31 to June 3, 2001, at The Elevated, as well as the Beaumont on North Halsted in Lincoln Park. "It became this bullshit little meaningless festival," Geary said. "Because one of the people who ran it, who will remain nameless, was embedded in the press as a freelancer and managed to get a hugely disproportionate amount of press for it as a legit thing. It became, 'Oh why are there two festivals?' There aren't. There's the real festival and there's a bunch of whinging wankers trying to denigrate the hard work of other people."

Sure enough, in the *Tribune*'s previews of the 2001 Chicago Comedy Festival, Allan Johnson mentioned[22] the Year-Round Chi-Town Comedy Celebration right alongside it, even comparing the anti-fest to the Slamdance Film Festival in one article and using a photo of Collier as the only accompanying image in another.[23] On top of all that, Johnson claimed that Collier wasn't trying to steal any thunder from the main festival, but was just trying to get on the radar of fans, as well as "industry types looking for new talent."

One thing I found interesting when I talked to comedians about the anti-festival is that nobody seems to be upset with Collier over any of this. In fact, all of the ire seems directed solely at Kozlowski. And I think there could be a few reasons for this. One is obviously because of Collier's position as the respected producer of The Elevated. And hey, maybe it is a decent point that the Slamdance Film Festival was founded in 1995 for filmmakers who couldn't get into the Sundance Film Festival and that the Edinburgh Festival Fringe is the world's largest arts festival and began as an alternative to the Edinburgh International Festival. But the comics who spoke to me about the anti-festival also seem to believe that Collier was motivated by his sense of loyalty to the scene, whereas Kozlowski's motivation seems to be that he just really wanted those Eric Idle tickets. (*Please. And really good seats*).

Whereas Kozlowski had enthusiastically accepted a Lewis Black guest-set on his self-produced show the year before, Collier defiantly turned him down. Hell, the reason Kozlowski volunteered with the festival in the first place, he told me, was to meet the comics coming in from out of town. It was Cayne Collier who rejected the festival. And it was the festival who rejected Kozlowski. And now he was looking for revenge.

"It just seemed like sore kid club," Matt Dwyer said. "Like, 'Oh, I didn't get picked for the football team, so I'll start my own football team.' God bless you for doing something and not sitting at home crying. But I was just like,

'You know what? Not everybody can play.' I never went to Montreal [Just for Laughs Festival]. I'm like, 'I guess I suck.'"

"I admire anybody that can get in front of somebody and make something happen for themselves," Carlson agreed. "But some of these comics had done the festival before and they just wanted to be in it every year. It was like, 'You can't be, man.'"

"I can understand why they did it," Golfman said. "I think because we used their venues, they felt they should have more say in the festival lineups and felt that the festival was about them when, in fact, the festival was for the city of Chicago and comedy fans from around the world that wanted to attend."

The twenty-year-old rift still seems pretty fresh for some of the comics from that era. Some still staunchly defend the anti-fest. Other comics still seem annoyed by it. "If I sat there almost losing my mind and life savings putting on a comedy festival and some fucking prick decided to throw on another one during the same time to piggyback off of all my advertising and hard work," Kinane said, "yeah I'd be a little bit pissed too."

It also seems like a lot of people who participated in anti-fest had regrets when they realized that it might not be a good look. It also seems like some spin doctoring also began in real time. "In future years," Deanna Isaacs wrote in *The Reader*, "Kozlowski and Collier say, they'll stage their event on a different weekend, so as not to look like they're competing with the original fest."

"Carl was backtracking about it when everyone got mad," comedian John Roy said. "[He said], 'No. It's not supposed to be an anti-festival.' Like, 'Of course it is. Why is it on the same date then? Shut up.'"

Some people have evolved on the issue over time. "At the time, that was the whole 'Hey, they're not local. Why are we calling it the Chicago [Festival]?'" comedian Emily Dorezas said. "I agreed with all of it. But I knew how hard Geary was working. So I didn't take a hard stance backing Cayne and Carl. But I've since realized that Geary was 100 percent in the right. It is impossible to produce one of those things, and you need to have people from out of town come in so it's an event. I just get it so much better now."

"Carl has apologized to me in the past about it," Golfman said, "so I don't really care."

And then there's Kozlowski himself. "I took a lot of heat on a message board the scene had back then," he said. "A lot of people saw it as a purely selfish move by me, and to some extent it was, but when I organize an event,

I truly try to make it the best I can make it. It started as revenge, but I did feel a sense of mission that our fest would actually feature *all* Chicago comics rather than a bunch of people flown in. Would I do the same thing now? I don't know."

Give Kozlowski some credit. The lineups were pretty solid for their era, as well as diverse. You know, like a modern festival would look. And they featured an impressive selection of South Side heavyweights, including Leon Rogers and Tony Scofield. And the biggest name, at least in hindsight, appears to be Deon Cole, who did the June 2 and June 3 shows at the Beaumont.

"One of the reasons we did that," Rogers said, "was because [the industry and the festival organizers] weren't checking for us [on the South Side]. Deon Cole and Tony Scofield are fucking legends. And *they* weren't getting looks. We were like, 'No disrespect to the guys who got on [the main festival] shows, but we're just as funny as them, if not funnier."

There's an old saying that goes, "Before you embark on a journey of revenge, dig two graves." Well, the anti-fest only lasted that one year. And the Chicago Comedy Festival ended after 2002 due to lack of sponsors and funding. Collier, Kozlowski and all the other CCF detractors got their wish after all. Chicago remained locals only.

"I'm very proud of what I did," Carlson said. "I wish it would have been financially successful for me. Because I'd probably still be doing it."

The festival wasn't all backbiting and self-sabotage. A few of the local comics picked up managers and agents or even made the jump to the coasts because of a positive response they received at the festival. And as you may have heard, someone at the festival was even given a development deal worth $250,000. If nothing else, the festival exposed the local scene to their "competition" in New York and Los Angeles, and it gave legitimate shots to a number of comics who were ready to be seen by the industry, without harming the comics who weren't.

"My deal is, you're gonna get one chance to be seen," Carlson said. "If you suck—and a lot of them sucked—you're not gonna be looked at again. Nobody cares anymore. You blew your wad and it's done. So be more than ready."

In the end, it might have been the scene itself that proved it wasn't ready to be seen by the industry. It needed more time, and it needed someone to show the way. And in one of the weirdest twists of fate for that young scene, and probably American comedy in general, the one comic from Chicago who was beloved by the industry really didn't love it back at all.

Chapter 11

DWAYNE

The praise is almost universal. "Dwayne was absolutely the one influence everybody had in common," comedian John Roy told me. "North Side and South Side. I mean, he was the one guy that every single person could agree, that's the funniest guy in the city. It was undisputed. No one would tell you anyone was funnier than him."

"I've watched Dwayne move a fucking crowd like Mickey Mouse in *Fantasia* with the water," comedian Mick Betancourt said. "I just watched him fucking move people like they were possessed, they were laughing so hard. It's him standing still with the wine in his hand, just like a catapult, just taut and hurling fireballs into the crowd. Masterful. Smart. Playful. It had all the notes that I really love in comedy."

If we're being completely honest, Dwayne Kennedy probably had no business being back in Chicago at these late '90s and early 2000s alt shows in the first place. He was way too talented to be there and should have been off in New York or LA becoming or staying wildly successful. Sure, he'd already done more in his career by 1994 than most of the comics in the scene would do in theirs. But he also seems to have had none of the ego or any of the drive that should have gone along with it.

"I started in the '80s, man," Kennedy told me. "I did *Showtime at the Apollo* in '88 and then I wound up in California in '89." Then he stopped himself abruptly. "You want to hear this story, Mike, or not?" And when I insisted that I absolutely did, he responded, "All right, man. I don't want to be that cat, 'Let me tell you a fascinating story about myself.' 'But nobody asked, sir.'"

Believe me, I was asking. Kennedy told me he started his stand-up career in Chicago and got his stage legs at places like the Comedy Cottage in Rosemont. And eventually, his friend Lance Crouther convinced him to make the jump to New York. It was in New York that Kennedy met a twentysomething Chris Rock, who, according to the *Chicago Reader*,[24] remembers Kennedy being funnier than everyone in that scene at the time.

Kennedy's memory of Rock in the late '80s, however, is slightly different. "When I first met Chris in New York, he would bomb all the time," Kennedy said. "*All* the time. But the thing is, you'd see him bombing at 9:00 at Catch a Rising Star. Then you'd see him bombing at 9:30 at the Comic Strip and then bombing at 10:45 at Stand Up New York. But here's the thing I realize in retrospect: he was developing. Not only just developing his act, he was developing that tenacity, that thing you need to pursue it. Me, I was so psychologically fragile, man. A great show would carry me for days. But then I wouldn't do it for days because I'd be high from that one show. But a bad show? I wouldn't go up again for weeks. And you realize that you just can't develop like that, not really."

Even so, everything still seemed to be moving along smoothly for Kennedy—at least at first. His *Showtime at the Apollo* tape was passed along to famed casting director Marc Hirschfeld, who got Kennedy a guest spot on the sitcom *227*, which then led to more guest spots on shows like *Amen* and *Seinfeld* in 1991 and then on *Martin* in 1992. "And then in '93, I kinda dropped out," Kennedy said. "I came back to Chicago. I started washing windows."

When I asked if something specific had happened that made him return, the answer Kennedy gave wasn't really what I was expecting. "I guess I was ambitious, but not *ambitious*," he explained. "I was never super driven. Maybe not as driven as I should have been. Rather than me addressing things like, 'I gotta really buckle down and do every club I can do,' I was always more of a reticent person. So I [said], 'Things aren't really happening. I'll just go to Chicago.' My first instinct is to always retreat."

"Dwayne was a living legend, even before [he came back to] Chicago," comedian Jen Kirwin said. "He's notorious. He's one of my best friends. I talk to him all the time, but he notoriously shoots himself in the foot time and time again."

"Literally everyone in comedy who knows him was like, 'How do we stop this guy preventing himself from becoming a mega-star?'" producer Mark Geary told me.

Brian Traynum and
Dwayne Kennedy,
The Elevated's third
anniversary show, 1999.
Cayne Collier.

"The best feeling in the world for me would be [to be] booked on a show and then the show was cancelled," Kennedy said. "So if you know anybody that's booking shows and cancelling them, give them my number."

That pattern of retreat, lack of ambition and disinterest in self-promotion may have prevented some career opportunities for Kennedy, but those same qualities also happened to land him in Chicago just as the alt scene was emerging awkwardly from the Comedy Bust of the mid-'90s. Maybe he could have been The Man in New York or LA if he'd wanted to be, but now he found himself in the uncomfortable position of being The Man in Chicago, whether he wanted the title or not.

"Everybody had left," Roy said. "Bernie Mac was gone. There was no one you could watch that was like, *good*. We had some guys that were all right road dudes that you could learn how to write a joke [from watching]. But there's nobody worth studying, except Dwayne. He was the only guy in the city that you could see consistently that you're like, 'Oh, now that's a guy that's got it all together.' We were all open mic-ers. Everybody was your level, except Dwayne and whoever the headliner was at Zanies."

"He's one of the few comics who can do politics and it's legit funny," comedian Sean Flannery said. "Like, he's not just preaching to the choir and value signaling. It's so, so funny."

"We were all chasing Dwayne Kennedy," comedian Matt Braunger said. "He was like Elvis."

We've seen how Kennedy helped make the Red Lion a popular open mic. And how his words of encouragement made a young Kyle Kinane stick with comedy after his first open mic. But before any of that happened, Kennedy also might have saved The Elevated from an early demise while the show was still only two years old.

On August 12, 1998, Kennedy appeared on *Late Night with Conan O'Brien*, and the broadcast happened to fall on the same night as The Elevated. And producer Cayne Collier told me that the comics and the audience from the show stayed at the bar afterward to watch Kennedy's set. The appearance couldn't have come at a better time. The Cue Club had been renamed Philosofur's just three months prior, and the management of the new upscale billiard bar wasn't sold on the DIY comedy show they'd inherited from their predecessor. "Cutting edge, independent stand-up wasn't fitting in their minds," Collier said.

But that night, with everyone at Philosofur's cheering Kennedy's televised set, the new manager finally changed his tune. "We talked," Collier said. "And he basically was like, 'I get it.' And I don't know if he said it or I said it, but it was something like, pointing to the TV and then to the stage: 'That guy was on this stage.' He finally got that what we were trying to build here was a place where he'd be saying and seeing much more of that."

Kennedy did *Late Night with Conan O'Brien* again in 2000. Once again, it was great. I mean, he opened with a pro-looting joke, which ends with the punchline, "Damn, baby, you think I'm made of bricks?" But the Kennedy joke that seems to get brought up the most in my conversations with comics now—a joke he told on his first appearance on *Late Show with David Letterman* in April 2002—was about the subliminal messages hidden in old Negro spirituals.

"I'm not real religious," Kennedy casually said, about two minutes into the set. "But I do like gospel tunes. I like Negro spirituals....I like 'Swing Low, Sweet Chariot.' That's a brilliant song, man. But you have to listen to it because it had more than one meaning. It was not just an ethereal aspiration to God. It also meant, 'Get ready, because we're getting ready to get out of here.' That was the code. It was like, 'Swing low, sweet chariot— the Underground Railroad is coming for us to carry us home. Or to Detroit or wherever it is you wanna be dropped off.'"

After a short applause break, Kennedy continued to build his premise. "You have to think," he said, "it took a brilliant mind to be able to write a song on that many levels. Because you know there were probably a lot of slaves who tried to *write* spirituals but just weren't really that good at concealing the message."

"It'd be like, [slave master voice] 'Hey, Joshua, why don't you sing that spiritual I hear you been working on?'" Kennedy continued before transitioning into the voice of a slave. "'Uhh, all right, massa. [Begins singing] Ohhhhh. Tonight at 8:30 gonna get some shovels and bash white folk in the heeaaad. What time?' [A call and response from the nearby slaves] '8:30.' Joshua's song writing career? Over."

The bit is more than twenty years old, and multiple comedians were cracking up trying to repeat it during their interviews for this book. So I guess I find it slightly unfortunate that the most often discussed and definitely the most infamous story involving Kennedy from around that time is about a collision, of sorts, between Kennedy and the scene's other most mythic figure, Bill O'Donnell.

The story has spent two decades now being exaggerated and conflated in a game of comedian telephone. But after hearing multiple versions, I believe there are three distinct parts to the tale and that the whole thing is best told by comedian Nate Craig, who saw the first two incidents happen and then succeeded in creating the third, however bad he feels about it now.

The first incident allegedly took place at the Chicago Comedy Festival in June 2000 during a Midnight Bible School show. And it didn't involve Kennedy at all. The lineup included pre-fame Fred Armisen and Zach Galifianakis. This same show got Chet Lactacious booked at Luna Lounge in New York City with his "Super Fans" Klan robe bit. According to festival organizers Dan Carlson and Stu Golfman, it also got Armisen booked on *Late Night with Conan O'Brien* and launched his career. And according to Craig, it also ended with a very memorable set from O'Donnell.

"You know how there's something really watchable about a comic that doesn't give a fuck?" Craig asked me. "Well, that's the most I-don't-give-a-fuck [thing] I've ever seen in my life."

O'Donnell's set began with what sounds like an especially hostile striptease, performed to the song "No Easy Way Out" from *Rocky IV*. And at one point, according to Craig, O'Donnell had stripped down to a lime green thong, and the vulgarity was escalating quickly.

"This is full health code violation," Craig said. "This is like 'shut the show down' territory. In the Chicago Comedy Festival. In a venue that's owned and operated by Second City."

It all appears to be part of O'Donnell's plan. "The part of [Andy] Kaufman's act that influenced me the most," O'Donnell explained, "was the antagonism of the audience, or at least the alienation of the audience. Everyone was preening for laughs, and it just struck me as kind of sad and desperate. So I liked the cringe factor—bombing, being offensive or just making them uncomfortable."

O'Donnell, you see, needed the crowd to strongly dislike him in order for the next part of the act to "work." And from the sound of it, he succeeded. According to the story, with the tension in the room at a high, O'Donnell proceeded to perform his version of the inspirational victory speech that Rocky Balboa gave to the hostile Soviet crowd at the end of *Rocky IV*, complete with O'Donnell's wife, Michele, translating the speech into fake Russian from somewhere off stage.

If you're not familiar with the movie, Rocky tells the crowd, "I came here tonight and I didn't know what to expect. I've seen a lot of people hating me. And I didn't know what to feel about that. So I guess I didn't like you much none either. During this fight, I seen a lot of changing: the way you's felt about me and the way I felt about you....What I'm trying to say is, if I can change, and you can change, everybody can change!"

Then, in the middle all of the chaos, came the coup de grâce. After the passionate speech, O'Donnell is said to have produced a toothbrush and jammed it into his throat until he vomited all over the stage. "I thought it was fucking great," Craig told me.

The second O'Donnell incident was also at Midnight Bible School. And this one does involve Kennedy. But this time, O'Donnell went on stage dressed as comedian Jeff Foxworthy and began by playing audio of Foxworthy's "You Might Be a Redneck" act over the PA.

"I bet Bill got more laughs [from Foxworthy's Redneck act] than [Bill] ever got," Mike O'Connell said. "No offense to Bill. It kills in 90 percent of rooms. Why not there?"

And indeed, as always, the bit got laughs. But this time, when the audio stopped, O'Donnell started berating the audience for laughing. "What the fuck do you hogs want up here?" is what Nate Craig remembers him saying.

"Keep in mind," Craig continued, "these are people who spilled over from the Mainstage show and the e.t.c. show. They could not get tickets to the Second City. They have now gone to Midnight Bible School in the Donny's Skybox Theater on the third level above Second City, the world-famous improv theater. These people were getting insulted by a guy who was not doing anything they were used to or that they'd ever expected. And this guy [in the audience] goes, 'You fucking suck.'"

The man was not an audience plant. He was just a regular guy who was not enjoying O'Donnell's performance. And apparently, this regular guy and O'Donnell exchanged a few more words until things got pretty tense in the room. A few people even left out of discomfort. And that's about the time O'Donnell allegedly decided to go after the man's date.

"Just ridiculous shit," Craig told me, when I asked what O'Donnell had said. "Like, mentally-ill-person-on-the-street-type harassment. And the guy comes on stage, and he gets right in Bill's face."

"The guy jumped on stage," O'Donnell said, "and [squared] up like, 'You wanna fucking talk?' People thought I was doing a Kaufman plant type thing. And I had no idea who this fucking guy was."

As this was happening, and this guy was ready to kill O'Donnell, somebody in the sound booth, for whatever reason, pressed play on the song "Fight the Power" by Public Enemy. And O'Donnell began to dance. "I rolled with it," O'Donnell said.

The angry guy was still standing right there in his face. But O'Donnell danced around him, playfully and mockingly. "Bill *really* wanted this guy to hit him in the mouth," Craig said. "He was like, 'Do. It.' It was *very* tense. It was not a good moment. It was just too much."

"It's the only time I ever got concerned we went overboard," Matt Dwyer said. "Also the only time I ever offered someone their money back because of something happening on stage. Any other time shit went too far, all I thought was, 'This is good word of mouth,' but I thought Bill was going to get killed."

But then it was over. Everything got defused. Dwyer walked the man out, and O'Donnell walked through the back. And as told by Nate Craig, the very next thing the audience heard was, "Ladies and gentlemen, Dwayne Kennedy."

I cringe picturing any comic having to perform in an environment like that. And Craig said he wasn't even sure Kennedy would come out. But we're not talking about just any comedian here. This is Dwayne fucking Kennedy.

"Dwayne walks out, like Dwayne does," Craig said. "Coolest head in the building. Not at all fazed by what Bill O'Donnell just tried to do. Definitely not impressed by the audience in that situation. Sits in the most tension that I've ever felt in any room I've ever seen in twenty-plus years of comedy. And I've seen some tense rooms. *Very* tense rooms. I've seen fights. I've seen people rush the stage. This was very, very tense. And Dwayne Kennedy just sips his wine. Sips it again. And starts in with, 'If you rush the stage. At the comedy show. To fight the comedian. You might be a redneck.'"

The room *erupted*. Dwayne Kennedy had taken the thick tension that everyone in the room was feeling and completely flipped it on its head with

Foxworthy's own catchphrase. And both the crowd and the young comedians who witnessed him doing this loved him for it.

To Craig, what Kennedy had done was magical. And he began to wonder if moments like that could be replicated. And I can tell it pains him to walk me through this, but the gist of his thought process was that he assumed Dwayne Kennedy could do absolutely anything on stage. So he wanted to manufacture a similar "lightning in a bottle" scenario where Kennedy would be forced to react to O'Donnell's mess again and inevitably say the perfect thing that needed to be said so he could save the day and make the audience erupt all over again.

To be fair to Craig, most of the young comics in the scene probably assumed the same thing. Mick Betancourt told me a story where Kennedy followed a set at Bible School where a comedian burned a copy of *Judy Carter's Stand-Up Comedy: The Book*, and when Kennedy came out he opened with, "You might want to think about reading that before you burn it."

"He never faltered," Kinane told me of Kennedy. "And I never want to encourage any heckling, but if somebody heckled him, oh, your night just got ruined, young man. Because Dwayne is gonna pick you apart in a way that's like, 'Is this part of the show?'"

"I relied on Dwayne's skill to do something that I thought was easier to capture than it was," Craig admitted, wincing at his early comedy naiveté. But then he paused for a moment, as if picturing what came next. "Although they did do it again at the Barrymore."

The third incident occurred on February 3, 2001, when Nate Craig brought Kennedy, along with Bill O'Donnell and a handful of other Chicago comics, to the Barrymore Theater in Craig's hometown of Madison, Wisconsin. This was the moment Craig had been hoping to create. He got to combine the best (in his mind) moments from the first two O'Donnell incidents into one show-stopping crescendo. And sure enough, when comics discuss this theater show now, the main thing everyone seems to remember was Kennedy having to follow O'Donnell after he intentionally vomited on stage.

"It was all over the stage and he had to perform in it. Or around it," O'Donnell said. "And Dwayne and I went sour....It hurt me because I always liked him. But I knew that he couldn't stand me."

"I still feel bad about making [Kennedy] do it, but he did do the same thing," Craig said. "Bill shut the room down. And then Dwayne came out and crushed. I remember it word for word. It was great. I loved it. But I didn't tell him what was coming. I thought he didn't need to know. I thought that's what he did. He was a superhero to me. I didn't know stand-up enough to know that that's not why you're doing this. You're not here to clean up people's messes. And Dwayne cleaned up my mess. And I'll never forget him."

I have seen grainy footage from that night at the Barrymore, specifically the moment Kennedy was introduced to the stage. And with the crowd sitting in a hushed tension, he opened his set by saying, "When you come out you think, 'Man, I hope the dude in front of me doesn't get buck naked and vomit,'" and then the camera zoomed in on Kennedy, who took a sip of wine while the crowd exploded in laughter.

"That's what you hope for," Kennedy continued. "We were talking about it backstage. I said, 'Man, what you gonna do?' He said, 'I'm gonna get buck naked and vomit.' I said, 'That's hack shit.'"

And when I played the clip for Craig, who hadn't viewed the performance in more than twenty years, he burst into hysterics. "So fucking cool," he said with a giant grin. "It's undeniably cool, dude. I'm sorry, Dwayne. If you ever need a kidney, you got one, buddy. Goddamn, dude. I fucking love that guy. Damn."

Dwayne Kennedy would go on to win Best Comedian at the 2002 HBO US Comedy Arts Festival in Aspen. He performed on *Letterman* again in 2003. He also had a *Comedy Central Presents* and a *Jimmy Kimmel Live!* set in 2003. But there was always a mystique about him. He was an enigma. I remember Geary telling me that if anybody wanted to book Kennedy on a show, they had to send a fax to his dad. And I've started referring to him as the Banksy of comedy.

"Dwayne Kennedy is arguably the best comedian any of us have ever worked with," Kinane said. "But that guy is like a ghost. All of a sudden it's like, 'Oh, Dwayne's on *Jimmy Kimmel* tonight. Does he live here? Is it a hologram?' Because that guy is happy to show up, blow people's minds and then disappear into a field after the show."

"I remember hanging with [writer/producer] Ali LeRoi at Dwyer's Midnight Bible School," David Stebbins said. "Watching Dwayne be brilliant as always, and [LeRoi] said, 'Dwayne is off painting fences and shit and every once in a while, he crawls out of his hole to show everyone how genius-level comedy is done. Then crawls back off.'"

"It really was like Mel Gibson from *Lethal Weapon*," Kinane said. "Like, he was great but he also went crazy and lives in a trailer on the beach or something. Nobody knew about his life, but if he was hanging out with you, you were like, '*Oh, man. This is cool.*'"

In a 2017 article[25] about Kennedy in the *Chicago Tribune*, where comedian Hari Kondabolu called Kennedy the godfather of the Chicago comedy scene, the writer also said that Kennedy is "almost impressively nonprolific in terms of recorded material."

"Dwayne recorded multiple records over the years that he never put out," Kondabolu told me. "He would dislike something about the recording or had some issue with who was making it and it would never come out. During one of his *Kimmel* sets, he promotes an album that never came out."

When his comedy album, *Who the Hell Is Dwayne Kennedy?*, did drop in 2020, CJ Sullivan told me he loved it so much that he pushes it on anyone he can. "Dwayne also inspires me," Sullivan added, "because he's somehow worse at promoting himself than any of us."

"I'm a little frustrated that it's not the biggest comedy album of the past five years," comedian Nick Vatterott said. "I feel like if a celebrity put out this album, nobody would shut up about it."

"I produced *Who the Hell Is Dwayne Kennedy?* along with W. Kamau Bell and Ahamefule J. Oluo, who did most of the work including recording and editing it," Kondabolu said. "We wanted to make this record because we knew if we didn't, it would never happen. For me, the idea of Dwayne's work somehow not existing for future generations to hear broke my heart. The jokes are too good and too important to disappear when he does."

"It really pisses me off," Geary said. "Dwayne Kennedy should be, like, a major name in American comedy. He really should. He is hands down one of the best comedians anywhere in America over the last ten to fifteen years. He's top drawer. But it's all down to him."

"Dwayne's an Emmy-winning[26] guy," Roy responded. "Dwayne has a Showtime special. *Letterman* appearances. Actual Emmys for writing for Kamau Bell. What do you want, Mark Geary? If there's no statue of him then it's not good enough?"

"Is Dwayne one of the best of all time?" Dwyer asked. "Fuck, yeah. So is that success—that he influenced fucking generations of comedians? That's *wildly* successful. And probably more rewarding than a mountain of money because that's a creative, and perhaps spiritual, reward. Said the atheist."

The scene benefitted from Kennedy because they valued his talent as a comic and his accessibility as a mentor more than they valued his commercial success. Why would they care about his TV credits? They saw him kill harder than everyone else. With smarter material than everyone else. And that changed all of them, and the way they thought about comedy, permanently.

Dwayne Kennedy. *Krystle Gemnich.*

"You just summed up Chicago, man. You just summed up Chicago," Mick Betancourt replied when I mentioned the scene valuing Kennedy's talent over his heat. "Are you good? Do you love this thing? Because everything else is, 'You're a jagoff.'"

"He couldn't see how successful he was to the people in the scene," Roy said. "They weren't judging him based on the whole history of comedy. Like, against Eddie Murphy. They were judging him against them."

I asked Dwayne Kennedy if there was anything in his career he would have done differently. He said he would have been more committed, more diligent and braver. In other words, he would have been like Chris Rock, bombing multiple times a night in order to develop.

"To aspire to be a great artist, man, you have to be open and sensitive and perceptive to the world around you," Kennedy said. "But that's a paradoxical thing when you then have to brace yourself for the onslaught of either no laughter...or criticism. It's like a duality, man. And it puts you in that quandary. So sometimes the most artistic people are the ones who aren't actually pursuing it."

Damn.

Chapter 12

THE DEN (BEGINNINGS)

The Monday night comedy open mic at the Lyon's Den on Irving Park Boulevard in Chicago's North Center neighborhood would become one of the most often discussed and well-respected rooms the city would ever produce. And if you would like to refer to it as the greatest open mic in the history of comedy, you'd get no pushback from me. In fact, any other claimant better bring some receipts.

According to Mark Geary, the Lyon's Den open mic started the week before he started his open mic at Red Lion Pub. But while Geary's show flourished immediately, the Lyon's Den was a little slower getting out of the gate. "What people don't know," Bill O'Donnell said, "is how bad the Lyon's Den was. The Lyon's Den was the worst of them all at that time. And it later became the best of them all."

The Three-Ring Comedy Circus, as it was officially known, was initially run by Tim Adamz, a comedy magician, and Jeff Carpenter, who was an improviser. And depending on who you ask, the show was also run by Andy Lurie. But the "rings" of this "three-ring" circus were initially a specific reference to stand-up, sketch and improv. That would change over time, but that's what the rings meant at the very beginning.

"The first week was particularly hilarious," Geary said. "Because the sketch and improv people found out what stand-up comedians are like. First, we're gonna do the stand-up, then we'll do the sketch and we'll end with the improv. There was me and another eight stand-ups go up and do three minutes. As soon as they're finished, the other seven leave. [I'm] the only one left, now watching some very fucking annoyed sketch and improv people who stood and supported the stand-ups. I think what they did the following week was switch the order to try and fix it. *Nope*, they're wise to that one. These are stand-up comedians we're talking about. We'll just be at the front of the bar getting pissed, and we'll come in when we're called. So I think the Three-Ring Circus was down to one ring after about four weeks."

"I would go on Mondays. And it was terrible, terrible, terrible," comedian Jeff Klinger said. "Like, three people. Including comics. It was bad. But I needed stage time. That's why I was going there every Monday."

Being one of the only consistent attendees of the terrible, terrible, terrible open mic was apparently a good enough qualification for Klinger to be offered a spot producing the show. He happily accepted. "I took a lot of pride in it," Klinger said. But then, as magicians often do, Adamz disappeared. "Tim Adamz was a working magician," Geary said. "So he went off on tour."

Eventually, Klinger brought on comedian Dan Kaufman to help run the show. The Three-Ring Circus concept shifted its meaning so that the "rings" stopped referring to stand-up, sketch and improv and started referring to the three guys who ran the show. "So then it became me, Kaufman and maybe Tim Adamz," Klinger said.

The new version of the show started to pick up steam. And once again, comics in the scene have different theories as to why. Geary credits the same implementation of guest spots that had given a bit of "intelligence to the anarchy" at the Red Lion. Now, every fifth spot was reserved for a more established comedian, who were often referred to as "ringers" or "rings" by other comics, just to add to the confusion of the three-ring term. "You can call them whatever you want," Geary said. "I invented the fucker. Klinger copied it."

"That was after we were already very successful," Klinger said of the reserved slots. "Because otherwise, we wouldn't have those comics coming in."

According to Klinger, if comics from Minneapolis or Austin were doing Zanies that week, they might come to town early just to do the show. "That's why that fifth slot was there," Klinger said.

One night, George Carlin dropped in, which definitely became part of the show's early lore. Even if he was just there to support his wife, Sally Wade, who was in town to perform at Zanies.

"All of sudden, I hear this voice over my shoulder," comedian Adam Kroshus said. "'Hey, is there a list here to sign up?' I'm like, 'I fucking recognize that [voice].' It's like meeting God."

"I talked to him," comedian Aaron Foster said. "He had a girl with him. You felt that, 'Hey, I'm trying to get some pussy' thing. I was talking to him for a little while. I'd say a good two, three minutes. 'Hey, how you doin'? I seen you on TV.' That type of shit. And then it was a great night. I mean, shit, *George Carlin*."

But then Foster made it abundantly clear that he's met, and is plenty comfortable around, much bigger stars than George Carlin. "Remember, I was at [legendary "urban" comedy club] All Jokes Aside," he told me, "where I'm sitting around Mike Epps. I was not star-struck by [Carlin]. He was just another dude."

Foster seems to be alone in that assessment. "Everyone went up and tried to do their A material," Kroshus said, "and I had a terrible set. I went up and just completely tanked it. I was all in my head. And he was sitting in the back of the room. And I think his girlfriend went up and then he left."

But not before giving one of the young comics a story he'd have for the rest of life. "I got to go up before Carlin, and he gave me some great compliments," Klinger said. But when I asked what those compliments were, he said it'd been twenty years and he couldn't remember. "It's in a [promotional] bio somewhere," Klinger said.

"People loved saying, 'Carlin said I was good,' and then they put that as credits," comedian CJ Sullivan joked. And when I reminded Sullivan that Carlin had been complimentary to Jeff Klinger, he realized, "I said 'people.' I mean 'Jeff.' I was gonna say, 'I've heard that story a thousand times.' And I realized that was him telling me a thousand times."

I found an old Klinger comedy bio that quotes George Carlin. And in it, the legendary comedian says Klinger is "One of the most entertaining and interesting comedians today, [with] an interesting choice of topics with a new and different slant that always keeps you guessing...my new friend." And yeah, you absolutely put that in your bio and tell people a thousand times.

Another theory as to how the show shifted from the worst open mic in the city to the epicenter of the scene has to do with the cultural shift that occurred after 9/11. "Weirdly enough," Kyle Kinane said, "9/11 had a lot of people showing up to open mics. Because that was the first major experience for a generation of people that were like, 'I better go to college and get a job,' and feeling unfulfilled. 9/11 happening made people reprioritize what they wanted to do with their lives. So I saw a lot of people show up to shows, either to watch and have a fun time or to participate. Because it was like, 'Fuck. I work in an office building and I'm unhappy. And that could just be the end of it. Oh, cool. I'm in debt and I'm middle management. Oh, I'm

Jeff Klinger and George Carlin. *Jeff Klinger.*

gonna fall to my death. You know what? I've always wanted to try stand-up. I think I better go do that now.'"

"You felt like you could die," Pete Holmes said. "I worked at the Bennigan's by the Sears Tower. Everybody was like, 'My friend in the FBI said the Sears Tower is a target and don't go to work on Tuesday.' That's the world we were living in. So we started getting a little bit bolder with our jokes and with our dreams."

In times of tragedy, the scene could also serve as the closest thing most people had to a community. "September 12," Kinane remembered. "It was a Wednesday. I went to Elevated. Because I didn't know where else to go. My sense of community was, 'I'm going to the comedy show.' There wasn't a show. But it was everybody sitting around, just having a talk about life. And it felt *good.*"

"What comedy has taught me as a whole," Pete Holmes said, "is you talk about it....We're all dealing with this thing that made us feel very unsafe. And everyone was talking about it. So CJ Sullivan was on stage at The Elevated, and he's doing a bit—a bit!—about how everyone has the same story. 'Oh yeah? You saw it on TV? You thought it was a movie? Yeah. That's *everybody*. Yeah. You couldn't believe it was happening and you called your mom? That's everybody's story.' Like, *that's* the angle. And he was doing it. He's in his twenties. He found what a room of top-notch comedy writers would have found. And he found it on his own. And he had the courage to do it like, the Wednesday, a week after. And I was just blown away."

American comedy had weathered a national tragedy and picked up a few converts along the way. And it's entirely possible that the tragedy of 9/11 had given a new sense of urgency to the comedians, as well as created a new wave of people who decided to try comedy for themselves. I might have been one of them, even if it was a subconscious motivation. Regardless, the scene was about to explode. But it wasn't long before one of the Lyon's Den's regulars experienced a tragedy of his own.

Chapter 13

KRO

I was stalked," Adam Kroshus told me, emphatically. "Genuinely stalked. Not bullshit stalked like people say, 'Remember that guy I met at the party last week, and he said he worked at Starbucks at Clark and Belmont? I went in there twice last week. Does that make me a stalker?' No, you just are interested in this person. I was flat-out stalked for three and a half years. I was *stalked*."

The saga of comedian Adam Kroshus and his stalker is such an entrenched part of the scene's lore that I think it's appropriate to take a bit of a detour to tell the full story. The woman in question was an open mic comic at the time. And before everything went down, Kroshus began to notice some strange behavior coming from her at shows.

"This woman was always standing in the periphery of my vision," he said. "I'd be talking to someone, and ten feet away, I'd notice this swath of blond hair, and this woman who would have a drink in one hand and the straw in the other, hitting her ice cubes in her drink and paralleling my movements. If I moved my head, she would move at the same pace that I was moving my head. So it was always in kind of the periphery of my vision."

That went on for a few months, but Kroshus never thought much of it until one Monday at the Lyon's Den when the woman finally approached him. "She comes up to me," Kroshus said, "and says, 'Listen, Adam. I've been meaning to say this to you for a long time, but I find you really attractive. And looking in your eyes right now is super intense. Could I just give you a hug?'"

Kroshus let her know that he wasn't interested in her, but he tried to be nice and they had a conversation for ten minutes or so. And that probably should have been the end of the whole thing. But instead, over the next several months, the situation started repeating itself. She'd express her interest, he would turn her down gently and then they'd do the whole thing all over again at the next show.

It was around that time that the Lincoln Lodge put on a Halloween-themed show, where the comics performed in costumes as various other personas. Kroshus happened to go up as famed prop comic Carrot Top. "One of the props was my high school yearbook," Kroshus explained. "It wasn't one of my high points of comedy."

When Kroshus retrieved his props at the end of the show, his yearbook was missing, although he didn't realize it at the time. Then, the following Monday at the Lyon's Den, the woman approached Kroshus to ask if he'd watch her set.

"I was like, 'Please go away. I'm not interested in you.' It started to annoy me a little bit," Kroshus remembered. "Half an hour later, show starts, [comedian] Brian McGannon comes running out from the other room and he's like, 'You gotta get in here right away.'"

"So I walk in," Kroshus continues. "She's on stage. She had taken my high school yearbook picture and she had blown it up to an eleven-by-seventeen copy. And she was talking about, 'Oh, and look at his smile. He looks so cute. But I don't like the direction of our relationship. I'm gonna light a sage candle because I'm a practicing Wiccan.' And no one's laughing. They're like, 'What is going on? This is bizarre.'"

Comedian Aaron Foster happened to be hosting the open mic that night. "Oh my God, that's one of my favorite parts of that goddamn place," he laughed. "We had a little round table up there. [She] puts the things on the table...and she wraps herself in cellophane. And you only got four minutes up there. And we're all like, 'Okay, what is she gonna do?' She takes this picture of Adam out and she said, 'I love Adam and I want to pledge myself to Adam.' And she had chocolate. She had mustard and ketchup. And she was spraying the shit on her body and wrapping it around her, and then she was yelling out this shit about Adam. 'I love you, Adam. I want to be with you.' And all this other shit."

"Three Mondays out of four in a month I'd go to Lyon's Den," Kyle Kinane said. "And the one I don't go, there's some lady wrapping herself in Saran Wrap pouring hot fudge over her nude body."

While the woman did wrap herself in cellophane and pour condiments on her body, Kroshus informed me that she didn't do it on the same night as the Wiccan ceremony. The act with the condiments happened right after 9/11, while the Wiccan ceremony was in early November. It's just that they happened so close in time that people tend to combine the two performances in their minds.

Either way, during the Wiccan ceremony, the comics at the Den initially seemed to think that this woman was attempting some type of performance art piece and that Kroshus was in on the bit. "I remember thinking, 'This is some weird avant-garde shit,'" Andy Lurie said. "I don't know where she's going with this shit, but *okay*."

"One night she does some kind of crazy, out-there type bit akin to something [Bill] O'Donnell or myself would do," Chet Lactacious said. "And it didn't work, but people were impressed that she did it."

It's interesting to me how "open mic comedian taking a bold new direction in her act" and "untreated mental illness" were basically indistinguishable from each other back in 2001, at least to the comics in the scene. But either way, Foster convinced Kroshus to go on stage immediately after the woman's Wiccan ceremony in order for him to respond.

"It was weird," Kroshus said. "She was talking about my dick and stuff. And I had never laid a finger on her. *Never*. Which makes it all the more strange. So I go up on stage. I say, 'Listen, I am not interested in you. This has to end.' She pulls a chair to the front of the stage and says, 'I want you to say it to my face.' People are confused."

Kroshus left shortly afterward, but at that point he still didn't know he was being stalked. The next time he saw the woman, she apologized for her behavior and then handed him an envelope. "I opened up the envelope and it's a bunch of confetti," he said. "Then I started putting it together like it was a jigsaw puzzle. And she had taken my high school yearbook picture from the night before and ripped it up into like, concentric one-inch-by-one-inch pieces. And I put it together and I was like, 'This is fucking weird.'"

Kroshus decided to look up more information about being stalked, and what he read startled him. "The most common sign of being stalked," Kroshus said, "was unsolicited phone calls, which I was getting at work and my home. And the second most common sign is a ripped up picture of yourself. And I was like, 'She's fucking stalking me. She's actually stalking me.' And from that, there was just a whole series of events that happened over the next three years."

The most often-discussed incidents were obviously the ones witnessed by other comedians. And one of those most often-discussed incidents happened to be in a setting that already sounds completely bizarre and ridiculous.

"We had a softball team," Kroshus said, referring to a ragtag group of comics who played in a no-glove sixteen-inch softball league. "We were named after SARS, which was the pandemic of that time." The team name was also an acronym for the Super All-Star Rocking Softballers—or some variation of that theme. And by all accounts, they were just as awful as their name. "We won all of three games," Kroshus said, referring to the multiple seasons the team existed. "The other teams were afraid of us because we looked like lunatics."

Guys played in jeans. Some had chain wallets and smoked cigarettes on the field. Another played with a cast on his arm. "Shawn Cole was out there shirtless, with soccer shin guards," Sullivan said. "He would yell, 'Blitz package!' He would try to block the hit like you're blocking a punt in football."

"Oh yeah. I loved the blitz package," Cole confirmed. "Keep the ball in the infield. Self-sacrifice."

"[Another comedian] was so high our first game," Brian Potrafka said, "I think he asked not to play. And on a popup, he collapsed under it. I was like, 'Yeah, this is how it's gonna go.'"

By all accounts, the worst player on this awful team happened to be Englishman Mark Geary. "Beautiful human being," Cole said of Geary, "but terrible softball player." And that's coming from an outfielder who once tried to headbutt a fly ball back into the infield.

"He wasn't very good at catcher," Potrafka said of Geary. "He could never catch anything, was his problem. Nothing thrown to him was ever caught. It was chased after and fetched. That hurt us."

Comedian Joe Kilgallon remembers playing against this comedian team when he was eighteen years old and a month out of high school. "We knew they were comedians because of the name and how bad they were," he said before adding, "I remember one of them batting with a boner."

"I never heard that one," Potrafka laughed. "That's great."

"Every team enjoyed playing that team," Kilgallon said. "Because it was gonna be a win and a lot of laughs."

With so much chaos surrounding this team, it almost feels appropriate that a stalker would get thrown into the mix. "We were in the dugout," Foster said. "I'm sitting next to Kroshus. I say, 'Man, what happened to your girlfriend?' He goes, 'I haven't seen her in a little while. I hope she gave up on me.' I stand up, turned around, that bitch is standing right behind him. I go, 'Oh *shit!*...She was screaming, 'You love me! Why are you doing this!?' I was like, 'Oh wow, man. I'm gonna stop teasing you.'"

"She showed up in disguise," Sullivan said. "We're out in the field and we heard a bunch of yelling. He calls the cops. Chicago cops come. The cops act like every other guy when they [heard Kroshus's story], 'So you fucked her? That's what happened, right?' He goes, 'No! I didn't! I shared a basket of fries with her one time at Lyon's Den! That was it!' And then the cop goes, 'Well for ten grand, I'll kill her for you.' A Chicago cop joke."

"I don't want to diminish what Kroshus went through," comedian Emily Dorezas said. "And it is bad. I am a total hypocrite because I'd be like, 'Oh yeah, Adam was horrible,' if Adam was stalking her. But I feel bad because I laugh at that."

"We all just totally dismissed it," comedian Sean Flannery said.

A pretty long time went by before anybody in the comedy scene actually took Kroshus's situation seriously. But if any one moment stands out as the turning point for when attitudes changed, it seems to be at an especially spooky night at The Elevated.

"This was almost two years into it," Kroshus said, "I was doing a set at The Elevated. I went out afterwards, and my car was parked under the L. And [comedians Pat] Brice and CJ [Sullivan] were smoking a cigarette, and we're just bullshitting. Nothing had happened. She wasn't there that night."

"Me and Brice are smoking a bowl," Sullivan corrected. "It's dark. But there's lights underneath the train tracks. It's very creepy. Chicago fog coming in. Smoke in the air."

"I get in my car," Kroshus said. "There's a big chain link fence behind them. So there's only one way to enter, one way to leave. I pull my car out and I notice this woman walking towards my car. She's wearing a wig, but she looks familiar. And she had these octagon Jan Brady glasses on. She had changed her appearance. And I was like, 'It's fucking [her]!'"

"It's like the girl from *The Ring*," Sullivan said. "She's running at the car. 'You love me!' and all kinds of weird stuff. And he's rolling up the window and locking at the same time. And he's trying to do a K turn out of a tight spot underneath the tracks."

"She opened my door," Kroshus said. "I had to slam it shut."

"You hear him yelling through the window," Sullivan said. "She's like, 'You love me!' And he's feeding into it going, 'You don't know what love means!' But it's horrifying. She's smacking the window. He finally peels out and gets out of there. Then she turns to us."

"I look in the rear-view mirror," Kroshus said, "And in the background, Pat Brice had jumped into CJ's arms in fear."

"He jumps up and I catch him," Sullivan said "We're like, *Scooby-Doo* style, when Scoob is terrified. And she walked right towards us. [She said,] 'Tell Adam blah blah blah.' [We said,] '*Okayyyyy*.' Fucking bolted back inside."

"I got home that night," Kroshus said. "CJ called me and was like, 'Yeah. This is bad.' He validated it. The other comics kinda fell into line and realized just how shitty the experience was. And that was a very key point in the process. But that was two years into it."

I specifically remember one night at the Mix open mic when the woman in question showed up and caused a giant scene right in the middle of the show. She was screaming Adam's name while he produced a restraining order from his back pocket and held it up at her like a crucifix to a vampire.

"It was really creepy," comedian Nick Vatterott remembered of the night. "I'd heard so many stories about it. And then one time I heard, '*Aaadaaam, Aadaaaaam.*' And it was like a ghost. All the other comics knew what was going on immediately. Somebody was like, 'That's the stalker.'"

Everything escalated from there. "She's laying on the ground, holding his leg, yelling, 'You love me! We're in love!'" Sean Flannery said. "You look back on all the chaos that was around us. And this was considered normal."

"I remember the cops tackling her to the ground outside and carrying her away," comedian Mike Wiley said. "That was the pinnacle."

According to Kroshus, that night at the Mix was the first night the woman violated her civil restraining order. "[Which] is just basically saying, 'Leave him alone,'" as Kroshus described it. It would take a while for him to build the case for a more substantial criminal restraining order.

That period took its toll on Kroshus—his mental health, as well as his career in stand-up. If Kroshus was performing, there was a decent chance the woman would show up and interrupt his set. As you might suspect, the whole experience made Kroshus feel a lot less enthusiastic about going out to shows.

"I wasn't doing nearly as much stand-up," Kroshus said. "This affected my trajectory. It really did. I cut my stand-up sets down by half. I simply wasn't going up as much because I was afraid of going out and seeing her."

"Adam Kroshus was The Man," Foster said. "He was one of [The Elevated's] favorite acts. That shit shocked him so bad that he just left the scene and quit doing comedy. And I feel like he's never recovered from that."

All told, Kroshus estimates there were ninety to one hundred separate stalking incidences from the woman in question. But eventually, after five arrests, including two in less than twenty-four hours, Kroshus got the criminal restraining order, which finally put an end to all the madness.

There is, perhaps, a grand finale to all of this. It came in the form of a video called "A Survey on the Crime of Stalking," which was put out by the Department of Justice in 2005. "It's the funniest video I've ever seen in my life," Flannery said. "This was actually at the behest of Biden, when he was a senator. They wanted to get better statistics around domestic abuse and stalking. As part of this effort, they were doing a video on how bad stalking is and how dangerous it is. And they were struggling to find men who had been the victims of stalking. But they found Adam Kroshus."

"He'll make you think that the [DOJ] picked his case out of all the stalking stories in America, flew him out, put him up," Sullivan said. "Turns out Adam's brother was dating the woman doing the videos. Anyway, the video is amazing."

"It's three women in a row telling the most death-defying, scary stories you've ever heard," Flannery said. "One guy had night vision goggles and would come into her house in the dark. The other lady had a [facial] scar from where her ex-husband slashed her. Atrocious stories."

"Her ex-boyfriend was some Green Beret who hid in the back of her truck," Sullivan said. "All these horrible, horrible things. And they cut to Adam."

"He's using a different voice because he's trying to sound sad," Flannery laughed. "He goes, 'It was really bad. I often got there too late to sign up for the Lyon's Den open mic. And I would have to perform in weaker spots.' And this is the best part. He goes, 'I have a condo that I own. I don't rent it. I own it.'"

Flannery sent me the video. He and Sullivan were only slightly exaggerating. It began with an overly dramatic piano soundtrack, which set the tone for Kroshus to tell his story in a delivery that looked like he was trying to force himself to cry. I did not want to find any of it funny. But the moment I found myself actually laughing out loud came when Kroshus began one statement in the persona of a misty-eyed stalking survivor, saying, "To this very day, every time I go home," and then he paused mid-sentence, moved his eyes up from the floor and locked eyes with his female interviewer—seemingly breaking character—in order to confidently add, "I own a condo in Chicago," before he remembered to be sad and slouched back in his chair to continue his brave story of survival.

"We had him tell the story at [the comedy show] the Blackout Diaries," Flannery said. "Then we played the video, and it got a lot of laughs."

Unfortunately, the saga of Adam Kroshus and his stalker still lives in a gray area in between comedy and tragedy, at least in the eyes of most of the comedy community who got to view it at a comfortable distance. When I interviewed Pete Holmes, he might have unintentionally explained why there was such a disconnect. "One of the things that I think [Kroshus] taught us," Pete said, "was that fully committing to an absurd premise *is* funny. It's not just what you're saying, it's the degree to which you're committing to it that is actually the joke."

Obviously, everyone feels sorry for the woman and her struggles with mental health. And everyone sympathizes with Kroshus for what he had to go through all those years. But somehow, the idea of Adam Kroshus as the victim of a female stalker felt like such an absurd premise that it actually felt like he was living out one of his own bits and fully committing to the performance along the way. Yes, it was a tragedy. But it was also funny in the exact same way that Kroshus was funny. And to paraphrase Emily Dorezas, nobody wants to diminish what he went through. But we feel bad. Because we do laugh at it.

Chapter 14

THE LINCOLN LODGE (BEGINNINGS)

From the mind of comedian Tom Lawler and the production know-how of Mark Geary, the Lincoln Lodge officially started on September 8, 2000, in the back room of the Lincoln Restaurant in North Center. It was essentially a nine-month gestation period after Lawler had approached Geary at Chet Lactacious's New Year's party to tell him his concept for a show.

That actual concept, at least as it's stated in an old program I saved from 2004, seems to be that a man named Dwight "Hairy" Heggenberger founded the Lincoln Lodge variety show in Muskegon, Michigan, in 1974 (stay with me). His show featured the top comedians, variety acts and musicians of the day. But in 1976, Heggenberger went missing, and then his venue burned to the ground. The only remains were a few signed photographs and some notes about the show. When those remains turned up at a swap meet in the mid-'90s, the current custodians of the Lincoln Lodge searched exhaustively for a new home. Finally, once they found the banquet room of the Lincoln Restaurant in Chicago, they were able to restore the Lodge to its exact period details, as specified by Mr. Heggenberger in his surviving notes.

Got all that? It's totally fine if you don't. It might even be easier to just tell you that in 2003, the *Chicago Tribune* described the show as "the kind of kitschy entertainment you'd get on a third-rate cruise ship, if said cruise ship was decorated to look like an Elks Lodge."[27] It might seem like an especially insulting review, considering that season of the Lodge featured multiple appearances by (pre-fame) Kumail Nanjiani, Kyle Kinane, T.J. Miller and Pete Holmes. But what the description does get across accurately enough

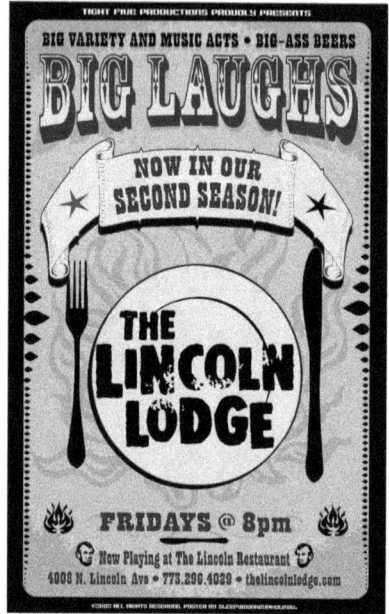

Left: Outside the Lincoln Restaurant. *Erin Nekervis.*

Right: The Lincoln Lodge season 2 poster. *Mark Geary.*

is that when you walked through those doors into the back room of the Lincoln Restaurant, you were transported into another world. Yes, it was kitschy. Yes, it was a throwback. But goddamn, they swung for the fences.

"It's more than a show, it's a destination," Lawler said. "It's basically a fake Shriners lodge. I definitely cooked up a fake history of the founder of the Lincoln Lodge, Dwight Heggenberger. That's the name that Oakland Coliseum's located on—Hegenberger Road.[28] So we put that in the programs, and we knew people were gonna read that and roll their eyes. Or it might give the media additional things to talk about. It makes it a little more interesting than just a show with some comedians that maybe you haven't heard of in the back of this restaurant. It's another layer."

"[Lawler] had big visions of trying to make it a really interesting show," Geary remembered. "He was like, 'I don't want to just see three boring stand-ups.' And luckily, I agree with that. I want it to smack me in the gob and be like, 'Wow, I didn't expect that.'"

"Anyone can come up with an idea for a show," Lawler said. "Finding a unicorn like Mark who can actually produce it and do it over and over again is something much rarer."

One thing Geary himself might not have expected (and/or smacked him in his gob) was that, unlike his previous venture at the Red Lion, the Lincoln Lodge was not a smash hit right away. "When the Lincoln Lodge first started, it was awful," Geary said. "We were gonna give it up after six months. We were like, 'This is total shite.'"

It probably didn't help that the back room at the Lincoln Restaurant had to be completely transformed for the show and then immediately torn down every weekend. That meant setting up the stage, the curtains, the lighting and all the AV equipment. "A lot of the production stuff from the Lodge comes from Red Lion," Lawler said. "Because the Red Lion's another room that had no stage, lights or sound system. Which you'd think would preclude it from becoming a place to produce a comedy show, but that does not hold [Geary] back."

It became so labor intensive that Geary, who initially alternated hosting duties with Lawler, decided that his efforts were better served solely on the production end. "My God, it took us four hours to set the room up," Geary said. "I was like, 'I can't host anymore. My brain is addled by the time I go on stage. I absolutely eat shit because of it. And then the whole show is screwed.'"

"Mark has no limit to what he'll put himself through to do these shows," comedian Mike Olson said. "I would show up and he's pulling stuff out of the ceiling tiles on a ladder and putting a whole stage together. I could never fathom the energy level that it took to do that."

"He ran all these cords through the drop ceiling," Lawler said. "Then he had lights that he would tuck into the ceiling as well. I'm not sure if it was legal at all, or safe. But that's what happened."

Even with a production-heavy show, the room somehow still managed to maintain all its pancake house "charms." "Even though he was filling the

Mark Geary sets up the Lodge. *Erin Nekervis.*

place," comedian John Roy said, "[the waitresses] never ever stopped yelling the drink orders. Even when it was sold out twice a week, they still screamed the drink orders like they were special and the show was lucky to be there."

"The waitresses all qualified for Social Security checks," Flannery said. "They would scream the orders. The beers all sucked. I don't think they ever cleaned the tap lines or anything like that. Were you the one who walked into the Lodge one time before a show and Mary was pouring Early Times whiskey into a Jameson bottle through a funnel?"

Ah, yes. Mary, the beloved, grandmotherly bartender with the Irish brogue who needed the drink orders shouted at her by the noisy waitresses. "Those waitresses and Mary, they were all characters in the show," Lawler said.

"That's what made it great," comedian CJ Sullivan said. "I don't even think Mary's from Ireland. I think she's from Cicero or something. She faked that accent for tips."

What's more, Mary had the loudest cash register anyone had ever heard. "That cash register was comically loud," Sullivan agreed. "Is this the beginning of Pink Floyd's 'Money' or something?"

It was a truly unique ambiance. And it served to remind everyone that absolutely none of it was supposed to be happening in this place. And maybe that's another reason it worked. When I asked the comics from the early Lodge period why they were willing to go along with such a difficult and outside-the-box show, it seems that it all came down to their faith in Geary.

"You want to be next to the person that's kicking ass," comedian Shawn Cole explained. "And Mark was doing it. He just kept making stuff happen. He just kept building it. He's in it forever. And you gotta love and respect that. And you might as well pitch in. If you're gonna be here and want anything from it, you might as well step to it."

"Geary put such a sense of importance around everything," Dorezas said. "And it's the same importance whether it's this two-by-four or Neil Hamburger's performance.[29] Everything is at 110 percent. And I think people put some prestige to that. It doesn't quite matter what Geary does. You just are like, 'Oh shit. This is serious. I don't know exactly what's happening, but this is big time.'"

Another labor-intensive aspect of producing the Lincoln Lodge was the wrangling of variety acts to perform on the show. "When we first started the show, me and Lawler used to cover all of these great, wacky events in the city," Geary told me. "If it was a backyard variety show, or a really good poetry thing, or spoken word, we'd be out there trying to get people to come do it at the comedy show....You need a dedicated body to pull that off."

"We're always poring through *The Reader* or *TimeOut*," Lawler told me way back in 2006,[30] "or working off word-of-mouth and checking out random puppet shows and loft parties for possible acts."

The Lincoln Lodge variety acts included Lord of the Yum-Yum, a vintage tuxedo–clad oddball who would frantically beatbox and growl and make other guttural scatting noises into a voice sampler until he produced his own layered and hypnotic versions of classical songs like "Flight of the Bumblebee" or Tchaikovsky's *1812 Overture*. All of this predated the comedic beatboxing compositions of Reggie Watts.

There was also the sketch duo the Defiant Thomas Brothers (Paul and Seth), who won "Best Sketch Group" at the HBO US Comedy Arts Festival in 2005 only to break up for unspecified reasons. There were magicians like Nate the Great, who would produce a live goose during his set. There were also weirdo musicians, including the occasional thereminist. The most successful discovery Lawler ever made for his variety performance was probably a twenty-one-year-old filmmaker named Jordan Vogt-Roberts. And we'll definitely be getting to his story later. But the most unsuccessful of the variety performances, through no fault of their own, almost convinced Geary and Lawler to stop doing the show.

For this story, you'll need to know that comedian Brian Potrafka was a bit of a wild card. But his wild card status is probably what led to him becoming part of (and subsequently getting removed from) Doug Stanhope's Unbookables tour years later. The overall opinion of Potrafka from the comedians I talked to seems to be that he could deliver a real spark of creative genius on stage. Or, to paraphrase Sean Flannery, Potrafka was a genius four to six beers in. But other times, maybe after that seventh or eighth beer, there could be some problems. As CJ Sullivan told me bluntly, "He was a real threat of violence all the time."

Potrafka, for the record, considers himself to be a teddy bear, which also happens to be my experience with him. Sure, he also told me a story about getting thrown out of the Denver Comedy Works while he was drunk and high on methamphetamines in the '90s. And that inevitably led to him fistfighting police officers and then getting thrown in jail for a week just prior to Christmas. But maybe we'll learn that Christmas was a trigger of sorts for Potrafka's bad behavior.

In December 2001, Geary and Lawler put on a Christmas-themed show, where Potrafka was to perform as Santa Claus. "I was mad because they had this Santa routine that I ruined," Potrafka said. "It was some anti-corporate rant, and there was supposed to be a part where I'm wearing a Nike T-shirt.

Like, I flip my beard up [to reveal the shirt underneath]. But I never do, so you never see the contradiction of my joke that I'm wearing a Nike T-shirt. So they're just like, 'Oh, he's just anti-corporate.'"

"He went up and he tanked," comedian Monte said. "I mean, completely bombed."

All these years later, Monte doesn't blame the beard as much as he blames the crowd for not getting Potrafka's humor. Or, I guess, he blames the musical variety act from that night for bringing in a crowd that didn't get Potrafka's humor.

"The closing act was this duo," Monte said. "They had nothing to do with the comedy scene. They weren't even a variety act that anybody knew. They had cute Christmas sweaters on. And they were doing really hokey singalong songs. And the house ended up being packed by all suburban moms. And of course, they didn't get Potrafka."

"He makes it sound like Donny & Marie up there," Lawler said. "I don't remember it like that. It wasn't corny. I found [the male singer] at Innertown Pub, which is this hipster bar [in West Town]. It was a little Wes Anderson twee maybe, but he had an appeal. And it might have been their second or third time performing [at the Lodge]."

"At the end of the show," Monte said, "these two are up there and they're killing with material that we're like, 'This is terrible. This is like a children's Christmas song.' And they're saying 'poo' and 'pee.' We're like, 'What the fuck?' And Potrafka's back there and he's drunk. And he has that glazed look over his eyes. And I go, 'Dude, if you go up there and you tackle these motherfuckers, I will buy you a beer.' And he goes, 'Wha?' And I go, 'Not only will I buy you a beer, I'll buy you a big ass beer.' And he goes, '*Really?*'"

"He was like, 'It'll make the show great,'" Potrafka said. "'They'll be mad at you, but it's for the greater good of comedy.'"

Potrafka, who was still dressed as Santa Claus, stumbled into the makeshift backstage area, where he threw open the curtain and bum-rushed the performers on stage. "I didn't think he was gonna do it," Monte said. "He grabs the girl first. And when he brings her down, he falls with her. And we're laughing. And Geary gets in my face, and he's screaming at me. I'm playing innocent. Potrafka gets up like a snake. He gets up from his waist without using his arms. He just peels up. And he looks, and the girl is still trying to play guitar."

"It was done with safety," Potrafka insisted. "Not like, a violent way at all."

"He slammed the guy," Monte said. "And Geary just went crazy. And everybody in the audience is freaking out. And we're laughing hysterically in the back. And then Potrafka just gets up. And he walks out. And the girl just starts playing guitar. They continued on like it was part of the show. And nobody knew what to do."

"At that point, I left the room and just sat with my head in my hands wondering what the hell was going to be next," Geary told *TimeOut Chicago* in 2009.[31] "We realized we'd given artists such free rein that at most of the shows it was just total anarchy."

"Oh, he was fucking pissed," Potrafka said of Geary. "He didn't hold a grudge long term. But for at least a month or so, he was pissed. He sent me an angry e-mail. It's water under the bridge, but yeah. He didn't take kindly to someone doing that."

"It was a sign of the schism between the show we wanted to produce versus what some of the comedians in the back of the room wanted the Lodge to be," Lawler said. "I felt very embarrassed about it, and it took me a while to not be upset with Potrafka about it."

According to Geary, there were two main factors in turning the show around from being "total shite" and "total anarchy" to becoming the "Nation's Longest-Running Independent Comedy Showcase." The first big change was that Geary stopped booking apathetic, unappreciative comics, and he doubled down on booking the comics who seemed to care about the show.

The second big change was the implementation of a seasonal "cast" to help promote and produce the show. And it evolved out of comics, like Steve O. Harvey and Josh Cheney, wanting to help Geary and Lawler (plus their significant others) set everything up and flier at L stops in the dead of winter. "I think Geary changed the game because he got people involved," comedian Mike O'Connell said. "Like Steve O. and Josh Cheney and those guys who were part of that group....That was a serious community of people with the same thinking. He got people invested in it. So it just got better."

"We had to get a lot more savvy about who we were booking and what our expectations were," Geary told *TimeOut* in the 2009 article, which was a preview of the show's tenth season. "Once that piece clicked into place, we increased our audience every year."

Mark Geary, Tom Lawler and the entire Lincoln Lodge cast were probably going to figure it all out no matter what. But I'm also guessing that the growth of the show had more than a little to do with the talent that was bubbling up from a certain open mic that happened to be only a block away.

Chapter 15

THE DEN (PEAK)

The first taste of success for the Lyon's Den open mic regulars came when comedian John Roy defeated Loni Love to win *Star Search* on February 6, 2003. Sure, the comics had already seen Dwayne Kennedy have some success over the years. But Dwayne Kennedy was always more of a mentor than a peer. Roy was still in his late twenties and only five and a half years into his career. He idolized Kennedy, just like the rest of them did. And Roy's victory (he won $100,000 and a development deal from CBS) could be looked at as a sign of hope for everybody else.

"It was a big deal," comedian Shawn Cole said of Roy's victory. "I didn't know [David] Stebbins. I knew *of* him. [Mick] Betancourt had some success.[32] I knew of Betancourt, and we met a couple times....I was genuinely excited when [Roy] won. I was telling people, 'This is awesome. We run with this guy. He just won *Star Search*. He just dumped Loni Love on her ass. He just broke the game. He cracked through.'"

"I was jumping up and down that he won," Brian Potrafka said. "Because it proved my theory. There were generations in the 1920s, [with] Hemingway and all these hip people. I thought we were one of those. And I wanted to prove I'm not an egotist or a biased fool. And this, to me, was like, 'Well, proves it.'"

"I couldn't believe that I had won," Roy said on *The History of Standup* podcast in 2019.[33] "And Arsenio [Hall, the host of the show] set me up in a weird way. He goes, 'Is there anyone out there that didn't believe in you that you want to kind of get back at now?' And I said, 'No, but I want to let everyone know out there in the Lyon's Den doing their set every Monday for free that if I can do it, so can you.' And then Arsenio loved that and then went, 'Lyon's Den! Lyon's Den! Lyon's Den!'"

The following week, Roy was back at the Lyon's Den open mic, where he was greeted with a standing ovation. "When he came in, we all clapped," Pete Holmes said. "And obviously we didn't plan it....We were so happy for him."

John Roy. *Erin Nekervis.*

"It was a real hero's welcome when John came back," comedian Emily Dorezas said. "Because it was like he had been to the top of the mountain, and he was still willing to talk to the little people."

Obviously, not everybody in the scene was thrilled for Roy. This was still a scene with a faction of comics that had completely rejected traditional stand-up. And John Roy was a traditional stand-up to his core. Unlike most of the alt comics, he got regular work at Zanies. And he told actual jokes with setups and punchlines. He just so happened to be really fucking good at it. And ironically, Roy's tight bits and professionalism were the things that impressed the new generation of alt comics entering into the bizarro Chicago scene after 9/11.

"John Roy would kill in a way that was important for us to see," Nick Vatterott said. "Like, 'Okay, there is another level of funny that, craft-wise, you need to understand.'"

"John Roy did extremely carefully written bits," comedian Robert Buscemi said. "It was syllable for syllable. Really, really powerful jokes."

"If John Roy blessed us," comedian Brooke Van Poppelen said, "it'd be like, 'Whoa, it's pro time.' Like, 'This guy is a fucking pro.'"

"He's the first [comic] I saw where I was like, '*Daaaaaamn*,'" comedian Ricky Carmona said. "'These are *jokes*.' Other muhfuckers are going up there and they're crinkling up their papers and they're stumbling on the steps on the way up and shit....But there were some people that it's just like, 'Man, I'm taking all of this in. Word.'"

According to comedian Bill Cruz, John Roy's *Star Search* win also caused an uptick in the number of comics showing up to the Den every Monday. "We would get people from the suburbs who had no idea what was going on," Cruz said. "They just wanted to try stand-up because they saw John Roy's thing. It was night and day."

"I walked in," comedian Nate Craig said. "I was like, 'What is this?' It was like a tour bus dropped a bunch of people off."

It wasn't long after his *Star Search* win that Roy headed out to Los Angeles. But the Den was increasingly creating new stars to replace him—at least in its own isolated bubble. And the person who probably inherited the mantle of "best traditional stand-up" when Roy left was a young, married, Christian comic from Massachusetts named Pete Holmes. In fact, in a 2004 article from a Chicago bar publication called *The Tap*,[34] Roy called Holmes "the brightest up-and-coming comic in Chicago" and said that he was "already demonstrating star-level talent."

If Roy only knew how right he was. And when Pete talks about his entry into the scene, he almost frames it as if the Den found him, as opposed to the other way around. And yeah, his first few days in the scene seem especially fortuitous. "A huge part of why I did stand-up," Pete told me, "is my stop on the train was the Irving Park Brown Line. And I would walk past the Lyon's Den every day on my way to the train, and [the sign out front] said 'Monday Comedy.' And I was like, 'What could that mean?'"

Pete told *The History of Standup* podcast that he would walk past that sign every day as if he were resisting its temptations. "Every day my route home was walking by, not just *an* open mic, *the* Chicago open mic," he said. "The biggest one. The cornerstone of what we're talking about was on my route home....I would walk past that place. And I would for months without even going in. One week, I walked in just to look. I just wanted to see the room. That was the first step. So I went in the back just to see if I could imagine myself going there. And then the next week, I sign up. I felt like I did all right. I thought I held my own."

By almost all accounts, Pete did more than that. "One of the most impressive people I ever saw was Pete Holmes," comedian Dave Odd told me. "I remember me and [comedian Jeff] Siena kind of whispering, 'Pete said he just started doing stand-up. There's no way he just started doing stand-up.'"

Pete Holmes. *Erin Nekervis.*

Perhaps even more fortuitous than his route home was who Pete Holmes met right away at his first show. "I walked in, and there was Robert Buscemi," Pete said. "And I asked him how it worked. And he became a very close friend of mine and a huge icon of the scene."

Robert Buscemi, who would in fact become a huge icon in the scene, got a relatively late start in stand-up. He was in his early thirties by the time he hit that first open mic at the Lyon's Den. Which made him about a decade older than Pete and most of the other open mic comics in the scene. Luckily, if any generational divide did exist, it was quickly negated when Buscemi developed his own style of absurdist comedy that was immediately embraced by the scene.

"When I started stand-up," Buscemi said, "I literally had no idea what I was gonna want to talk about. But I immediately created these fictional characters. And immediately, other comedians responded. They would kind of go, '*Ohhhhhh.* He's doing something different.' And it was titillating to other comedians. I've never felt like I was a particularly good chronicler of my life, or storyteller about a night some friends and I went out, but I feel like fantastical dreamscape stuff or really strange, tiny jokes, I can do that. So that's what I did."

Buscemi had been audio-taping his early sets, and when he listened back, he began to notice a stage persona beginning to emerge in his performances.

Robert Buscemi. *Krystle Gemnich.*

In an interview I conducted with him back in 2006,[35] Buscemi compared the experience to "a negative emerging from the chemicals in a photography darkroom. It was sort of magical....In a way, it was the most mundane thing ever—like seeing your reflection in a mirror. I remember the day it happened. I just heard the guy I wanted to be emerging on tape—the timing, the material, everything."

"There's certain magical comedians," Pete said, referring to Buscemi, "that when everything is just aligned—the scene, the year that it was, where we were with absurd comedy, where Rob was in his life...there was just nothing funnier than watching him do 'Meat? Meet Meat!'...[Everyone] agreed, in Chicago, that it was the funniest thing in the world."

The bit, or chunk, Pete is referencing begins with Buscemi renting a U-Haul van to drive to a slaughterhouse in order to intercept its low-grade remnant meat before it "dumpsters it." It's already wildly off-kilter as a premise. But in the hands of Buscemi, it serves as a vehicle for him to craft a surreal, funhouse-mirror fantasy where he has invited all his friends over to his home for concoctions like "thick intestine gravy" and "squirrel peppers," and they all cap the night off by soaking their feet in a huge trough of beef stock while they watch the sun set over his valley. "That's living, right there," Buscemi tells the audience in his syrupy rural, central Ohioan twang. "That's what that is."

"It's important to me that the captures be humane," Buscemi says, segueing into one of his early signature bits. "I like a quick capture. Any drawn-out kill, you get that final fear-flush of adrenaline, gives the meat a tartness that I don't particularly care for. So I like a quick kill. And I like to be involved. Because I think it's more direct contact with what you ingest. So I'll frappe a puffin, frog gig a wood sprite. I'll pepper a wild boar's nose and sneeze-kill it. You know? Eat its fur. Which is a great source of um, fur. Or I'll dig a pit, just in nature somewhere, lay down spikes and put a rug over it. Because any animal that doesn't know there shouldn't just be a rug lying in nature? That's dinner, is what that animal is."

"Or if I'm out, just in social intercourse with an animal at a party or something," Buscemi continues, really stretching the audience's limits for the absurd, "I'll spill my kerosene martini between an animal and its shell and go to light its cigarette for it, and flash-fry them right there at the party. *Fwooof.* Beware turtles, armadillos, medieval knights. I will turn you into a self-contained scalding soup cauldron. That's my promise."

And then the coup de grâce. "I think my favorite, though, is to kill meat *with* meat. To me, it seems green. Or red and whatever meat color. Grayish. But it's green, ecologically circular, to kill meat with meat. I have this high-powered sling shot. I'll sling-shoot a frozen meatball at an animal's temple. Just *whap*. Because I think it's mete that meat meet meat. You know, it's like *whap*. Meat meet meat. You know? Meat meet meat. Meat? Meat? Meet meat. I will mete out meat to meat. That's what I'm saying. Bet your sweet peters I will."

"Meat? Meet Meat!" which is on Buscemi's debut album, *Palpable*, is just as brilliant as it is idiotic, as if the smartest person in the room is telling you the dumbest thing you've ever heard. But within bits like these, Buscemi managed to take his outsider status—his age, his accent and his look—and use it to create a believably ridiculous comedic persona, as well as a surreal comic poetry all his own. Nobody else was doing anything like it. And it made Buscemi the hippest guy in every room in the scene.

The critics noticed too. Allan Johnson of the *Chicago Tribune*—who notoriously hated alt comedy, loathed Midnight Bible School and barely mentioned the Lincoln Lodge in anything he wrote—called Buscemi "clever and sophisticated"[36] in one article and "daring and fearless"[37] in another, as well as "worthy of such big-time fests as the US Comedy Arts Festival and the Montreal International Comedy Festival."

Johnson *got* Buscemi. He got the character Buscemi was trying to portray, and he got that it was all being done with a heavy wink to the crowd. "He could easily be the next big Chicago comedian," Johnson wrote of Buscemi in 2005. And I think everyone in the scene would have enthusiastically agreed.

That was who Pete Holmes, who actually would go on to become the next big Chicago comedian, met his first night in stand-up. But the already fortuitous story of Pete Holmes gets even crazier from there. "And then the next night, I did the Cubby Bear [open mic]," Pete told *The History of Standup*. "And I met Kumail."

Kumail Nanjiani, who is currently a movie star, grew up in Karachi, Pakistan. But at age eighteen, he came to the United States to attend Grinnell College in Grinnell, Iowa. And after graduation, he took an IT job at the University of Chicago. And then apparently, he went about crushing at every open mic the city had to offer.

"Kumail and Pete Holmes were two guys that the first time you ever see them on stage, you're like, 'All right that fucker's gonna be famous,'" Dave Odd said. "Because there's no way they can't be."

"When we first met Kumail," Matt Braunger told me, "he had one eyebrow around his whole head....But also had funnier jokes than most people. Speaking in his second language."

Not only was Nanjiani (who did have a pretty wicked unibrow back then) a gifted joke writer. But apparently, because everyone's mind was still on 9/11, the War in Afghanistan and/or the War in Iraq, the fact that Kumail was a brown person who mostly *didn't* talk about any of it on stage impressed the comics in the scene even more.

"Kumail was starting right after 9/11," Kyle Kinane told *The History of Standup* podcast, "and to see him coming in with a Pakistani accent and not addressing it, not doing easy jokes about 9/11. Like, 'No, you're just a good comedian.' He's like, 'This is a joke about me reading someone's crossword puzzle over their shoulder on the L and about what the plural of octopus might be.' I'm like, '*This is great.*'"

While Pete Holmes, Robert Buscemi and Kumail Nanjiani all started the same week, a few of the other Den's stars—Kyle Kinane and Matt Braunger—would be heading out to Los Angeles. And when I asked Jeff Klinger, who had been running the Lyon's Den and had watched every performer who came though the scene, who he thought was the best comedian in Chicago during his time there, he didn't hesitate to say, "By far, Matt Braunger. I was like, 'This person is the next Will Ferrell. He's unstoppable.'"

"I remember thinking, 'This guy is like Robin Williams,'" Buscemi said of Braunger. "I was like, 'Somebody needs to see this guy'…I saw greatness in him really early."

Braunger had come to Chicago to perform in plays. This led to him to improv and sketch and then ultimately to stand-up. It apparently came naturally to him. "[Braunger] came in and it was like, 'Who the fuck is this guy?'" Kinane said. "How dare you be from sketch and be funny?"

"I often think about Braunger's last show," Dorezas said. "Because that was a big deal.

Top: Kumail Nanjiani. *Krystle Gemnich*. *Middle*: Matt Braunger. *Krystle Gemnich*. *Bottom*: Kyle Kinane. *Erin Nekervis*.

And Kyle was gonna move either right before or right after. So there felt like a shift, but we were all like, 'They're now gonna go be megastars.'"

Kyle Kinane, who had begun his stand-up career as a "fucking punk-ass Cramps wannabe," was now one of the most respected comics, if not *the* most respected comic, in the scene. "He was The Guy when I got there that everybody talked about," Nick Vatterott said. "I have like, thirty-five memories of my eight years in Chicago. And that's it. It's confined to thirty-five. So it's weird which things my brain has decided to remember. But I remember the first time I saw Kyle."

"That dude was other level," Carmona said. "I remember one time Kinane ran on stage just wearing cutoff jean shorts and that's it. And was like, '*Whoooooo!*' And doing this thing about how Chicago people, when it's a winter day and it hits forty, we act like it's a ninety-fucking-degree day. And I was like, 'This is great.'"

"Anybody can get drunk and take their shirt off at the bar," Pete Holmes said. "He would get drunk, take his shirt off and then go on stage and then *kill*. I still get a little star-struck around Kyle."

Matt Braunger, Kyle Kinane and John Roy all headed off to LA. And they were accompanied by Jeff Klinger around the same time. This also meant the reins (or, I guess, "Rings") of the Lyon's Den open mic would be handed off as well. And they eventually wound up in the hands of comedians Steve O. Harvey and Josh Cheney. In a hot room like the Lyon's Den, this essentially made "Steve O. and Josh" the first two comedians every new comic in the scene would meet going forward. And they would make a huge and lasting impression.

Steve O, who happened to have the best mattress commercial joke in the history of comedy, was also somehow even funnier off stage. "He was the funniest guy when we'd go play cards," comedian David Angelo said. "It'd be fifteen comedians there. And really funny comedians too—[Sean] Flannery, CJ [Sullivan], all those people were there. And it was no question, Steve O. Harvey's the funniest guy at the poker table. It was a guarantee."

Steve O. Harvey. *Krystle Gemnich.*

"He was just really quick," Angelo continued. "On the [annual comedian] canoe trip, we went into this restaurant in Wisconsin. The waitress is counting all of us. She's like, 'Eight?' And Steve goes, 'No. We haven't. That's why we're here.' I mean, that was the time difference too. There was no delay, and I was just like, 'This guy is so funny.'"

That quick wit, along with his kindness, made an intimidating scene feel a lot more welcoming. "The beauty of Steve O. Harvey is he had the ability to make everybody his best friend," comedian Darren Bodeker said. "He was attentive to you when he was in your presence. He would listen to what you had to say. Your opinion mattered, and so you felt good and special. And I think everywhere he went he was kind of everyone's best friend."

"Steve O. Harvey was the first guy who was like, 'You want to go get some food?' And I was like, 'Oh my God, yes. Of course,'" T.J. Miller told me. "And he took me to a diner. And I was asking questions. And I remember thinking, 'This is a big moment [for me]. This guy is one of the Chicago luminaries. He's a *titan*. And I'm sitting here eating hash browns with him. Oh my fucking God.' He was just so smart, so knowledgeable and so nice."

Steve O's partner in the sound booth was Josh Cheney, who happens to have the best impression of a dancing Muppet that you will ever see. Cheney, who was from the Chicagoland area, had known that he wanted to be a comedian since age eight or nine. "I was counting down the minutes and

Nate Craig and Steve O. Harvey. *Cayne Collier.*

days until I turned twenty-one, [when] I could get into a bar and perform," he told me. And from the very beginning, Josh Cheney performed in a suit.

"[Cheney] always wore a suit and tie," Andy Lurie told me. "And nobody gave him grief for it. Nobody ever said, 'What are you doing? Why can't you look like you failed the audition for Nirvana like the rest of us?'"

I asked Cheney how many suits he owned in his suit-owning prime, and with a big smile, he said, "For sure, nine. And at least one tux." He did it for a mixture of reasons. Partially because of the suit-wearing comics he grew up loving, like Groucho Marx and Bob Newhart. He wore them partially because he believed it showed respect for the audience, which was important to him. But also, he wore suits on stage because it just made the whole thing a little more ridiculous.

"I grew up loving Leslie Nielsen," Cheney explained. "And that super dry sense of humor. The fact that he was dressed in a suit, saying those ridiculous things in *Airplane*, *Naked Gun* and any other movie. That disconnect was like, 'How could somebody who looks like a very serious businessman from the '50s be saying and doing these things?' That in and of itself is more ridiculous and more funny."

This version of the Lyon's Den was what I'd wandered into in my own business suit in the summer of 2003. And it was the open mic I would attend almost every Monday night from January 5, 2004, until the Lyon's Den had its final show just over six months later.

During that brief period, I was forced to unlearn everything I thought I knew about comedy. And I had to watch, listen and learn from the very best comics in the scene while also taking note of "what to never do" from the very worst. This was my education. And I honestly feel like I went to Comedy Harvard.

One of the very first nights I went to the Den, I walked into the men's room, where I bumped into an apologetic Nick Vatterott, who was duct-taping a dozen fully inflated white balloons to his body. I remember laughing to myself and thinking, "This place is so weird." And then seeing Nick go up on stage to host the show, where he convinced the room full of people to sing a football-themed version of "Frère Jacques," in the round, while he popped the balloons.

"I had written twelve one-liners," Vatterott explained to me, seventeen years later. "But I was like, 'I don't want to just do one-liners.' So this is what you saw when you walked in. I was like, 'Every time I tell a joke, I'm gonna pop a balloon. I want to see how many jokes I can tell in a certain amount of time.' The time, the sands in the hour glass, were going to be having the audience sing this song [to the tune of 'Frère Jacques'] 'Larry Csonka, Larry

Csonka, Dan Dierdorf, Vinny Testaverde, Dick Vermeil.' So I got the whole audience to sing that song. And it's me popping all the balloons, doing one-liners."

"It's so funny," he added. "I have a very vivid memory of you coming into the bathroom while I was trying to manually put these balloons on."

The bathroom duct tape interaction notwithstanding, Nick Vatterott has one of the least glamorous beginnings to his comedy career that I've ever heard. "I was in Columbia, Missouri," he told me, "and just living on somebody's couch for a year. And not going to school in a college town. Just *really* being the worst type of person."

Nick Vatterott. *Krystle Gemnich.*

About once a year, there would be a stand-up contest at Deja Vu Comedy Club in Columbia. "And I would do that, lose and then wait until the next year to get up a second time," he told me. "I didn't know you could just start a show."

Vatterott eventually decided that he should do something more productive with his life. So he signed up for a class at Second City and drove straight to Chicago in his Volkswagen Bus. And after a few wrong turns, Vatterott managed to pull up to the Second City Training Center with only minutes to spare before his first class.

Nick Vatterott. *Erin Nekervis.*

With no job and no place to stay, Vatterott wound up living out of his minibus for his first two weeks in town. But once he got a little more settled in, he began inquiring about the local stand-up scene. And when he was told about the Lyon's Den, Vatterott decided to make the trek the very next week.

At first, Vatterott assumed that the front bar area was also the showroom for the open mic. But after he was directed to the back, he pulled open the curtain and began to hear laughter, which grew louder as he entered. Then he saw comedian Mike Wiley on the stage. And Wiley was killing. "It was just packed, and people were screaming and laughing," Vatterott remembered. "I was like, 'Oh. *This* is the Lyon's Den.'"

"I was on stage when Nick Vatterott showed up?" Wiley deadpanned when I relayed that story. "And he's still doing it?"

Over the next few years, Vatterott would provide some of the most original and celebrated moments in the scene's lore. But at first, he got known as the guy who would pop in late into the night and blow the minds of the last five drunk people who were still there.

"This happened every week," Robert Buscemi said. "Nick Vatterott would come in. And nobody was still in the room....But he would perform the most elaborate, wild, ambitious, comprehensively written [pieces]. And I have never seen him glance at a note once. Ever. He'd come in with a costume sometimes. And you'd have to grab four drunk people so he at least had four people to perform to. And it was just brilliant, through the roof, every time."

"I was so impressed with Nick," comedian Becky Garcia said. "Because I would never see the same set twice. The capacity for that brain. It's beyond. It's just limitless. I can't think like that. I don't know anyone in the world who could."

Besides his reputation for coming in late and blowing people's minds, Vatterott also got a reputation for never repeating the same jokes twice. To the point that Mike Burns told me that he would run into the back room of the Lyon's Den any time he knew Vatterott was about to perform. "Because you're gonna see something special," he said. "And that's not to slight anyone who did more conventional stand-up. But they were gonna do those jokes again, probably next week or at another show you saw, but Nick Vatterott could be up there for one time only singing about Yoda and tuning a guitar while popping balloons out of his ass or something."

Vatterott partially sees his prolificacy and penchant for experimentation as symptoms of a larger psychological issue. "I had this very OCD thing happening," he told me. "I wanted to do five new minutes, or three and a half, or whatever it was, every week. And as soon as I left the stage, I started figuring out what I wanted to do next week."

He gave himself strict rules regarding his act, including never allowing himself to repeat the same joke at the same venue. He would also never repeat the same joke twice in the same week. He would, however, allow himself to save or sandbag specific jokes for upcoming weeks. And sometimes, he would hold on to jokes for months without using them, just because he wanted to be able to sleep at night.

Nick Vatterott. *Erin Nekervis.*

Vatterott was smart enough to know that there wouldn't necessarily be three and a half minutes of new jokes that were worth telling every single week, so sometimes his self-imposed new material rules would open doors for Vatterott to experiment or play with the form. No new jokes this week? No problem. He'd just do something else to get a laugh.

Sometimes Vatterott would perform three and a half minutes of straight stand-up. Other times, he might, say, sit in a closet for hours, only to emerge as a ventriloquist dummy. "There was one night where Nick Vatterott sat in a closet next to the stage for like, two hours," Cheney said. "And waited for [comedian] Brady Novak to do his set....And Brady came up on stage and was like, 'I'm gonna be doing my new act. It's gonna be a ventriloquist.' And Brady took Nick Vatterott out of the closet and put him on his lap like he was a ventriloquist dummy."

Novak was a former collegiate pitcher who was about six-foot-six and three hundred pounds. And Vatterott was about a foot shorter and less than half his weight. It was a ventriloquist bit after all. "The movie *Chicago* had just come out," Novak said. "And they have this ventriloquist scene with Renée Zellweger and Richard Gere....I was like, 'Nick, you should be a ventriloquist [dummy]. And I'll play the Richard Gere part.' And then we improvised a lot of it."

When they got to the show, both of them put their names in the hat (or probably the plastic beer pitcher). Vatterott drew number 6 and Novak got number 20. "[Vatterott] goes, 'Let's do number 20,'" Novak said. "So he wanted to wait in there for twenty people, which made it even better."

"It's not funny if I get pulled sixth," Vatterott explained. "It's funny if I'm in there for twenty comics."

In the end, it was a perfect Lyon's Den set. And one that could have only paid off like it did in a show with that many comedians and an audience that stayed the entire time. When Vatterott was revealed, the crowd erupted in laughter and appreciation. Then he and Novak killed for four straight minutes. And then, for no apparent reason, they left the stage acting like pterodactyls.

"That's when comedy was the most fun," Vatterott said. "And you could only do that at the Lyon's Den."

A lot of comics saw that set as if a gauntlet of weirdness had been thrown down by Novak and Vatterott. "I'm gonna use a bullshit Mike Tomlin quote that he uses all the time," comedian and Steelers fan Ken Barnard said. "Iron sharpens iron. Because, for me, as a person who likes weird stuff, you see Nick Vatterott sitting in a cabinet playing a ventriloquist dummy two hours later. That sort of stuff is like, mind-blowing. And [I think], 'How weird can I get?' Everybody [was] pushing each other to be as nuts as possible. That room was just thrumming with that energy. Not everybody was weird, obviously, but weird really worked there."

"[Weirdness] was rewarded," Van Poppelen said. "There was pressure, in a really good way, to be different and weird."

One of the first thoughts I had when I rewatched the clip of Novak and

Brady Novak. *Krystle Gemnich.*

Vatterott performing the ventriloquist bit was feeling bad for whatever poor open mic-er had to follow them. I can imagine a scenario where everyone in the audience was still recovering from that performance. And then some awkward twenty-four-year-old had to get up there and say, "So dating is hard," right after. But that might just be me speaking as a former twenty-four-year-old who had to follow Novak one time as he stood on top of a stool on stage, put a cigarette out on his crotch and then threatened, in his booming voice, to dive into his pint glass of water below him.

This was what the Lyon's Den was like. Every Monday, comic after comic. Since this was Comedy Harvard, an important part of that education for newer comics was to see people killing with all different types of styles across the comedy spectrum. And in addition to Pete Holmes and John Roy, there were other comics doing really well with traditional stand-up. And the name in that category who got mentioned in my interviews about as frequently and as reverently as the comics who are currently famous was Nathan Trenholm.

"Dave Odd would have us do [comedy] contests," Pete Holmes said. "If I went after Nathan Trenholm, I would win. If I would go before Nathan Trenholm, I would lose. It was like voting for a sweetie pie or a naughty devil. And if you're at a bar on a Tuesday night, chances are you're gonna vote for the naughty devil. And he was great. We were always friends. But because he was always beating me at contests, I was like, 'I gotta work harder. I'm not as funny as Nathan.' So that actually motivated me. It's not a great fuel to run the machine on, but a little bit of a healthy competition with somebody was helpful."

The other comedian who gets mentioned the most frequently in Lyon's Den conversations wasn't marrying improv and stand-up like Nick Vatterott and Brady Novak, and he definitely wasn't a traditional stand-up in the mold of John Roy, Pete Holmes and Nathan Trenholm. He wasn't even necessarily an anti-comedian like Chet Lactacious or Bill O'Donnell. He was a force of nature in a category all his own by the name of Shawn Cole.

"That whole 2001 to 2004 era, everyone was struggling to out-anti-comedy each other," Dave Odd said. "Their whole thing was being as unfunny as they possibly could be. And the only person who ever did that well was Shawn Cole. Every comedian within a mile would rush into the room to see what he was doing."

"I remember seeing Shawn Cole," Novak said, "and going, 'There's no way I'll be that funny. Maybe I'll be funnier than some of the other people.'"

"He would physically make me hurt all over," Becky Garcia said. "The back of my head would start pounding, and I felt like I was gonna vomit because I would laugh so hard."

"I would come in to see Shawn Cole," Brooke Van Poppelen said. "And be like, 'I feel nervous. This is exciting. I don't know what he's gonna do. He's really frightening.'"

"He was physically intimidating as fuck," Buscemi said. "He would put one leg up on the stool. Like a medieval painting of the devil. It was crazy. It was so funny and scary and overwhelming."

Cole's signature bit, which I'm confident will make zero sense when you read it, began with him asking the crowd if they loved their bodies or if they loved rock-and-roll. That was the choice. They couldn't have both, he assured them. They had to choose. "It's probably a bit about censorship," Cole told me. "Or it's probably just nuts."

I'm pretty sure Cole knows it's the latter. In the next part of the bit, which negates the first part entirely, Cole tells the audience that he's figured out a way to love his body *and* rock-and-roll. Then he begins a song. Well, it's probably more of an animalistic bellowing than a song. But it begins with the mouthing of guitar noises. And the whole thing roughly goes, "*Brenenenenenowww. Brenenenenenenow.* I got a strong back, I'll be a good man for you tonight, woman!" And then he points at his crotch and shouts, "Want to see it *spit?* Point it straight to hell!" And every comedian in attendance would be losing their minds laughing.

"I can't imagine anyone thinking that's comedy," Vatterott laughed. "But if you saw it live, it's one of the funniest things you'd ever see."

"Oh my God, we would *scream* laughing," Buscemi said.

Like I said, it probably makes no sense to you. But sometimes Cole would only tease the bit, much to the frustration of the other comics who loved it. Sometimes he would pause in the middle of whatever he was doing in his set and ask the audience, "Can you imagine if any of this was real?" There were also a variety of stage names he used. Some were mundane, like "Brawny Daniels." Others were wildly inappropriate, like "Gary Rape." And one time Cole was hosting the Crush open mic, and an older guy kept badgering Cole to go up earlier in the night, so Cole finally brought him up to the stage as "Old Casket Face."

"Whenever he introduced me," Garcia laughed, "he's like, 'This next gal: Boy is she dumpy. Here we go.'"

"I don't know if I made this clear," Cole told me. "The entire thing was fuck-around time."

"He was the epitome of, 'Just do what's funny,'" Vatterott said. "It doesn't have to be jokes. It *can* be jokes. But what is funny to you? Because a lot of times jokes will follow that. But he was up there doing what he thought was funny. And we did too. He was our favorite person to watch."

Of course, the person who probably gets brought up in Lyon's Den conversations as much as any of the now-famous or semi-mythical figures from the Chicago scene is a comedian by the name of Michael Strauss. And he might actually deserve more credit for turning that Monday open mic into the hottest room in the city than anyone. He performed under the stage name of Thomas Mayonnaise. But everybody knew him as Tommy Mayo.

The first time Strauss performed at the Den was back in the bleak early days when nobody came. "It was three comics that night," he told me of his first time. "The audience was my five friends and one other couple. It was not popping off."

A little while later, Strauss got a job waiting tables at Hugo's Frog Bar on Rush Street, where he met and worked alongside another aspiring comedian who went by the name Nathan James Lee. Strauss and Lee decided to start attending the mic together, which by that time was already significantly better than the first time he performed.

"That was when I had severed my finger polishing a wine glass at work," Strauss said. "I remember coming out of surgery. Like, on that Monday. And that was the first time I went up as Tommy Mayo. And I don't know if the drugs were really strong or what, but I decided to keep Tommy Mayo because I never thought Michael Strauss was funny. It was too German sounding. And I was just looking at every angle."

The one angle that definitely worked for Strauss, and for Nathan James Lee, was inviting all their coworkers to the show. "All our friends just wanted a place to go after work," Strauss explained. "We just started inviting everybody at work. And everybody was showing up every Monday."

This was an open mic where forty comedians would sign up every week. And names were drawn out randomly from a pitcher before the show. When I ask comics from the Lyon's Den era which spot on the list they thought was ideal, there's a large contingency of people who thought the numbers 10 to 15 or 10 to 20 were the absolute sweet spot. I happen to be in that camp. However, I also had to be out the door for work the next morning by 7:00 a.m. So I would often go home if I drew higher than a 30. But apparently if a comic fought through their urge to leave, they would be handsomely rewarded.

"The sweet spot is between 10 and 20," Kumail Nanjiani said on the *Box Angeles* podcast[38] in 2015. "And then it's bad from like 20 to 35. And then people leave and then new people come in.…There were these two guys who started doing stand-up, who were these handsome guys who worked at a douche-y restaurant. So they would bring all their beautiful friends around eleven.…It was just a fucking great time."

"There was a different scene at that hour," Vatterott said. "When Mayonnaise showed up with his crew, then it would get this second wind every week."

"They'd get off work and every person that worked there would come in," Dorezas said. "And I'm telling you, you didn't want to be anywhere near spot 1 through 20 on the list. Because around 20 to 23, like, 50 people would come in....It was night and day. And a crowd brings a crowd. So it was wild how consistent that group would show up and be a really great audience. And massive."

When I asked Josh Cheney, who saw more comedy at the Lyon's Den than anyone else, what his most memorable Lyon's Den moments were, he also brought up a Tommy Mayo story. "The night Tommy Mayo was blackout drunk," Cheney began. "And he put a milk crate on his head and ran into the audience. At full speed. And took out the first three high-top tables of the audience....I don't think anybody got injured. But if you had dropped that milk crate from a three-story building, it would have smashed in the same way that this smashed off of his head."

"I did a *Jackass* audition bit," Strauss explained. "There was a milk crate on the back of the stage. And all I said was, 'This will cushion my fall if I jump off this stage.' So I put the milk crate on my head right at the last second. I jump off the stage. My knee hits the speaker on the stage and I flipped upside-down. Broke my thumb. That was a good night. It was worth all the pain."

"He was a wild card," Van Poppelen said. "He didn't know what he was doing. Other than cocaine. He was fucking batshit. But I liked hanging out with him."

In the end, the legacy of Tommy Mayo is probably more about the crowd than the comedy. "Maybe I brought the crowd," Strauss said. "Maybe I brought the energy. I know from what I heard, everybody started wanting to go on later because they knew the room was gonna fill up again. God, I don't know. Did I really have that much to do with it? You already had all the talent. You had your Bridos and your Mike Holmes and your CJ Sullivan and Brady Novak. Vatterott. T.J. Miller. Kyle Kinane. I mean, you know the names."

Maybe he's right. Even though he's being overly generous by naming me with the rest of the other names. Especially since I was such a late arrival. But Mike Holmes and I moved to Chicago, just blocks from Wrigley Field in the fall of 2003, right around the time of the infamous Steve Bartman Cubs playoff game. And once we arrived, we didn't really hit the ground running, to say the least.

Chapter 16

2004 (BEGINNINGS)

After I moved to Chicago, it took me three months before I tried stand-up there and then another month to do it again after that. I'd love to tell you I was busy with work or doing other productive things with my time. But I was mostly just too intimidated to start doing comedy in Chicago. And so I didn't. And neither did my roommate, Mike Holmes.

It wasn't until Christmas 2003, when my sister gave me a book called *How to Do It Standing Up* by Barry Dougherty, that I finally got the motivation to give stand-up another go. The book emphasized the importance of stage time to aspiring comedians. And that meant finding open mics. And honestly, I'd never heard anyone say any good things about open mics before that. I'd only heard comedian Orny Adams talk shit about open mic-ers in the Jerry Seinfeld documentary *Comedian*. So that pro–open mic mentality was a revelation. And I made it my New Years resolution to begin heading out to every comedy open mic in the city. And when I got back to Chicago after the holidays, I prepared a speech in my head, where I would tell Mike Holmes I was going to do stand-up with him or without him.

The speech didn't last long. It turned out that Holmes had been thinking the exact same thing. He agreed to go to open mics with me, and we headed to the Lyon's Den together on the very first Monday of 2004. This time, it went okay for both of us, and we celebrated our achievement when we got home. Probably more out of relief than anything. I remember Holmes saying, "We just made a room full of people in Chicago laugh!" And that was a big deal for two intimidated kids from Iowa.

The next night, we trudged through a foot of snow and subzero temperatures to attend a much smaller open mic at a bar called Piano Man in Wrigleyville. "Coldest night of our lives," Holmes remembered. "It was like a fifty-mile-per-hour wind too. It was like, 'All right, I'm taking this seriously now. This means I want it.'"

The second week at the Den, I drew a number in the sweet spot. I'd walked in, threw my name into the pitcher and had it drawn around number 15 on the list. In other words, it was the perfect chance for me to have my comedic coming out party and make a name for myself in the scene.

After my name was announced, I went on stage, grabbed the mic, took it out of the stand and proceeded to eat a proverbial bag of shit for the next three and a half minutes in front of a packed house. It was an absolute flatline. Not a single nervous giggle or even a cough. The only thing I remember hearing was after I said my final punchline, Robert Buscemi blurted out, "Ah, *jeez*," from somewhere along the back wall.

It was brutal. Every bit of confidence I'd built up in my own abilities over a year of sets in Iowa was completely out the window. Now I wasn't even sure if I was good enough to be there. And on top of that, when I saw all the weird off-the-wall shit that did really well, it confused me even more. I felt like I no longer had any idea what was funny or what I could do on stage that would make people laugh.

"The Lyon's Den could be great," Pete Holmes reminded me. "It could also gut you."

While I was being gutted, Mike Holmes was having the exact opposite experience. At least in my own mind. The third week in January, he absolutely murdered at the Lyon's Den and was approached by comedian and prolific comedy show booker Dave Odd about being a part of his Edge Comedy shows. At that point, Dave Odd might as well have been Lorne Michaels to me. I'd been to his Edge Comedy website. I'd seen his show lineups. And I just assumed that he was some kind of comedy impresario. And he actually was in his own complicated way.

Week by week, I was starting to get to know more of the comics and starting to do a little better on stage. Eventually, I even got two bits to kind of work. One was a joke I'd written with Holmes in college, where I made fun of the VH1 series *The Fabulous Life Of*. It was a little too weird for Iowa City, but it was just weird enough for Chicago. And the second bit came to me after that fateful night in the summer of 2003 when Holmes and I checked out the Lyon's Den for the first time.

After that show, and after the pep talk I gave Holmes, we smoked a little weed back at his sister's apartment. And I got so high that I wrote a joke about seeing two raccoons having "gay raccoon sex" that I found so hysterical in the moment that I couldn't believe I'd reached such impossible levels of comedic brilliance. The next morning, I saw a piece of paper with my own handwriting that said, "Listen up, fuckers. Party time is over."

The joke was obviously useless. But after the same thing happened a second time a few months later and I invented some joke about shearing sheep (yes, I'm serious), I created a new bit where I went through the worst jokes I'd ever written while I was stoned. It was basically just a device for me to do Mitch Hedberg–style jokes. But it worked. Neither the *Fabulous Life Of* thing or the weed bit were great. But at least now I had *something* and could build from there.[39]

Around that time, I decided that my three goals in comedy were to do The Elevated and the Lincoln Lodge—the two prestige booked shows in the city—and also to host the Lyon's Den. If I'd done all three, I'd know that I'd made it in the scene. And in April 2004, I crossed the first one off the list when I hosted at the Den. Granted, I got "asked" to host because Steve O. Harvey had walked up to a table where I was sitting with Mike Holmes and comedian Mike Wiley and said, "The person who was supposed to host tonight cancelled. Did any of you want to do it?" And then he physically turned to Holmes hoping that it would be him who volunteered. But before Holmes could answer, I happily blurted out, "I'll do it."

I'll never forget the confused look on Steve O's face. But I was determined. And to his credit, he let me do it. He was even complimentary afterward. I was really proud of that accomplishment, if you can call it that. It all sounds so minuscule now. And the reason they had rotating hosts in the first place was because the "Rings" thought it was such a tiring, thankless job. But I knew you had to be good to be asked, which is why I wanted to do it. And other Lyon's Den comics have told me that their first time hosting was just as big of a deal for them as it was for me.

"That felt like Carson calling you over to the couch, to be asked to host the Lyon's Den," Nick Vatterott said. "That was the biggest nod you could possibly get at that point....When Steve O. Harvey asked me to host the Lyon's Den, I passed on it. Because I told him I wasn't ready. I remember him laughing like, 'Okay, well let me know when you're ready to host this *open mic.*'"

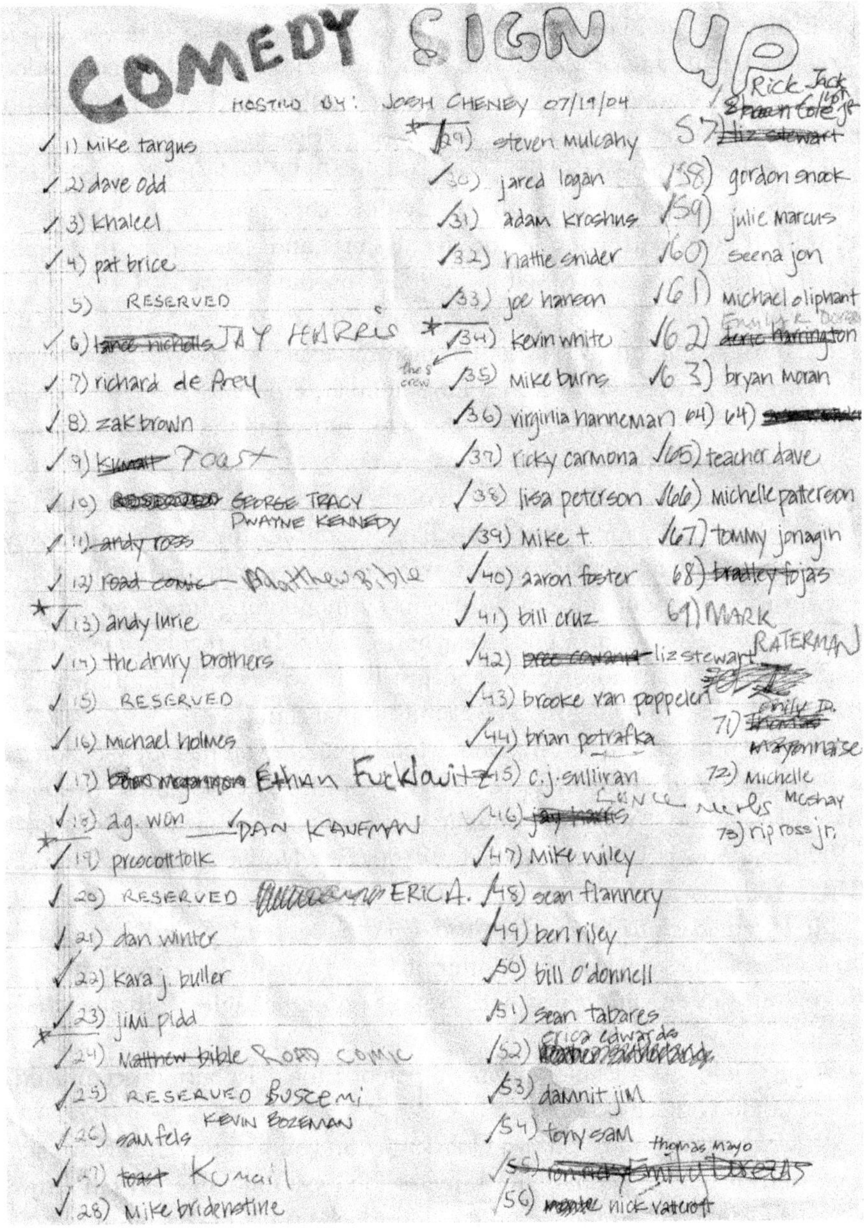

COMEDY SIGN UP

HOSTED BY: JOSH CHENEY 07/19/04

1) mike targus
2) dave odd
3) khaleel
4) pat brice
5) RESERVED
6) lance nichols JAY HARRIS
7) richard de Arey
8) zak brown
9) Toast
10) GEORGE TRACY DWAYNE KENNEDY
11) andy ross
12) road comic Matthew Bible
13) andy lurie
14) the drury brothers
15) RESERVED
16) michael holmes
17) Ethan Fucklowitz
18) a.g. won DAN KAUFMAN
19) prescott tolk
20) RESERVED ERICA.
21) dan winter
22) kara j. buller
23) jimi pidd
24) Matthew bible ROAD COMIC
25) RESERVED Buscemi
26) sam fels KEVIN BOZEMAN
27) toast Kumail
28) mike bridenstine
29) steven mulcahy
30) jared logan
31) adam kroshus
32) nattie snider
33) joe hanson
34) kevin white
35) mike burns
36) virginia hanneman
37) ricky carmona
38) lisa peterson
39) mike t.
40) aaron foster
41) bill cruz
42) liz stewart
43) brooke van poppelen
44) brian petrafka
45) c.j. sullivan
46) LANCE NICHOLS
47) mike wiley
48) sean flannery
49) ben riley
50) bill o'donnell
51) sean tabares
52) erica edwards
53) damnit jim
54) tony sam
55) thomas mayo
56) nick vatterott
57) liz stewart
Rick Jack 16th
58) gordon snook
59) julie marcus
60) seena jon
61) michael oliphant
62) Emily K. Dorezas
63) bryan moran
64)
65) teacher dave
66) michelle patterson
67) tommy jonagin
68) bradley fojas
69) MARK RATERMAN
71) emily D. mayonnaise
72) michelle mcshay
73) rip ross jr.

Final Den signup, 2004. *Josh Cheney*.

"If they ask you to host the Lyon's Den," comedian Ricky Carmona said, "you feel like fucking *Goodfellas*. 'Did I just get made? I think I just got made.' Because you've gone from 'I don't know anybody here, I'm just here to do my thing.' To 'Hey, we trust you. Take it for a drive.'"

The last ride for Lyon's Den came on July 19, 2004. Josh Cheney hosted a massive, drunken blowout with seventy-three comedians on the lineup. We all walked away with commemorative T-shirts and plastic cups that read, "Lyon's Den Chicago Farewell Tour 2004" on the front and "GOING OUT ON TOP" on the back. The greatest open mic in the history of comedy got its proper sendoff. But pinning down the exact reason, or reasons, for the Den's greatness has proven a little difficult, especially since the results couldn't really be replicated when the show moved to the former home of Coyle's Tippling House shortly after.

Although I did have fun listening to comics try to explain it anyway, I think a lot of them had some pretty compelling reasons for the show's popularity, and some may have actually gotten pretty close to the mark. But like most articles written about this era, I'll begin by mentioning the talent. "I was there every Monday for a good year and a half," Den regular James Fritz said. "I would walk down there and just be blown away and intimidated. Because, I mean, the talent level was nuts at that thing."

"A regular day at the Lyon's Den, Monday night, you had forty-two acts. Right now, you'd probably have to pay over $1,000 to see those people," Aaron Foster said. "You start counting who they are. Hannibal is gonna be a $100 ticket now. T.J.'s gonna be $50 to $60. Pete Holmes, Kumail. That's a $70 to $80 ticket. A lot of them cats."

"If I went back to Lyon's Den today, I'd be scared," Kyle Kinane said. "If it was of the same caliber. Matter of fact, if you had a reputation, then sights were set on you. It was like, 'So-and-so's a headliner.' 'Really? Let's see it.'"

"You would see all kinds of incompetence too," Robert Buscemi said. "Let's not kid ourselves."

"It was an open mic," Shawn Cole said. "So you had these really wicked gear shifts where you could have three or four real fun comedians in a row, and then you'd have someone up there just lock up the brakes on the whole thing. So it was interesting that way too."

"For a lot of people," Mike Wiley said, "that was their night to do stand-up. So for a lot of them, it's like, 'I have to put 100 percent into this. Because otherwise, I'm not gonna get back on stage for another week.' And that pushed people to do their best and compete with each other. It wasn't necessarily that there were better comics. Because there weren't many places to do stand-up. The Lyon's Den became the place."

"All of you guys were super grateful and didn't take it for granted," post-Den comic Joe Kilgallon told me. "So when you got your chance at the Lyon's Den, you're more focused, you're more motivated to go up there and bring the walls down. When you have great shows every night, you're gonna phone them in a couple times."

"The highlight of my week was going to Lyon's Den," Sean Flannery said. "That's what made me a good stand-up. Because there was a lot of healthy competitiveness there. You knew everybody else was gonna have new jokes, and it was this pressure. Good pressure, I felt, to always be writing new jokes. And they had to be interesting. And original. Because that's all that usually got laughs there."

"The scene was everybody pushing each other," comedian Nate Craig agreed. "If you kept doing the same bits, it was not cool. Nobody was gonna rush in the room to watch you."

Then there was the bar itself. "The architecture of the Lyon's Den was important," Pete Holmes said. "Because there was a front area and a back area. And it really felt like two different rooms....We have the hang area. So that's fostering the community. And we have a tight, small, dark, low ceiling, good PA back room."

"There was just something so magical about being at that place," Dave Odd said. "The Lyon's Den was one of the few open mics, probably in the world, where comedians don't [say], 'Okay, I did my set. I gotta go run to another open mic now.' They're like, 'No. I'm gonna stick around.' Because it was more about the camaraderie and hanging out with other people and being around. There was such an electric vibe there."

"We all did each others' shows," Eric Acosta said. "But Lyon's Den was homeroom. Like, Dave Odd's group, Elevated, Lodge. On Monday nights, [we'd all be in] homeroom. Everybody's at the Den. And then through the week, we'd go back to our own territories."

"That open mic night at the Lyon's Den had drink specials that were staggeringly unprofitable," Jared Logan said. "Two-dollar bottles all night. Okay. You know what? Ignore all that shit....The reason people came to the Lyon's Den open mic was for two-dollar bottles of beer."

The success of the Lyon's Den was obviously the sum of many parts. Yes, the talent level was high. But it was made exponentially better by the fact that everyone had been so desperate for something like it to exist. And once they got it, it became the center of a community. It also became a beacon to anyone who'd thought of trying to perform stand-up. And if any new comic wanted the respect of their peers, they had to constantly be generating new material instead of lazily phoning it in. So some people got really good in a hurry. And yes, there were also two-dollar bottles of beer, a front bar hangout area and nobody had anywhere else to be.

"You guys were spoiled," Joe Kilgallon said. "You had what everyone who's ever been in that room told me was the greatest open mic ever. And when that ended, where do you go from there?"

"Then Lyon's Den closes [and] relocates," Eric Acosta said. "It's not really the same thing. Around '04 or so. There was this lull. I was like, 'I gotta get out of here. Because Chicago's on a down arrow right now.'"

Just to put things into perspective, the Lyon's Den open mic was so good that when it moved a few miles south to Crush (later known as Mix Bar) in Lake View, the drop in quality convinced one of the scene's best comedians, Acosta, that it was time to head off to Los Angeles because Chicago was drying up. But for new comics like David Angelo, who had moved to Chicago shortly after the Lyon's Den closed and had never seen the room, the open mic at Crush was still the greatest thing in the world. And honestly, it was probably just as good, if not better, than any open mic in the country at that time too. It just wasn't *The Den*.

"Every Monday there was that open mic [at Crush], which exists nowhere else in America," Angelo said, "where the scene would come together and have a fun time. Everyone would show up. It would be fifty people, and you knew all of them. And then there'd be some audience. But there were enough comics, and they'd all hang around. That spoiled me on open mics. Every other open mic I've ever been to was a complete nightmare. Because there's no community to it. And that one had a community."

"I remember being so disappointed when I arrived in New York," Logan said. "Because there were plenty of open mics. But the comics didn't listen. Many of them were poorly attended. So instead of the Lyon's Den, fifty people in the audience, you had fifteen comics who aren't really listening. And so you couldn't incubate the material so quickly. You had to wait until you were getting booked a lot in New York before things really started to gel. In Chicago, things would start coming together very fast."

"The worst part of being a comedian is the open mic years," Angelo said. "Because everyone is really weird and it's the hardest time. But everyone is also the least practical. All you have to do is [say], 'Let's just have fun,' and the open mic will be fun. It's all it takes. I don't know why it's such a mystery. So that's truly the secret of Chicago, as far as I'm concerned, was you had

A) good open mics, so you could do a minimum of one good show a week. And then B) that's how you became friends with everyone. Every scene in America could elevate themselves if they just did that."

In 2004 and 2005, a new comedian in Chicago did have the opportunity to do multiple shows per week, including a decent number of booked shows. Some, like the Lyon's Den and then Crush, could be great. So could The Elevated and the Lincoln Lodge, and later Chicago Underground Comedy. And the rest, which were usually abysmal Boschian hellscapes, were put on by Dave Odd.

"Obviously, I hope you have a whole Dave Odd chapter," Brooke Van Poppelen told me. And I do have a whole Dave Odd chapter. Because, like it or not, there's really no real way to not have a whole Dave Odd chapter.

Chapter 17

A WHOLE DAVE ODD CHAPTER

Without Dave Odd," comedian Jared Logan said, "I think there is no Chicago scene that would have even launched some of the talent that it launched. Or as many talented people as it launched."

"I have a ten-dollar bill in my kitchen, framed, that Dave Odd handed to me," Pete Holmes said. "And it's presented proudly."

"I'll give him this," comedian Eric Acosta said. "He's a hustler. I could never flier and secure rooms. And I would never get out there and pound the pavement and get that stuff done. He got rooms. He put shows on. Good for him. But he's kind of a creep."

The story of Dave Odd and his involvement in the Chicago comedy scene is as complicated as it is integral. But it all begins in late 1997, shortly after Dave turned twenty-one and started heading to the city's open mics. One of the first comics he met was John Roy, who was also pretty new at the time. "His act was kinda disturbing," Roy remembered. "He used to talk about killing all his childhood bullies. Like, having them jump into the pool, but hit glass and die. And Dave was gloating at them from the diving board. It was a really weird Joker kind of bit. He was a school shooter that shot zings instead of bullets."

And then something happened that made Dave stop coming around. "I don't really want to get too into it," Odd said, "but I obviously had some personal issues at that time. I ran into a tremendous roadblock in my life in May of '98. And then didn't return to comedy until 2001."

The exact details of that roadblock have been the subject of countless conversations, speculations and rumors among comedians ever since. However, I've found absolutely nothing concrete or corroborative to support any of the things I've been told about the situation second- or thirdhand. And since Dave didn't want to tell me his version of what happened, it's probably not fair to let a bunch of comedians give their twenty-four-year-old hearsay versions of what happened either. "It's one of the few things in my life that I take very seriously," Odd said, without going into specifics. "It really did change me, fundamentally, for the better."

What is important to our story, for now, is that when Dave returned in 2001, he wasn't welcomed back with open arms by the gatekeepers of the scene. "A lot of people were mean to him," comedian Monte said. "I, specifically, was very unkind to him when he first came around. I remember calling him a creep and being an asshole to him. Or saying, 'What are you doing around here, dude? You know people don't like you.' Which is real shitty, and I shouldn't have done that."

"Maybe Dave Odd got his shit together and has reconciled with his past," Kyle Kinane said. "I'm not really sorry for making jokes at his expense. But also, fuck, what if you never let anybody live anything down that they've done, if they've tried?"

"I use to have beef with him over it," Adam Kroshus said. "But I've let go of it. He paid his debt."

The first order of business for Dave after he returned to the scene was acquiring a new stage name to distance himself from his past. "I went to the Red Lion Pub," Odd said. "And one of the first people I talked to there was [comedian] Pat Brice. He was super nice to me right off the bat. I'm like, 'Hey, I'm just returning to stand-up, and I want to use a stage name.' And I was like, 'I was thinking of using Odd.' And he's like, 'Dave Odd. That has a good ring to it.'"

The name change probably helped, but it definitely didn't move the needle with anyone who remembered what happened in 1998. So the unfortunate irony of Dave Odd's situation is that if he hadn't experienced that self-described roadblock, and if he hadn't been ostracized by the scene because of it, he also probably wouldn't have needed to create Edge Comedy in the first place. "I wasn't getting booked at the premier shows," Odd told me in 2006.[40] "So I decided, 'Why beg and grovel to get stage time when I could just start my own thing?'"

Dave Odd would certainly start his own thing. He would start it repeatedly and consistently over the next decade and a half. And the very first show that

Odd ever produced took place at the Lyon's Den on Tax Day 2001. He called it the "Idiotically Ridiculous Show" or "IRS." But since Tax Day also happened to fall on Easter Sunday that year (and perhaps was a harbinger of things to come), exactly nine people showed up.

Undeterred by the low turnout, Dave began a monthly show at the Beat Kitchen in North Center shortly after. "I was gonna do each show as a theme show," Odd said of his Beat Kitchen run. "And the first show was called 'The Edge'…It was just supposed to be a raunchy blue show. It was a great show. And the booker for the Beat Kitchen was like, 'We'll give you a show every month. Why don't we just keep it the Edge Comedy Show? That's good'… And by the time that run was over, the Edge Comedy Show just kinda stuck."

At the end of 2001, Allan Johnson, the comedy critic at the *Chicago Tribune*, wrote,[41] "Dave Odd's comedy empire grows and grows." And Johnson listed "various Tuesday and Thursday-Sunday shows at Miska's Backroom Nightclub" in Roscoe Village that Dave was running, as well as a new Tuesday room at the Tender Trap in Chicago Heights. And at that time, that must have sounded like an absurd amount of shows for one person to produce. By contrast, The Elevated's Cayne Collier and the Lincoln Lodge's Mark Geary were only producing one show apiece. But Dave was just getting warmed up.

Besides Miska's and the Tender Trap, the *Tribune* also listed Edge Comedy shows at Oasis One-Sixty in Chicago Heights and Elbo Room in Lake View in that first year. Then, in 2002, Odd was running shows at Rockhouse Grill in Rolling Meadows, Knock Out's in River West, Dizzy's Bar in Grayslake, Nite Cap in Portage Park, the Algonquin Roadhouse in Algonquin, the Chase Café in Rogers Park and then back at the Lyon's Den in North Center. That September, Allan Johnson called[42] Odd a "Comedy impresario" who had been "quietly staging productions in and around Chicago for the last year-and-a-half." *Quietly*, I'm guessing, was the operative word. But still, it is a staggering amount of shows.

In 2003, Johnson called Odd a "maverick" producer.[43] And sure, the show listings for that year were even nuttier than the year before, with shows at Chase Café, Knock Outs, the Four Treys in Roscoe Village, Aliveone in Park West, Zella's in Sheffield Neighbors, Trader Todd's in Lake View, Brisku's Bistro in Horner Park, Hi-Tops in Wrigleyville, Holiday Club in Wicker Park, Mark 2 Lounge in Rogers Park and Jefferson Tap in West Loop Gate. And I'm guessing there were a ton more. I had even popped into an Edge Christmas show at Mullens on Clark in Wrigleyville as an audience member. It was practically unavoidable. Edge shows were everywhere, and fliers for Edge shows were littering the streets.

If you were to glance at the show listings in the *Tribune* in early 2004, you would see that Tuesday nights had the Edge Tandem Comedy Show at Wise Fools Pub in Lincoln Park and Thursdays had the Edge Comedy Dungeon at Super Bowl in Melrose Park *and* the Edge Comedy Lounge at Holiday Club in Buena Park. On Friday, there was the Edge Comedy Showcase at Brisku's Bistro *and* the Edge Comedy Contest and Showcase at Chase Café. Saturdays had the Edge Underground Comedy Club, also at Chase Café. And Sunday was the Edge Comedy Joke-Off Showdown at Mullens on Clark.

"He did so many shows," comedian Joselyn Hughes said. "So many bad shows."

In total, Odd estimated that he put on shows in more than one hundred different venues, with at least twenty in the city proper. There was a major catch to all of this. Because of the sheer number of Edge Comedy shows in existence at any given time, the quality of those shows often suffered. "They were almost always disastrous shows," Robert Buscemi said. "You'd always swear to yourself you'd never do another one, and the next week, there you are."

The other reason the quality of Odd's shows might have suffered is because he would book just about anybody to perform. And when a producer's policy is to book just about anybody, they can put up some real stinkers, from brand-new open mic-ers to the absolute dregs of the scene nobody else would book. Of course, that open door did have some upsides. Odd can truthfully boast that he was the first person in Chicago to book T.J. Miller, Pete Holmes, Kumail Nanjiani and Hannibal Buress, along with many, many others. "I was the first guy to put everybody up on stage in Chicago," Odd said. "Even the shitty people."

"A lot of these comedians started their own rooms because Zanies was the only game in town," Odd continued. "And if you want to get into a club like Zanies, you gotta do auditions, get a recommendation, jump through all these hoops, send in tapes and keep checking back to get it. And then, when the show they're producing goes well, they're like, 'Well, if you wanna get into our show you have to get recommendations, and send in tapes, and do auditions and jump through all these hoops.' It becomes the same thing. So when I started producing shows, I was like, 'I'm never gonna be this exclusive club.' Which means that not every show's gonna be perfect."

When I asked Odd to estimate how many comedians he gave stage time over the years, he put the number in the 1,500 to 2,000 range. He could have told me any number and I would still guess that he made an impression on all of them. It seems like every comic who got their start in Chicago during the Edge Comedy era has a story about the first time they were approached for a booking by Dave Odd. "Dave came over and he goes, 'You were really funny. Would you like to do my show?'" Nick Vatterott said. "I was like, 'Wow. I'm a real stand-up comedian.' And then he turned around and walked up to another guy who did *okay* and was like, 'Hey. You were really funny.'"

"[He approached me] right when I got off the bus," comedian Fay Canale joked. "He was the first person to come up, with no emotion in his face, and say, 'Nice to meet you. I'm Dave. Buy my pamphlet.' Those shirts though. Mwah."[44]

As for my own first encounter with Dave, it was at that Mullen's on Clark "Edge Christmas" show that I attended as an audience member in 2003. One of the comedians made small talk with me before the show, I mentioned that I'd moved to Chicago to do stand-up and it was only a matter of time before Dave walked up to my table to see if I wanted to go on stage that night, sight unseen.

He must not have liked what he had seen, by the way, because when Mike Holmes and I started going to shows regularly the next month, Holmes got booked at Edge shows for an entire month before I finally asked him to put a word in for me with Dave. I must be the only person in the history of the Chicago stand-up scene who had to ask Dave Odd for a set. But he did let me go up at his next show at Wise Fools Pub, where I met another comic who had just started named Jared Logan.

Logan had moved to Chicago in 2003, sight unseen, after graduating from the University of Memphis. "I knew, because I'd been a theater major," Logan told me, "that the Steppenwolf Theatre was there. And I think my plan was, 'I'll be one of America's greatest thespians or a stand-up comedian.'"

Even prior to meeting Logan, I knew who he was because Mike Holmes would come back from his first Dave Odd shows and tell me about this guy who was beating him in comedy contests and how funny he was. Even in his first few months in comedy, Logan was absolutely crushing. And the first thing I think of when I picture Logan from those early Edge shows, or any shows from that era, was his closing bit: "Killgore, the Murder Trooper."

"Women have it harder than men," Logan would start. "If you disagree, watch commercials that are targeted at little girls. A commercial for, like, a toy or a game for a little girl always seems like it came from another world where feminism never happened. A commercial for a game for a little girl always sounds like [in an over-the-top, saccharine delivery], 'Hey girls! It's the Shop 'Til You Cook Game. The only game that combines shopping and cooking, the only two things a woman is good for! Move your cheerleader token around the shopping mall searching for the ingredients to make the perfect dessert. Don't land on the career path or eligible men will think you're a lesbian.'"

"And then toys for boys," Logan continued, "are just as evil, but in the exact opposite direction. It's always for some action figure. And it's always got some badass song to go along with it. And it's always horrifying. It's always like [he begins aggressively and maniacally shout-singing], 'Killgore, the Murder Trooper'! He uses guns to shoot his enemies in the face with acid! And he drives a truck made of snakes made of metal! If your mom won't buy Killgore, you must cut her!"

There were other variations. But the results were always the same. This joke, in his hands, at his volume and intensity, would absolutely decimate a room. And good luck to anyone who had to follow him.

I specifically remember one night at the Lincoln Lodge when Logan said, "Thank you! Good night!" and left the stage while the crowd was still fully, uproariously reacting to his performance. Josh Cheney was hosting the show and had to stand there and wait for them to settle down before he said, "Yeah. We got stuff like *that.*"

"I remember seeing him," Monte said. "This was when Jared had just started. All eight pistons were firing for Jared. And he was high energy, sweaty, hair flying everywhere, intense, the crowd literally laughing so much that it's getting hot in the room. There's so much respiration because Jared Logan is on fire and he's killing."

The night I met Logan at Odd's Wise Fools show, I had a good set and actually tied him in the comedy contest voted on by the audience. And it was pretty much off to the races from there. I did Edge shows all over the city for the rest of 2004. And most of those nights, I'd be on lineups right alongside Logan, Mike Holmes and Mike Burns, who became my first friends in the scene.

I would love to pretend that I became friends with those guys at the Lyon's Den because it sounds a lot more glamorous, but deep down I know we're friends because of Edge Comedy shows. And almost none of those shows were glamorous. In fact, two of my most vivid memories from this period come from Chase Café in Rogers Park, where the stage in the small front room was just a semi-sturdy coffee table. And after one particularly brutal show in that room, Holmes and I discussed whether we'd made a mistake by

THE PERFECT AMOUNT OF WRONG

moving to Chicago instead of Minneapolis, where another guy we started with in Iowa City was already getting paid emcee work at the local club. And presumably not on a coffee table.

The other vivid memory I have from Chase Café is of Kumail in the cavernous back room of the building, performing in front of two of my coworkers, who also happened to be the only two people in the audience. His whole set was just taking a Superball that he'd found somewhere and winging it off of the walls and letting it ricochet wildly around the empty room. And honestly, it was a still a pretty good set.

"Many of [Dave's] shows were dog shit," Logan said. "But some of them weren't. Sometimes there was an audience of twenty-five or thirty people. And they laughed. So every once in a while, he had a great show."

Logan is right. And I still remember the ones that were great. My absolute favorite of all the early Dave Odd shows were the birthday roasts he put on at Holiday Club. Back then, roast shows were not nearly as prevalent as they would become, but Comedy Central had been airing yearly Friars Club roasts since 1998 and had released its own wildly popular roast of Denis Leary in 2003. So when Dave did his own version at Holiday Club a year later, I was pumped. I loved the old-school format, I loved writing those mean jokes about the other comics, and on my twenty-fifth birthday, Dave even put on a birthday roast for me. Well, it was a co-roast with Kara Buller, a comedian whose birthday is the day after mine, but still.

The dais for my portion of the roast included Mike Holmes, Burns, Logan, Dave and Tommy Johnagin. And I got so many of my old college friends and coworkers to show up that the room felt packed. I specifically remember Burns's filthy set making my old college roommate, Rob Johnson, laugh so hard that he had to run to the bathroom to throw up. The jokes were vicious, but the comics had actually taken the time to craft entire sets about *me*. And that was truly the first time that I felt like I was "in" with, or accepted by, the scene. Or at least my own tiny little corner of it.

I knew that Edge shows were still the minor leagues of the comedy scene. Or at least that was the not-too-subtle perception at the time. For the most part, new comics took the stage time Dave offered, initially out of ignorance of his past and then out of necessity. "At that time, that's drama I don't give a fuck about," comedian Ricky Carmona said. "'Do you have stage time for me? Cool. I don't want to get caught up in any of that extra nonsense. That's not my business.'"

"My goal was to get on stage every night, and Dave was a huge part of that," Tommy Johnagin said. "I'm very grateful....But he was an odd duck....You open his trunk and it's full of mushrooms. Or ghosts. He's a different guy."[45]

All the drama surrounding Dave seemed reinforced daily on the scene's official Yahoo! message board, which was called "chichahahago." And the name was admittedly fun. It was just the experience that was not. Or to quote Kyle Kinane when I brought it up, "Man, what a rotten place."

In the days before a social media comment section was the most toxic and unhealthy argue prison on the Internet, there was a thing called Yahoo! Groups, which was ostensibly just a bunch of discussion boards for various communities. But in the case of this particular community discussion board, it was really just an open sewer of negativity.

"That was before MySpace or any of that," comedian CJ Sullivan said. "That was a prelude to all things Internet. Because Geary's hope for that thing was, 'This is how we can promote shows, an opportunity that can be a positive thing. There's gonna be a community. You can ask questions about managers and shit like that.' And it just turns into hate-filled speech, misogyny and racism, and people just attacking each other."

"It only takes so much effort going onto Twitter and being like, 'You suck,'" Johnagin said. "But when you said, 'You suck' on there, you had to sign into three accounts."

"It was always rough-and-tumble, with plenty of bantz, as we say in England," Geary said. "But as soon as Dave Odd joined, it hit its heyday and became the all-out brawl we remember fondly."

Nobody rushed into more public arguments or held more public grudges than Dave Odd. "I think it's just something within me," Odd said. "I kinda seek out drama."

"He'll walk right into the fire," Darren Bodeker said of Odd. "If you hate him, he's still gonna go there and take the slings and arrows....He's one of those kind of guys."

"I still do that today," Odd said. "But now it's about politics."

"If you go to his Facebook," Bodeker said, "he is calling people Nazis all over the place. Just a flamethrower. I see him nowadays, and he says, 'I don't know how long I have to live. Because they're gonna get me.' He's living in that mindset."

"I carry a can of bear mace with me at all times," Odd said, "a switchblade pocket knife, and a flare gun in my pocket. Because I always have these people threatening me. I don't trust Nazis."

Possibly due to a lack of Nazis in the scene, Odd mostly aimed his haha board displeasure at the shows and social circles from which he felt excluded.

That often meant lobbing insults at Mark Geary. Or at the booking politics of the Lincoln Lodge and/or The Elevated. Later, he'd launch attacks against Chicago Underground Comedy. Dave would even get into it with me, which I admit I enjoyed. But the greatest of all the blood feuds in all of chichahahago message board history has to be between Dave and his archnemesis, Andy Lurie.

"It was the perfect storm," Sullivan said. "These guys were the heavyweight champion of long, unnecessary diatribe prose. It would be like one thousand fucking paragraphs. And there's no one there to stop them. There was no blocking from use or muting or any of that shit. Good God, your inbox would be full."

It all seemed to stem from a personal relationship gone bad. "We were really close friends," Odd said. "And I remember exactly what caused the problem. We were doing a show at a barbecue joint [in West Town]. This was around 2002. So I had Kumail in the show."

"This was early for Kumail," Lurie said. And yes, it's probably important to point out that in 2002, Kumail would have been very new in the scene. But it was also the direct aftermath of 9/11, and the entire political climate that came with it.

"When we got there," Odd said, "there was a whole family having a reunion, a Black family. So we tried to do a comedy show. And nobody was there for the show, but there's this table of twenty people. So Kumail got on stage, and one of the people in the family reunion called him 'Camel' or something like that."

"There's a crowd in the front row that just wanna say, 'Hey, what's up Al-Qaeda?'" Lurie said. "And as with all Edge shows, when there was hecklers, 'Get Lurie. He'll go up there.'"

"Lurie says to me, 'Watch. I'm gonna fix this,'" Odd said.

"I was good with hecklers," Lurie said. "So I decimate these motherfuckers."

"He swaggers up on stage and he goes, 'Hey Black people, shut the fuck up. Hey everybody else, here's comedy,' or whatever," Odd said. "And it immediately just turned into everyone screaming and yelling. And the manager of the restaurant had to comp the entire group. It was probably $1,200. And obviously I was pissed off at him. He lost us the room. And of course he blamed it on me."

"The main reason it got canceled," Lurie said, "was because Dave went up to everybody eating and went, 'Hey, we're doing a comedy show. Would you like to pay ten dollars?' or something like that. 'No. I don't care how good the show is, if I came here to eat ribs, don't foist a fucking show on me.'

That's why the show got canceled. Not because I stood up to some hecklers that attacked Kumail. Even if that was the reason…they were making fun of Kumail because he was Pakistani. So 'Lurie, go get 'em.' Well guess what, I did get 'em. And if that is why we got [canceled], sorry. You sent me out there to attack them, which I didn't mind doing."

For Lurie, it seems less about the specifics and more like a last straw. "I was tired of his bullshit," Lurie said. "So whenever any argument would start on the Chicago board, I'd just be like, 'Nah.' We didn't have the term 'gaslighting' back then, but, 'I'm not gonna take your lying, manipulative bullshit, and I'm gonna lay out why you're an idiot and bury you with the truth.' Then he'd try to fight back."

"The posts were a piece of art," Brian Potrafka said of Lurie's replies, "because they were so long and well composed."

"Some say Lurie's *still* typing," Kinane joked.

I suppose we are talking about a guy whose signature bit was fifteen minutes long and titled "River of Porn." But the fighting would usually continue until someone brought up Dave's past. Which was always dangling there like the ultimate trump card to win any argument. But Dave would invariably start a whole new skirmish within the week, and the entire pattern would repeat itself. Surprise comedy you didn't ask for, every night of the week. So I suppose they were kind of like mini Edge Shows in themselves, right in your e-mail inbox.

"The issue Dave had was he was such a misanthrope," Logan said. "[He] hated human life so completely and other people so completely. But that's part of what I find so funny about him. It is very funny to be an impresario, someone who is trying to maintain diplomatic relations with all these different venues and all these different comics. You have to really be a people person. Dave, I think, loves reptiles more than humans."[46]

On November 12, 2004, I performed at the Lincoln Lodge for the very first time. And I was more proud of that one show than of every show I'd done in Chicago to that point combined. My parents had come in from Iowa to see the show, which was the first time they'd ever seen me perform. They even had the program from the night's show matted and framed for me, and it hangs proudly on the wall of my office. This was the major leagues, as far as I was concerned.

"For all of us," T.J. Miller said, "the first step, and in some ways the most important step, was getting booked at the Lodge."

"Getting to do Lincoln Lodge was the crown jewel," Burns agreed. "It was not like any other show that I ever saw in Chicago. The Lincoln Lodge was a fucking produced *show*. You had that to look forward to every week."

The Lincoln Lodge cast. *Back row, from left to right*: T.J. Miller, Tom Lawler, Robert Buscemi, Steve O. Harvey and Ken Barnard. *Front row, from left to right*: Eric Drury, Dan Winter, Jason Drury, Bill Cruz and Reilly Lambert. *Mark Geary*.

"Is there a better feeling," Ken Barnard said, "[than] walking through that back parking lot, walking through that weird long hallway, opening up that door, and the show's already going on? You see who's on stage. Everybody's back by the bar. Just that whole feeling. How many dozens of times you did that and always, always felt excited? Even if you weren't going up. You're gonna laugh. You're gonna have a huge beer. You're gonna have some fucking waffle fries. There was no better Friday night. No better night of the week, in my time in Chicago, than walking through the back of that greasy spoon."

The Lincoln Lodge was a professional operation. When you walked in, someone in a fez handed you a program and took you to your seat. They had professional lighting and a projector for videos. There was even a Man on the Street segment with a live feed into the showroom from a correspondent just outside on the sidewalk being live-filmed on a handheld camera.

According to the Lincoln Lodge's Tom Lawler, "Man on the Street started in Season 4, and it wasn't until Season 5 that we were able to consistently execute this segment without a major technical failure." So if it didn't work, that was part of it too.

One of the best Man on the Street performers in my era was Ken Barnard. "He has this crazy energy, and that bit needs it," Lawler said. "Because you're usually not working with a lot out there. There's very few pedestrians on that stretch of Lincoln. And it's like doing comedy in space, as far as how little you can hear. You're almost playing to complete silence. So he brings all this energy. He was great."

"I absolutely loved doing it," Barnard said. "Obviously, it's great when somebody is walking by in twenty-degree weather and you can actually get something out of them, but even when there's nobody out there, it's usually a lot of fun. One time, there was an old CVS shopping cart. And there was nobody out there, so towards the end of the [segment], I just hailed a cab and tried to get the shopping cart into the cab. He was so pissed, but the audience seemed to really love it."

"My favorite Man on the Street," Geary said, "was when Zak Brown was host, Kumail was the Man, and it was a blizzard. And I said to Shawn Cole, 'Listen, there's gonna be nothing happening out there. I need you to come out after about a minute and just make something happen'…So [Kumail is] out there. It's just a mega-blizzard blowing down Lincoln. And Shawn Cole comes walking down the street and he's got no shirt on, and a bottle of MGD in his hand. And the host doesn't recognize it's Cole. So he's like, 'Kumail! Stop that guy. He's gotta be interesting.' And the next thing, Cole does a psychotic meltdown act, smashes the beer bottle on the side of the building and threatens Kumail with it. And then I'm [holding the camera and] laughing. But at that point…I [made the] camera all jerky like *Blair Witch*, and then I pulled the feed out and killed the mic.…I walked back in and [Zak] was on stage going, 'What should we do?' And I just got on the God mic and said, 'Everything's fine, Zak. Carry on.'"

Like I was saying, it was a professional operation. Then Geary would play "Always Look on the Bright Side of Life" by Eric Idle (not Michael Palin!) at the end of each show, and then everything would be torn down as the comics headed next door to Resi's Bierstube to drink fancy German doppelbocks or pay two dollars for a random "mystery beer." This was all juxtaposed by Dave Odd's Edge Comedy shows, where I stood on coffee tables and performed for nobody. And I thought the more I got to do shows like the Lodge, the less I had to do shows like Dave's. The irony probably being that without that stage time Dave provided, I wouldn't have gotten good enough to feel like I no longer needed him.

So, what is the legacy of Dave Odd? "He was awesome about putting up young comics," Mike Holmes said. "He really was. We would have had half the stage time without him."

"I do appreciate all the stage time he gave a bunch of people," Tony Sam said. "Obviously, it seemed like it came at a price."

"It came at a big cost," Bill Cruz said. "There were so many times that we went into different bars and said, 'Hey, I'd love to start an open mic here,' and they'd go, 'No. Dave Odd was here a few years ago. I don't want anything to do with stand-up.' That was across the board. It took a long time for Chicago bars and comedy to recover....You had to wait until those bars went under new management and those people didn't know who Dave Odd was."

"The most important commodity you have as a comedian, especially when you're starting, is stage time," Andy Lurie said. "And thanks to Dave, I was getting forty-minute sets when we were still fighting to get a five minute set....And I will always be grateful for that." And that's coming from his biggest nemesis.

Through all this, I haven't really discussed Dave as a comic. But he was the one consistent element at all these shows. "My favorite reaction to get from an audience is the groan, followed by laughter," Dave said, which pretty much sums up his act. But I'll give you my favorite Dave Odd joke anyway.

"You ever get those things in the mail with the missing kids on them?" Dave would ask. "The picture of the missing kid from his yearbook or his Sears family photo. And then right next to that picture, they have an age progression picture of what that kid would look like now. And they do it with computers or whatever. And I always thought that was very dishonest. I always thought the age progression picture should be a skeleton tied to bricks under a lake."

"I'm being dead serious, and people fight me on this and say I'm remembering wrong or I'm crazy," Logan said. "Dave Odd's jokes were very well written. They were very funny. And nobody gave him credit for that."

"I really respect Dave Odd as a joke writer," T.J. Miller told me in 2006.[47] "Nobody's going to say otherwise. He needs to stop bringing snakes into bars though."

"There's a little secret fan club of his comedy," Robert Buscemi said. "I love his jokes....It was good stuff. Boy, man. He ran these shows and they were, gosh, they were just *bleak*."

I closed out 2004 with "The Edge Stand-Up New Years Eve Spectacular" at the chain fondue restaurant the Melting Pot. People had dressed up and paid special rates for their big night out, and absolutely none of them had expected or wanted stand-up comedy to be part of their evening—let alone stand-up about dead kids at the bottoms of lakes. It was a fitting end to my first year in Chicago comedy. And things could only go up from there.

Unbeknownst to me, the bar for alt shows would be raised yet again in 2005, this time courtesy of the young, newly wedded husband-and-wife team of Tony Sam and Brooke Van Poppelen. Soon there would be a Tuesday night show to surpass The Elevated and rival the Lodge for the best in the city. And just like the entire post-2001 scene as a whole, there are people who argue that all of it started with Dave Odd.

Chapter 18

CHUC

In January 2005, Allan Johnson of the *Chicago Tribune* attended the first Snubfest, a tiny four-day comedy festival held at the Cornservatory Theatre in Lincoln Square meant to highlight performers who got rejected from more important festivals. And in his coverage, Johnson especially gushed over Robert Buscemi. That's the article where Johnson said Buscemi was worthy of the Aspen and Montreal comedy festivals, while calling him "clever and sophisticated" and a "pleasant surprise." The article's headline was even "Snubfest's Buscemi the Odds-On Favorite."

It all still feels like a shock to Buscemi. "It was like, three feet of snow outside, accumulated," Buscemi said. "And there were eight people in the audience. And three of them were other performers. There was *nobody* there. But there was a journalist from the fucking *Chicago Tribune*, and he gave me really, really, really good press." All of which infuriated the Lincoln Lodge's Mark Geary.

"Allan Johnson writes about all this great Chicago talent that's in a shitty festival, not the Lincoln Lodge," Geary said. "I am fuming. I get my wig off at [Lincoln Lodge co-producer] Tom Lawler and go, 'Why is the Lincoln Lodge not front and center as the place that is making this happen?' So Tom, being the nice guy that he is, pitched Allan Johnson the idea of doing an article. Not about the Lodge, but about the scene. So Allan Johnson goes, 'Okay. I'll do an article about the scene.' So we're like, 'Okay, when's the photographer coming to the Lincoln Lodge?' And they're like, 'They're not. Because we went to another show.'"

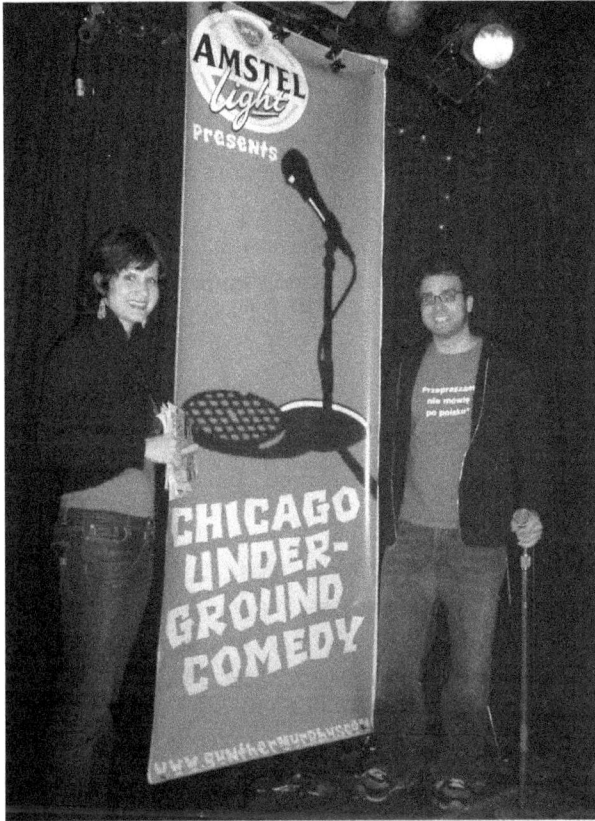

Brooke Van Poppelen and Tony Sam at Chicago Underground Comedy, 2005. *Kristy Mangel.*

The show that the *Tribune*[48] had chosen to photograph was not nearly as established as the Lincoln Lodge, to say the least. "I had a couple shows at a sandwich shop in Evanston," Dave Odd said. "It only ran for four to six weeks. And we performed on a little two-foot-by-two-foot plywood thing they built....Allan Johnson from the *Chicago Tribune* was doing a story about the Chicago comedy scene, and the cover of that story was Tony Sam on stage at my show called 'The Chicago Underground Comedy Club.' That was what we called the show at this sandwich shop. And I don't think the article was especially flattering. [It said,] 'Comedy can be in any shitty place.' Whatever. And then he died of a brain aneurysm."[49]

"Instead of having a picture of a comedian in front of a full house," Geary said, "with a properly produced professional show and a real microphone, you have a man standing on a milk crate in the middle of a shitty bar on a Tuesday night. And that finished me with Allan Johnson. Because I was like, 'You came into this with an agenda. And your agenda was, 'Look at these plucky little outsiders with their fucking milk crates and their shitty guitar amps. They're trying really hard, but they'll never be Zanies.'"[50]

"Now I obviously got my wig off yet again," Geary said. "But Tony Sam really got his fucking wig off. Because he's the idiot on the milk crate. So he decides he's gonna do something about it."

"I remember everybody was giving me shit about that," Tony Sam said. "They're like, 'Oh, look who's the face of alternative comedy'...I left work and I went around the corner and I bought a copy and was I like, 'Holy shit,' and I showed my mom."

"The first thing he does is come to me and says, 'Can I be on the Lincoln Lodge cast?'" Geary said. "I say, 'Sorry Tony, but there's no room.' So he takes the article to the owner of [the Lake View music venue] Gunther Murphy's and says, 'Look at this. There's a comedy scene started. You should do a show.'"

"I'm pretty sure that's what happened," Odd agreed.

Both Odd and Geary are probably wrong. But in fairness, Geary's Lincoln Lodge and Odd's Edge Comedy shows had the most to lose from the emergence of Tony Sam's new show at Gunther Murphy's, which Tony called Chicago Underground Comedy. Plus, the article was Mark's idea and featured one of Dave's rooms, but Tony Sam was the only person to benefit. At least in the minds of Mark and Dave. So I understand their frustration. "If we'd have let Tony Sam join the Lodge cast," Geary said, "ChUC would have never happened. I mean, I wasn't a dick about it. I thought him and [Tony's then wife] Brooke [Van Poppelen] were fucking awesome. But there was no room at the inn. That's the story we talked about earlier....When there's no room at the inn, people go, 'F this inn. I'm gonna create my own inn.'"

When I looked at the article in the *Tribune*, the name of Odd's show was actually the Edge Underground Comedy Club, which was a name Dave had also used for a show at Chase Café. So the caption for the Tony Sam photo reads, "At places like The Edge Underground Comedy Club at Fusion in Evanston, comics such as Tony Sam find a willing audience—if not much of a stage." Then the sub-headline reads, "Thriving underground scene puts the edge back in comedy." And the article came out on April 8, 2005, exactly one month before the first Chicago Underground cast meeting at Bad Dog Tavern.

The repetition of the term "underground," plus the photo of Tony Sam published just a month before a Tony Sam–produced show called "the

Underground" had its very first organizational meeting seem to indicate a correlation between the article and the show. And when the first listing for ChUC went into the *Tribune*,[51] Allan Johnson noted, "We wrote a story about this very scene weeks ago, and to show how much we're on the curve, here's a new showcase of such talent that's scheduled to be on display every week." But even if Tony *didn't* use that article to sell the show to Gunther Murphy's, I'm still grateful for whatever they did use. However, the origin story of ChUC is actually a bit more complicated, especially since the version told by Geary and Odd leaves out one major player entirely.

The true story of Chicago Underground Comedy starts with a Sunday open mic at Bad Dog Tavern in Lincoln Square run by comedian Brooke Van Poppelen. "The open mic at Bad Dog was born out of one of my millions of bartending and waitressing jobs over the years," Van Poppelen said. "I waitressed the front room. And I'd run up between serving tables and host [the show]. It was wild."

The show picked up a pretty big fan along the way. "I think I showed up at Bad Dog Tavern in early 2005," Kristy "K-Rock" Mangel said. "I had recently gotten separated from someone I was married to. I was twenty-seven, so I was pretty young....And I was cruising the neighborhood bar scene to be out of the house. So it was just a Sunday night randomly at Bad Dog with a friend of mine. And we were just having beers. And they started setting up a PA. At the time, I didn't know who 'they' were. But some kids were setting up a PA system in the front of the bar, and I happened to be sitting right there. I got ambush comedy'd for my first show."

That has got to be the most enthusiastic response to ambush comedy in the history of the world—not just in that moment, but in her next five years of photography, blogging, website managing and magazine publishing. "I was like, 'Oooh, what's this fun thing that's happening?'" Mangel said. "I'd been a music kid my whole life, so being around live events was a really natural and fun thing for me. So my friend, being a responsible adult that he was, [said], 'Well, it is 9:00 p.m. on a Sunday. I'm gonna get going.' And I was like, 'I'm gonna stick around and see what happens.' And that was my very first time seeing underground comedy in Chicago....I quickly was like, 'This happens every week? Holy shit. I'm gonna be here.'"

Around that time, Van Poppelen also met the talent booker from the Abbey Pub in Irving Park. "They hit it off," Sam said. "And [that talent booker] co-booked Gunther Murphy's. So she said, 'We're looking to do something different. We have a sponsor, Amstel Light, [and] we can get them behind helping produce the show. And we're like, 'Hey, that sounds cool.'"

Tony commissioned the official logo. "The first idea for the show was just to be called 'The Underground,'" Sam said. "Somehow it morphed into the 'Chicago Underground.' And then it accidentally became 'Chicago Underground Comedy' because we enlisted Andy Ross, who was a really funny comedian and really talented artist....And he came back and it said, 'Chicago Underground Comedy.' And we're like, 'Well, let's call it that because I don't think he's gonna redo it.'"

Next, taking a cue from the Lincoln Lodge, the show got a cast of its own. "It was everyone who was nice to me and who I thought was funny," Van Poppelen said. "And who seemed to be working really hard for the right reasons. And obviously, people who were just killers."

I was lucky enough to be in that initial cast. Probably because I was at Bad Dog every Sunday. And it was also around that time that my apartment also became a social hub of sorts because of a writing game that Mike Holmes, Jared Logan and I had begun playing every before the open mic. "We just didn't have enough shows," Logan said. "But we were obsessed. All we wanted to do was stand-up comedy. So we would sit around, generating material with each other by playing this game where everybody threw a topic into a hat, you pull the topic out, everybody has five silent minutes to write about the topic and then you shared what you wrote. And look, it was a game because you're hanging out with your buddies and you're just trying to make them laugh. And you're probably smoking weed sometimes and having a couple beers. And people said it was nerdy or embarrassing and I'm like, 'I don't know, man. I became a professional stand-up comedian.'"

None of us are quite sure how the "game" started. "I believe it was all my idea," Logan joked. "I will say I was used to that kind of game because I came from four dorky years as a theater major. So it didn't seem weird or odd to me to do something like that."

The writing game actually caught on pretty quickly with a select number of comics who also didn't mind how dorky it was. And every Sunday throughout 2005, there'd be a full house of comedians over at our apartment on North Greenview playing the game. I even had "Greenview Writers Guild" T-shirts made and distributed to the regulars just in case the whole thing wasn't already dorky enough.

Everybody was getting jokes out of this exercise, or they wouldn't have kept coming back. I certainly did. And I also got a weird sense of pride whenever I'd see comics doing jokes on stage that I knew they'd written in my living room. My all-time favorite writing game joke might be the bit Logan wrote for the topic "Summer" that went something like, "Have you ever gone skinny dipping in the Talaveras County Reservoir on a warm June night in the summer of 1995 with Mindy Tutwiler? Because if you have, you're the one who *murdered* her."

Besides the jokes themselves, the writing sessions led to some pretty funny moments of their own. One of these was the first and only time T.J. Miller came to the game. When it was time to go around the room and say what we'd written, T.J. began reciting a string of dark one-liners that were completely off topic from whatever was pulled out of the hat. When his jokes fell flat in the room, T.J. suddenly began pretending his notebook was trembling uncontrollably, and then he began making over-the-top panicky noises until a copy of Dave Odd's five-dollar stapled-together joke pamphlet fell out. Once everyone realized he'd just been reading Dave's jokes verbatim, the room erupted in laughter. T.J. had basically come there just to do that bit. And then he left shortly after.

The other story that gets brought up the most with the writing game has to do with a comedian who went by the name Jay Harris. "We're talking about a guy who was a bit older than us," Logan said. "Maybe he was just trying to pass time. I think he was a single guy without anyone in his life. And so he had open mics. And a notorious bomb-o terrible comic. I think I can say that and not get into any trouble. Sorry, Jay."

If it sounds like Logan is being overly harsh, just know that Jay Harris bombed so consistently that the open mic regulars actually started to enjoy his act a little bit. So when his name would be announced at the Lyon's Den or the Mix open mic, comics would begin shouting for "Diamond Jay" and making the diamond hand symbol associated, at the time, with Jay-Z's Roc-A-Fella Records. In the parlance of the times, it was known as "throwing up the roc."

"He's a very conservative-looking man," Mike Burns, the originator of the "Diamond Jay" nickname, explained. "I thought it was funny to call him something that was flashier than he was. There's poking a little fun. It was fun to throw up the roc. And Josh Cheney [who frequently worked the sound at these open mics] played a lot of [Jay-Z's] *Black Album* as intros, so that probably was on. We were sitting there and all probably threw the roc up. And he liked it. You get bored seeing people doing the same act every week. You'd have to make these little side games to make things exciting."

Harris became known for telling one specific joke, in every set, about a trip he took to the fast-food chain Popeyes. In the bit, the cashier asked Harris, "Do you want your biscuit?" And since his meal came with a biscuit, Harris asked the cashier, "Why? Do *you* want my biscuit?" And I think that was the entirety of the bit. He had better jokes, but the biscuit thing is what he became known for because he did it in every set. "Jay Harris did the biscuit joke [at the Lyon's Den]," comedian Mike Wiley said, "but instead of doing the punchline, he just held the microphone out and the entire audience shouted, 'Do *you* want my biscuit?' And it was magical."

One weekend, "Diamond Jay" came to the writing game. The very first topic drawn out of the hat said, "Burger King" on it. So everyone tried to come up with bits inspired by the topic and then started sharing and getting feedback on what they'd written. When it was Diamond Jay's turn to share his jokes, with absolutely zero irony, he said, "So you know how I have that joke about Popeyes?" And everybody was like, "Obviously." And Jay nodded and said, "Anyway, I was thinking, Burger King has biscuits. So instead of Popeyes, it could be Burger King." And everyone stared at Jay in disbelief for about five seconds before we all just fell on the floor laughing.

Around that same time, Jay Harris got to open for Mitch Hedberg as a "special guest" at Zanies Vernon Hills. And Dave Odd was booked as the feature. It happened to be the same week that we threw a going-away party for Mike Burns at our place. This would have already been a memorable night for me since Burns was one of my first friends in the scene. But I also knew that thirty-something miles north, my favorite comedian was performing with Dave Odd and that people like Diamond Jay were getting chosen for guest slots. Actually, Allan Johnson of the *Tribune* said that, as a special guest, Harris was "fine but not special."[52] Which is the opposite of what he was, which was god-awful, but *spectacularly* special for that very reason.

During the party, I got a phone call from Dave. When I answered, an unmistakable voice on the other line said, "Hey man, it's Mitch." And I lost it. "I remember having him call you," Odd said. "I remember you pushed through the crowd of people at your place and everyone was like, 'What the fuck's wrong with this guy?'"

It's basically true. I feel like I reacted to the phone call about the same way a teenage girl would have reacted if her favorite boy band member called her. Once I realized I was on the phone with my hero, I set off in a mad dash to find Mike Holmes and hand him the phone. I'm not exactly sure why. Maybe it was because Holmes and I had spent so much time listening to Hedberg's albums together. Or maybe I wanted a witness for this monumental moment in my life. But in the process of rushing through the party, I accidentally spilled beer all over a young comic named Hannibal Buress, who had also opened for Hedberg earlier in the week.[53] And when I finally handed my phone to Holmes, he answered by saying, "My roommate just handed me the phone in such a manner that I'm going to assume this is Mitch Hedberg."

"You walked toward me like God was on the phone," Holmes remembered. "Also, thanks for that."[54]

Since Burns's going-away party was in early March, and the first Chicago Underground Comedy show was on May 31, 2005, part of me has always assumed that if Burns had still been in town, I would have never been asked to be a part of that show. My second thought is, *Jesus, he missed out.*

ChUC was fantastic from the start. It gave me the most consistent and valuable stage time I'd ever had in my life. As much as I loved the Lincoln Lodge, I only got to do that show three times a year at that point. Everyone on the cast of ChUC was

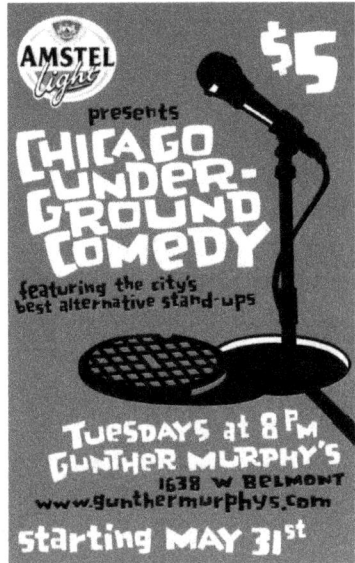

Original ChUC flier, 2005. *Author's collection.*

performing at Gunther Murphy's, to a packed house, twice a month. For every comedian involved, it felt like a great leap forward. All in the back of a rock venue, brought to you by Amstel Light and Chicago's Pizza.

"We came out of the gate with free pizza every fucking week and a fucking keg of free beer for anyone who wanted to come to our show," Van Poppelen said. "And I was like, 'We're taking this up a notch, bitches.'"

"It started great," Sam said. "It really delivered on what we wanted it to be....The promotion, the sponsors, the pizza, the giveaway, and the show was only five dollars. I can't think of any other show on a Tuesday night that could pack a room with that many people."

"ChUC was one of the greatest parts of Chicago and of the scene," Vatterott said. "I felt like that was the last tentpole—Lyon's Den, Lincoln Lodge, Elevated and then Tuesday needed a tentpole. And it really felt like a party every week."

"Chicago Underground Comedy was gigantic," Logan said. "And I think that frankly it did eclipse the Lodge and became the better show."

Only three months into the show's existence, ChUC took its show on the road when Mike Holmes set up a show for us at Jokers Night Club in Cedar Falls, Iowa. I made the trip alongside Holmes, Brooke, Tony, Jared and Kumail. We made a pit stop at the *Field of Dreams* movie site in Dyersville.

And we all stayed at the home of Mike's parents in nearby Waterloo. Holmes's parents came to the show. My parents came to the show. A local woman who sold her own porn DVDs came to the show. It was a memorable trip, to say the least.

The other reason the trip was so eventful didn't have much to do with the show at all, but it would greatly affect ChUC going forward. "We went to Northern Iowa," Sam said, "and I'm pretty sure that's the trip that [Brooke and I] realized that we didn't want to be married anymore."

The news spread quickly. I remember Holmes taking me aside and whispering, "I think Brooke just told Tony she no longer loved him in my sister's childhood bedroom." And I don't remember seeing Brooke much after that trip.

"I just stopped showing up to Chicago Underground," she said. "I let [Tony] take it over. It became its own thing. I was like, 'Well…I don't feel welcome there. Every time I go there's gonna be stupid drama.…It was really traumatic, and it's why I ran away from Chicago immediately. I was homeless in New York for a few weeks. That's how bad I wanted to get away from Chicago."

With Van Poppelen gone, Sam focused all his energy on producing the show, which now included an unofficial photographer and chronicler in Kristy "K-Rock" Mangel, who had made the jump from Bad Dog Tavern. "I remember Brooke and Tony saying, 'Hey, we got this showcase starting [at] Gunther Murphy's. You should check it out,'" Mangel said. "Literally, almost every night of the week, I was just out and about. And of course, quickly people got to know me as the girl with the camera…and it evolved from there."

K-Rock's rise to prominence in the scene is still pretty amazing in hindsight. "She was, like, a local who loved to drink and hang out," Van Poppelen said. But with MySpace exploding in popularity in 2005, as well as YouTube bursting into the public consciousness at the end of the year, everything about the way comedy was consumed was about to change. That would be true for the next step in K-Rock's evolution. And it would also be true for me. Like it or not, social media had arrived, and nothing would ever be the same again.

Chapter 19

2006

On January 11, 2006, my old college roommate, Rob Johnson, sent me an e-mail about an idea he had for a blog site:

Mike,

Why should MySpace make all of the money from OUR blogs? What do you think about me setting up a domain and Web site, and you rounding up your closest comedian friends and making a blog [site]? I can run the Web site & get advertisers, and the funny people can be funny. We can split the profits in some equitable manner. At the very least, we'll have fun and have a place for all of your comic minds to run wild. Best case scenario...this could generate some $ for us. Let me know what you think...

−Bill (Gates)

Rob had recently moved to Chicago, and Mike Holmes and I were letting him crash on our couch until he figured out his job situation. During his time in financial limbo, Rob had become pretty immersed in the comedy scene, regularly attending at Chicago Underground Comedy and the Lincoln Lodge. "It was so obvious that something special was happening there," Rob said, "and even though I wasn't performing, I just loved being a part of it."

After Rob convinced me that he was serious about the blog site, I suggested we ask Mike Holmes, Jared Logan, Kumail Nanjiani and Mike Burns, who

Blerds launch party, 2006. *Back row*: Kumail Nanjiani, Pat Brice, Jared Logan, Nate Craig and CJ Sullivan. *Front row*: Rob Johnson, Prescott Tolk, Mike Bridenstine, Mike Holmes, Sean Flannery and Jordan Vogt-Roberts. *Forest Casey.*

were my closest comedy friends at the time. When all of them seemed receptive to the idea, Rob told me to ask even more comics. So, one night at ChUC, I asked Pat Brice, Prescott Tolk and Sean Flannery if they'd also be interested in joining. I considered those guys to be three of the heaviest hitters in the scene (Prescott had just been on Comedy Central's *Premium Blend*), and I was actually a little nervous about asking them. Surprisingly, they all seemed interested. Then, after seeing Nate Craig perform at ChUC, Rob thought that he would perfect for the site as well. And then CJ Sullivan expressed interest in joining, and everyone thought he was great, so he rounded out the initial group of ten comics. After going back and forth about potential website names, we eventually settled on Nate's idea: Blog Nerds, or…Blerds.[55]

Initially, Blerds was just supposed to be a blogging site. Blogs were a pretty big deal at the beginning of 2006, and video sites like YouTube were really just getting off the ground. I remember sitting in a booth in the front of Gunther Murphy's after the ChUC holiday show when Kumail told me about YouTube for the first time. *Saturday Night Live* had a Digital Short called "Lazy Sunday" that everyone was talking about, and he told me that's where I could watch it. That same Christmas, my parents happened to buy me an iMac, which featured built-in music and video editing software. I became obsessed with making songs and videos, even though I was mostly excited to use them in my live stand-up sets and didn't realize that they could be uploaded to YouTube or MySpace. All of that focus was about to shift. And two days after our group decided on the Blerds name, I played a video on stage and, in the process, wound up having one of the most consequential sets of my career.

It was March 17—St. Patrick's Day in Chicago—an epic day of binge drinking for a decent portion of the city. I was scheduled to perform at the Lincoln Lodge, but during the day I got "St Paddy's Day in Chicago drunk" watching no. 3 seed Iowa lose in the first round of the NCAA Basketball Tournament by a buzzer beater to no. 14 seed Northwestern State.

When I got to the Lodge, Mary, the beloved grandmotherly bartender of the Lincoln Restaurant, took one look at me and yelled "*Coffee!*" as Susan, my favorite waitress, rushed a fresh pot over to help sober me up. I was a mess, and Lodge cast member Steve O. Harvey was loving every minute of it. He even playfully heckled me about Iowa's loss from the "God" mic in the sound booth during my set. Everyone was so nice to me, even though I'd shown up trashed, and I'm not entirely sure why. Maybe they felt bad about Iowa losing. Maybe getting drunk in Chicago on St. Patrick's Day is considered both festive and respectful. I just know that I was way too drunk, and everyone seemed way too okay with it.

If I were to see a clip of the set now, I'd probably hate myself for being so sloppy on stage. But in my head at the time, it was magical. I had a new fake catchphrase bit I was doing, where I'd yell, "Bang! You're pregnant" after my jokes. And for whatever reason, everything just kind of worked that night. Over the next week, I was getting MySpace friend requests from people with "Bang! You're pregnant!" as the greeting on their profile. A new comic told me that everyone in his office was saying the catchphrase to each other now. It felt nuts. Especially since nobody had ever reacted that positively to anything I'd ever done before.

Also in the crowd that night at the Lodge was a twenty-one-year-old Columbia College Chicago film student named Jordan Vogt-Roberts. And when the show was over, he approached me because of the video I'd played at the end of my set and asked if I worked on a lot of film projects. The truth was I had no idea what I was doing and had just kind of started messing around with iMovie three months prior. But for some reason I told him that yes, I did do a lot of film projects. And he suggested we collaborate some time. "Sure," I remember thinking, "I'll never see you again in my life."

Mike Bridenstine and Jordan Vogt-Roberts, Blerds photo shoot, 2006. *Forest Casey.*

It was a week or so after meeting Jordan at the Lincoln Lodge that I saw he was scheduled to be a variety act at the show. That's when I decided to check out his MySpace page and saw a spec video he'd made for "Shake Your Rump" by the Beastie Boys and was absolutely blown away. So was Tom Lawler from the Lodge. "[Lawler] proceeded to track me down about showing the video at the Lodge," Vogt-Roberts told me in 2006.[56] "We got to talking, and by the end of the conversation, I was booked to do ten minutes as the variety act.... After that, I approached you, Señor Bridenstine, after one of your sets and talked about filming junk. One month later and the slippery behemoth of the Chicago comedy scene pulled me into these murky waters."

That's a quote from somebody who was not getting enough sleep. But oddly enough, it was right after meeting Jordan and seeing what he was capable of that the guys in Blerds started suggesting we also make videos for the site's launch party. I've thought a lot over the years about how fortuitous the timing of everything was, from Rob's initial e-mail all the way to meeting Jordan at the exact moment I did. Everything just lined up perfectly for no apparent reason.

"For better or worse," Vogt-Roberts told me, "I'm always in producer/ director mode, and I'll see locations, people or opportunities and know I want to work with them or make something with them. The Lodge was one of those moments."

That April, Jordan started directing the first Blerds videos for our launch party. The general theme of the entire project was that the comics would do their stand-up bits, and the scenes would cut away to act-outs of whatever they were talking about in those bits. The initial batch of videos sat quietly on the Blerds website for the time being.

The site went live at the end of the month, complete with the launch party at Sopo Lounge in Lake View with a thirty-dollar all-you-can-drink special. The night before, the Comedians of Comedy (Patton Oswalt, Maria Bamford, Brian Posehn and Eugene Mirman) had come into town and performed at the Logan Square Auditorium. And in Kristy "K-Rock" Mangel's fan blog, *Five Drink Minimum*, from April 30,[57] she wrote, "I don't have the words yet for the Blerds party last night. I will say this, however: the 10 min. of video that they screened trumped two hours of *Comedians of Comedy* the night before, in terms of sheer brilliance and hilarity. Nights like that remind me again and again that I am living a blessed life."

Initial responses to the Blerds site and videos were overwhelmingly positive within the scene. I even got an e-mail from T.J. Miller shortly after we launched the site that just said, "Holy fucking shit, dude. This is fucking awesome, man. It looks fucking great. Goddamn. When did you guys do this? Fuck. Shit. What the fuck am I doing with my life?" And then he came over, frantically pacing around my apartment and repeatedly telling me that we were sitting on a gold mine.

When it was clear that T.J. wanted to join the group, I thought it would be a no-brainer. The only reason he wasn't initially asked was because he always seemed too busy. He was in Second City's Touring Company. He was in the cast of the Lincoln Lodge. He was shooting national commercials and doing a video project of his own called Very Bad Porn. But when his name was brought up to the group, there were some people who were adamantly against his inclusion. The knock, at that point, seemed to be that T.J. was pretty ambitious, and people feared he would use the group to serve his own purposes and then discard it once he got what he needed.

I wasn't aware of any of the T.J. drama yet, but anyone paying the slightest bit of attention could have seen the ambition. I think T.J. might have even been aware of that perception of himself when I interviewed him on my MySpace blog in June 2006, and he joked, "I'm honored to take [Blerds] over now," before he added, "No, I think it's amazing. When I first saw it, I thought it was hilarious. It's a great idea. I'm really excited to be a part of it....Those are the funniest dudes in the scene."

T.J. Miller hosts a burlesque show, 2006. *Krystle Gemnich.*

The reason T.J. was eventually voted into Blerds, of course, is that he was also undeniably talented. "I saw T.J. Miller do a set at the Lyon's Den one time where he only did crowd work," Jared Logan said. "And it was still, to this day, some of the most impressive crowd work I've ever seen....It wasn't mean crowd work like you expect. When you think crowd work, you think of Don Rickles. And that was what I thought of when a comedian starts talking to the crowd. T.J. did this very funny improvised material.... And then someone who was interrupting his set—a heckler. And instead of being mean, or taking them apart, he ended up bringing this girl on stage. And by the end of it, he proposed marriage to her."

I know exactly which set Logan is talking about. It's still one of the most impressive sets I've ever seen as well, even though we're both talking about a five-minute open mic set from a twenty-two-year-old. But yeah, he was *that* good, even back then. "They gave him the light after five minutes," Logan continued. "And he was crushing so hard that—I mean, he really was bringing the house down. Like, *bringing the house down*—that he looked at whoever gave him the light like, 'Are you kidding me?!?! Just let this continue.' So T.J. from the beginning, was very clearly extremely talented."

"I know there's some complications with T.J., obviously," Pete Holmes said, referring to T.J.'s well-documented public troubles over the years. "But when I watch myself do crowd work, or Kumail do crowd work, almost anybody from Chicago, I'm like, 'There's notes of T.J. in there,'…[If] someone [in the crowd] goes, 'I've heard this one,' most comedians in the '80s and '90s would be like, 'I'm sorry, looks like we have a drunk on our hands,' or something like that. And T.J. would do what I would still do—and I learned it from watching him and his improv technique, in general—was to be like, 'I love that

T.J. Miller at Chicago Underground Comedy. *Erin Nekervis.*

this guy comes to the show to let us all know which ones he's heard and which ones he hasn't'…And when I watch a lot of us, especially when we're improvising, I'm right back at Hi-Tops watching T.J. before I knew him. He was sort of merging Chicago improv and Chicago stand-up….T.J. taught me a lot of things."

"I didn't know how to approach a crowd or improvise on stage until years after I saw T.J.," Logan said. "So [Pete's assertion is] definitely true….I think that what T.J. really did was, because he had that improv background in addition to a stand-up background, he wasn't trying to think of jokes, he was just playing the scene. So instead of, 'No, you idiot,' it becomes, 'Yes, And.' That's how I think he did crowd work….He was using the basic keys of improv very well."

"I was such an improviser that I was able to do a scene [with hecklers]," T.J. explained. "The idea is to re-contextualize their behavior. What they would do [in the '80s and '90s] is have stock lines for hecklers. 'Hey, buddy, I don't go down to your job and slap the dick out of your mouth.' And those were the ways that you handled it—you shut it down and you're back to your jokes. My jokes sometimes would be meandering, or I'd be improvising. And so I couldn't shut somebody down and then go back to these formulaic, setup/punchline jokes. And so I would run with it."

When I gave T.J. the "I've heard this one," example that Pete used, without skipping a beat, he launched into the scene with the hypothetical heckler.

"Oh you must be a really good father," he started. "Your kid comes home and is like, 'Dad, look what I drew.' [And the dad says,] 'Seen it. I've seen better giraffes when I draw them accidentally in my sleep. This guy fucking sucks. Let's get another round.' And so the kid would be like, 'Dad, why did Mom leave you? Oh, I know why. Because I walked in on you and Mom, and you had your pants down and she said, '*Seen it*.'"

"I sort of make this scene," T.J. continued. "And there's too much going on for somebody to be like, 'Hey, fuck you, man. My wife didn't say that.' Because it's all fake. So there's really nothing for them to try to jump back into."

That skillset is part of the reason that, in early 2006, it just kind of felt like T.J. was about to explode onto the national scene. So I figured any association with him worked in Blerds's favor. Plus, it felt like every single article I was reading at the time about comedy had to do with either blogging, Internet videos or the alt scenes in New York or Los Angeles.[58] So I truly felt like we were poised for success, in the right place, at the right time in Chicago. And if America wanted alt comedy, I thought, there was no better place to look than our little scene, where we'd been proudly anti-club for an entire decade.

"We didn't give a fuck about Zanies," Pete Holmes said. "When I was hosting at Zanies, I knew the headliners were closing their sets, even though I'd never seen them before, when they started talking about the G-spot."

"Going to Zanies," Kyle Kinane said, "all those big dudes from the '80s would come in and do the same act that they were doing [in the '80s]. It was dated the first time I saw it. Two years later, I'm seeing somebody do the same headline act and the same dead look in their eyes because they have no desire to connect to an audience. And I'm watching the audience get younger and give less of a shit about what's happening and realizing, 'Well, this was an expensive and boring night out.' And great, now you've created disinterest in stand-up in general. So I would love to get into Zanies and be like, 'Hey, guys. Just to let you know, there's people your age that are doing this and care about it at all these bars and venues across the city.' But I didn't get that opportunity."

"Kyle Kinane left town without having been booked at Zanies," the Lincoln Lodge's Mark Geary said. "Kumail left town never having been booked at Zanies."

"Zanies wouldn't book anybody [in the scene]," T.J. Miller said. "And it wouldn't matter anyway. Because no one you knew went to Zanies."

"It's so interesting," Mike Burns said an hour and forty-seven minutes into our interview. "I didn't even think of Zanies in the entire time we've been talking. At all. I didn't expect you to bring it up. It wasn't even an option. So you looked down on it."

"It forced us to work on our own and create an independent comedy scene," comedian Mike Wiley said. "Because we knew, 'The clubs aren't gonna have us. We need to do something on our own.' And I think that was a good thing, to be honest."

"I think that's why everyone had their own original voice," comedian James Fritz said. "Because everyone was just being a true, authentic-but-heightened version of themselves and what made them be unique. Because you weren't trying to land jokes to tourists at fucking ChUC. It wasn't about moving mozzarella sticks or remembering to plug the drink special. You could take big swings."

The night with the biggest swings I'd ever seen to that point was the one-year anniversary of ChUC on May 30. I specifically remember thinking that it was the greatest comedy show I'd ever seen in my life. And I remember thinking it *in the middle of the show*. The next day, Kristy Mangel blogged,[59] "By the end of the show, the energy in the room was probably the highest I have ever experienced." So it definitely wasn't just me who felt that way.

Jared Logan as Oedipus. ChUC Halloween show, 2006. *Krystle Gemnich.*

Everyone in the cast was on fire that night. But the moment I remember thinking it was the greatest show I'd ever seen was after Nick Vatterott did a set as "Johnny Tough Guy," where he berated the audience and then left dramatically through the crowd, only to have to return multiple times because he'd forgotten something somewhere in the room. I believe he did a version of it in his 2021 special, *Disingenuous*. But that night at ChUC, it worked so perfectly that I thought he'd had the set of the night. I just didn't see how it could be topped.

Later in the night, David Angelo did a set as "The Ghost of Chief Grey Fox," which was a disembodied voice on the "God mic" doing Native American–themed Borscht Belt–era material like, "How many Mohicans does it take to change a light bulb? None. They conspire with the French in the darkness of night."

"It was a snapshot of a different era that hopefully there's no footage of," Angelo laughed. But multiple people still brought that set up fifteen years later as one of their favorite they'd ever seen. It absolutely decimated the room. And it was all just smoke and mirrors, as they say—sound effects and spooky stage lighting. Nobody was even on stage.

That first year of ChUC had definitely normalized the idea of a comedy collective, which also informed the development of Blerds. But while ChUC was initially headed by Brooke Van Poppelen—and included Kara Buller, Renee Gauthier and Allison Leber in its cast—I have to admit that it never occurred to me that Blerds had begun with ten white dudes, a white male director, a white male producer and that Kumail was the only example of diversity in our entire group. Even so, that might have had more to do with the demographic breakdown of the North Side scene than any other factor. "When we did it," Sean Flannery said, "[the scene] had to be, like, 90 percent white dudes."

"Nobody was thinking about inclusion or diversity at the time," Logan said. "Or, excuse me. *We* weren't. There were people, at the time, thinking about that."

"You were just a collection of freaks who made some videos," James Fritz said. "You didn't have a production company behind you. I think if it went to series, you might have grabbed a broad or two. Or put Kumail in a wig and been like, 'Is this diversity?'"

Maybe the most telling evidence for how many women were in the scene around the time would be a sign-up sheet from the Lyon's Den or the Mix open mics. The most famous of those lists, the last night of the Lyon's Den, had seventy-four names on the signup, and only ten of those names were

SpitFire, 2006. *Clockwise from left*: Allison Leber, Becky Garcia, Hattie Snider, Renee Gauthier, Joselyn Hughes, Hannah Gansen, Kara Buller and Fay Canale. *Krystle Gemnich.*

women. And I would guess that only five of those performed regularly in the city. Two years later, when Blerds started, the number had ballooned to eight.

In mid-2006, Kristy "K-Rock" Mangel helped organize a collective of Chicago's female comics called SpitFire. "I wanted to just see more women doing stand-up," Mangel said. "I was like, 'Y'all should work on more stuff together so I can see you perform more.' And they were like, 'Yeah, I love that idea. You can help produce it.' And I was like, 'I actually don't know how to do that. But all right, cool. I'll try to do that.'"

SpitFire wasn't the only new project being spearheaded by K-Rock. In July, the *Apiary*—a blog site dedicated the New York comedy scene—launched a sister site in Chicago known as the *Bastion*. Mangel was the obvious choice to become the site's senior reporter. It really almost feels inevitable—the very first post[60] on *Five Drink Minimum* stated that she wanted her blog to be "a site akin to the *Apiary* in NYC." And in just over three months, that had already come to fruition.

Elizabeth McQuern was tapped to be the site's editor. "We did not know each other at the time," Mangel said. "[Nate Sloan of the *Apiary*] reached out to both of us and pitched us this idea of becoming a subsidiary of this New

York blog that would be more of a web 'zine style, more serious journalism. Not just a fan blog, but doing interviews, doing background research, writing essay-style about a show or two. That's how it started."

The site launched on July 10 with an interview of T.J. Miller[61] and immediately became the newspaper of record for the Chicago comedy scene. One of the first stories the site had to cover happened in late July, when the Montreal Just for Laughs Comedy Festival (or JFL) announced its highly sought-after annual list of New Faces. The New Faces were the young, up-and-coming stand-ups deemed ready to be introduced to the entertainment industry. And success at the JFL festival could mean representation, six-figure development deals and a shot at fame and fortune. That year, the list included Adam Devine, Morgan Murphy, Reggie Watts, Roy Wood Jr. and, as a bit of a shocker to the entire Chicago comedy community, Hannibal Buress. Or as the *Bastion* put it, Hannibal had "skipped to the front of the line"[62] with his selection.

Hannibal Buress at The Hideout, 2007. *Krystle Gemnich.*

Among the names Hannibal had skipped over were Kyle Kinane, Matt Braunger, Pete Holmes, Kumail Nanjiani and T.J. Miller—none of whom had done Montreal yet. Or Aspen, for that matter. And just to put things into perspective, Hannibal hadn't been selected to be one of nineteen comics in the cast of ChUC, and nobody batted an eye. And I would guess that if you surveyed the comics in the scene at that time, nobody would have said he was their top pick to go to Montreal. At least not in 2006.

At this point, I should mention that in the lore of the scene, Hannibal is often portrayed as a guy who started as an especially struggling open mic-er who then became one of the best comedians of his generation through his tenacity and hard work. But besides the fact that every new comic gets better with stage time, and the fact that it's probably a little unfair to speak critically of a twenty-one-year-old comedian no matter who they go on to become, the timeline of when Hannibal arrived in the scene (June 2004) and when he's documented as killing at both Zanies and the Lincoln Lodge (March 2005) leads me to believe there may be a healthy amount of comedic exaggeration in the retelling of his origin story. So the true story of Hannibal Buress is a bit more complicated.

Hannibal Buress at Chicago Underground Comedy. *Erin Nekervis.*

Hannibal grew up in the West Side neighborhood of Austin and began his comedy career as a nineteen-year-old college student at Southern Illinois University Carbondale in 2002. The following year, Buress was selected as one of eight nationwide finalists in the college division of the Laugh Across America Comedy Contest, which earned him an all-expenses-paid trip to the Las Vegas Comedy Festival.

Reflecting on the experience a decade later, Hannibal told the *AV Club,* "I really did benefit early on from starting on a college campus. I was able to start in such a supportive environment, to the point where it was easy to get press and people knew me in Carbondale as the comedian within the first year and a half of me doing comedy....But also I think that, on the flip side, that made me think I was a way better comedian than I was. I would come to Chicago on breaks and then bomb it up."

Be that as it may, there were still established comedians who saw greatness in Hannibal early on. "I was doing a show down at Southern Illinois," South Side comedy staple Leon Rogers told me of his first time meeting Hannibal. "I was the host, and I remember Hannibal walked up to me and said, 'Yo, could I get a guest spot?' And I'm like, 'Cool, man. No problem.' And when he went up on stage with his deadpan style and his satire, that shit was over the kids' heads. The comics were on the side fucking rolling. But the students were like, 'Man, get this motherfucker off stage.'"

"Some of the shows I would open on campus would be Black comedians coming down," Hannibal told the *AV Club*, "so it would be a mostly Black audience and Black students. I did all right for those crowds....But I learned quickly that it is a different energy and a different level of expectations, and there's no room for failure performing for a Black audience. If you don't get them right away it's tough winning them back even if you're doing top-notch material."

Rogers knew that all too well. "I chastised the fuck out the audience," he told me. "I said, 'That was pure comedic timing genius, deadpan style. In about two to three years, that muhfucker's gonna be making a lot of money. And all you little girls out here that's shunning my little dark-skinned, bow-legged brother, y'all gonna regret that shit.' And then about two years later, he's on a late-night talk show. But I saw [his potential]. When I heard the jokes, I was like, 'This muhfucker is hilarious, yo.' And just to see him continue on and do his thing, I'm proud of him."

When I asked Rogers if there was anything specific he saw in Hannibal that made him see his potential, he was quick to respond. "Hannibal was *different*," he said. "Immediately when he's talking on stage, you start going through your mental rolodex of comedians. I was like, 'This dude is like a Black Steven Wright.' That same type of deadpan humor. I was like, 'Yo, I've never seen a brother do that shit before.' It was amazing."

Hannibal also had an early fan in T.J. Miller. "The only person who did as many sets as me was [Hannibal]," he told me in a story that sounds strikingly similar to the one Dwayne Kennedy told about a young Chris Rock. "What made Hannibal so successful is that he had this Teflon confidence. It did not matter what people thought about his stand-up. It was so much more about getting the work done and doing it again....He would do three sets on a Tuesday, three sets the next night, and I would do the same thing."

Leon Rogers and T.J. Miller were two of the early adaptors. But the most telling anecdote of how Hannibal was viewed by the North Side scene just prior to his JFL booking might be the story of his first Lincoln Lodge set in 2005. At that time, the show's policy was that if a new comic wanted to get booked, a cast member had to vouch for them. "If you want to come to a cast meeting and fight in the corner of someone to be booked, you do that," Geary said. "I would let them win if they lobbied hard enough."

"So T.J. Miller lobbied for Hannibal," Geary continued. "And everyone's like, 'He fucking sucks. He talks too slow and he's not funny....And T.J.'s like, 'No, dude. He's the future. He's amazing. Put him on the show. I'm vouching.' Against everyone else in the room."

"I don't remember exactly," T.J. recalled seventeen years after the fact, "but I'm positive that I would have gone to Geary and been like, 'This guy works so hard. He'll do so well in this room. He's got to be part of *this part* of the scene.'"

"So we put him on the show," Geary said. "Hannibal goes up, murders, kills—of course. And T.J.'s just looking at me, 'You're a twat, aren't you Geary?'"

"He did a set and absolutely fucking crushed it," Lodge cast member Ken Barnard confirmed.

"It was amazing," Lodge cast member Bill Cruz added. "I'd never seen that kind of turnaround happen that fast."

So I guess it wasn't just the Black crowds who could make it tough on a comic if they didn't win them over right away. "I can only say this because Hannibal is *Hannibal*, and people know who he is, and they have no idea who I am," Jared Logan said, "Hannibal, when I saw him the first couple months, kinda sucked. He would bomb pretty bad. And then one day, it just flipped. And it wasn't a year. It was like, a couple months. And then suddenly it was like he found the cadence or the rhythm that he needed. Then it was kill city from then on."

"You know when you accidentally hit 1.5x the speed on a podcast?" Brooke Van Poppelen said. "He did that with his act."

"I think it was a crossroads and the devil sort of situation," Pete Holmes said. "I could probably find the e-mail Kumail sent where he said, 'You'll never guess who's funny now.' And it was a clip of Hannibal."

"He was terrible," T.J. said. "But he was still funny. None of us—*none of us*—were like, 'That guy should stop doing comedy.' There's just something about him."

"I know that Hannibal doesn't like when people talk about him being bad at one point," Dave Odd said. "But it's a compliment to go from painfully sucking to an amazing comedian. I can't think of a better compliment."

Whatever his starting point was, it is absolutely fair and accurate to say Hannibal got *significantly* better in his first year in comedy in Chicago, to the point that his transformation has become legendary within the scene. Sure, some of that legend has probably been exaggerated in people's minds over time. But it does make for a better story. And while all the other comedians who "made it" from around that time (Kyle Kinane, Matt Braunger, Pete Holmes, Kumail Nanjiani and T.J. Miller) were said to be great right away, Hannibal's drastic improvement sets him apart for that exact reason. And for comedians struggling to find their own footing in the scene, Hannibal's lore also provided a sense of hope that they, too, could make significant improvements. And since a lot of those comics *didn't* also become Hannibal Buress, Chicago's Patron Saint of Stage Time, it might explain why his work ethic has taken on such a mythical status as well.

"Hannibal was an incredible hustler, man," comedian Aaron Foster said. "That muhfucker would do three or four mics a night, and he never had no *car*. One time I drove from the Lyon's Den to out west somewhere, and he showed up. I said, 'How'd you get here?' He's like, 'Man, I took three buses and, you know, [rode] a camel,' or something. I was like, 'Wow. This dude is serious about this shit.'"

"I remember calling Hannibal once to ask where all he went up," comedian Robert Buscemi told me, "Mind you, I was a *hustler*. I was performing most nights—three or four booked shows a week and one or two open mics. So he starts listing the shows he's doing. 'I start at a 5:00 p.m. poetry thing on the North Side where they'll let me go up, then they'll give me five minutes at a student-run improv jam at the Cornservatory, then I go west to an open mic that's mostly music, then the stand-up shows start at 8, and I'll hit this one and then that one and then head south and then back north.' He lists like six shows and we're not even to 9:00 p.m. on a Monday....I've always remembered that story as exactly what it takes to get what you want."

The date of Hannibal's first Lincoln Lodge appears to be March 25, 2005, which is just over two weeks after Allan Johnson of the *Tribune* called him "unexpectedly special" after his guest set for Mitch Hedberg. So Hannibal was obviously turning the corner by that time. But killing at the Lincoln Lodge and having a great guest set at Zanies don't get anybody selected for Montreal. The truth is, to complete his evolution, Hannibal probably needed to spend time in New York, which he did for the first few months of 2006, where nobody had seen him struggle.

"In New York, he just did better," Mike Burns said. "Maybe he just needed a fresh start. Sometimes you see someone so much that you don't see their progress."

"My theory is, he went to New York and had to scream over everybody, so he learned how to be more vocal," Mangel said. "Because he was so timid and quiet when he was in Chicago....Or maybe we saw him at mics so much and we were all drinking and partying and we weren't listening." After he got New Faces, everybody was listening.

In late October, the other big industry festival in the world of comedy, the HBO-sponsored US Comedy Arts Festival in Aspen, put on a showcase at the Lincoln Restaurant so it could scout for talent. In its preview for the show, the *Bastion* also noted, "Ambitious comedians should also show up at 7 PM that night for a seminar led by HBO's Senior Producer for Festival Talent, Kirsten Ames."[63]

I was one of those ambitious comedians in attendance. And during that Q&A session with Kirsten Ames, someone asked if she would advise a comedian in Chicago to move to New York or Los Angeles. In the moment, I remember thinking it was a dumb question. Kirsten Ames was the festival's New York–based scout. Of course she was going to say New York. But her answer floored me. "Move to LA if you want a career," is what she said. And it felt like a room full of jaws hit the floor at the same time.

I remember the moderator, Tom Lawler, asking, "So...*not* New York?" seemingly to double-check that she'd meant to say what she'd just said. But Ames doubled down. "*Go to LA if you want a career.*"

It just so happened that the next day I would be flying to Los Angeles for the first time in my life. I had been dating Renee Gauthier, who had just moved to LA. And we had agreed to try to make the long-distance thing work. Now I'd be traveling there with an entirely new mindset. Until that Q&A, I feel like everyone else in the scene had been talking about moving to New York after their time in Chicago. Pete Holmes had moved to New York and seen a decent amount success. Mike Burns and Brooke Van Poppelen were there too. But that answer from Kirsten Ames changed things.

There were obviously a lot more factors that went into the big migration west, and I'll get into all of them soon. But Kirsten Ames lit the initial spark. The funny thing is, three years later, I saw Kirsten at the airport in Montreal when I was a JFL New Face alongside Pete, Kumail and Renee. And when I reminded Kirsten of that Q&A at the Lincoln Restaurant, she replied, "I said to go to *LA*?!?!? I think I would say something different now. Are you sure I said LA?" And when I said I was 100 percent positive, she winced and said, "Is everybody...happy?"

A lot of those moves out west would occur in 2007, including my own. And as 2006 came to a close, I remember a lot of people feeling like major things were on the horizon. In August, after T.J. Miller and Prescott Tolk put on their two-man show at the Upright Citizens Brigade Theatre in New York, the *Apiary*'s headline read, "New Talent Discovered: T.J. Miller!"[64] And the post referred to him as "The Golden Child of Chicago" and said he "has all the markings of a comedy megastar." And that was affirmed in late December when T.J. was selected to be part of the US Comedy Arts Festival in Aspen.

Another selection for the Aspen festival that year was Kyle Kinane, who had become the final addition to Blerds in September. "I asked to be in Blerds," Kinane said. "Seeing these videos, I'm like, 'Aww, you guys are doing this in Chicago? *Fuck*. I'm sitting in LA just failing night after night.'"

Like Kinane, Blerds had begun to take off a little bit by the end of the year. I got interviewed in the *Bastion*,[65] as well as *TimeOut Chicago*,[66] and in December, I

Kyle Kinane at the Lincoln Lodge.
Erin Nekervis.

got interviewed for a big article about Blerds in the *Chicago Tribune*.[67] We did fun photo shoots. We booked shows at rock venues and set up a big New Year's Eve show in a collaboration with the Lincoln Lodge. We got a manager, who set us up with spots at the DC Comedy Festival, and a booth at the NACA National Convention in Nashville. Things were moving fast for us—probably a little too fast.

The landscape was changing in and around Chicago. And in the middle of everything, Chicago Underground Comedy had moved locations from Gunther Murphy's to the Beat Kitchen. And The Elevated—the show that basically launched the entire scene a decade prior—was officially passing the torch. And this time, it was for good.

Chapter 20

THE ELEVATED (END)

I n August 2006, The Elevated celebrated its ten-year anniversary. That kind of longevity made it one of a kind, at least in the Chicago scene, where the Lincoln Lodge was the only other independent show over five years old at the time. And then on December 6, the *Bastion* announced,[68] rather unceremoniously, that The Elevated was going on a hiatus while the show's producer Cayne Collier searched for a new venue. That venue never came. Collier's room, which had served as the inspiration for every Chicago alt show in the late '90s and early 2000s, was unfortunately no more. And it is perhaps even more unfortunate that most of the comics in the scene at that time had never seen the show in its full glory.

"It was definitely dying," comedian Joselyn Hughes said. "Especially at the *end* end. You'd walk in and there'd be three people there. And one of them would be talking to the bartender the entire time. It was *rough*."

"It tapered off and waned," Elevated regular Robert Buscemi said. "It was past its biggest moment....It used to be *the* place. By the time I came around, it was still a big deal. But it was changing."

According to Collier, the peak years of The Elevated were from 1996 to 2000 and again from 2002 to 2005, while the rough years fell somewhere between 2000 and 2002 and again from 2005 into 2006. The show had started at the Cue Club in 1996, which became Philosofur's in 1998 and then finally became Cherry Red in 2001. And the final incarnation was not a good fit.

"You'd be up there," Brooke Van Poppelen said, "and you'd be like... 'The crowd is precisely 50 feet away from me. In one booth and two tables

Cayne Collier at
The Elevated's
tenth anniversary
show, 2006. *Krystle
Gemnich.*

on the other side of this fucking auditorium that's meant for raves.' It was cavernous. I saw a lot of amazing shit happen there. I loved when I had opportunities to get up there. But as a budding producer, I was like, 'This room is so fucking wrong.'"

On top of all the venue changes, and the terrible fit with Cherry Red, there was also the fact that 80 percent of the show's existence was before the advent of MySpace. "There was no social media," Elevated regular Nate Craig said. "You were promoting a show with fliers. Underneath, behind and around the corner from the Diversey L stop. It was not easy to get people out, even if you had a built-up brand."

There were departing waves of performers, as well as departing waves of DePaul students who had frequented the show. There were battles with bar managers and serious bouts of depression, not to mention one of the largest and most destructive natural disasters in American history. "When Katrina hit," Craig said, "[Collier is] from New Orleans, so he had to hit the road and make money. He had to send a bunch of money home so that his family was taken care of."

There are exponentially more reasons through its run that this show should have failed rather than succeeded. And yet it continued to chug along for a full decade when no other show had come close. Maybe the true value of the show was never in its commercial appeal to begin with.

The greatest example of what The Elevated's later years could produce is Nick Vatterott's 2010 television debut on *Late Night with Jimmy Fallon*. In his stand-up set, Vatterott pretended to forget the next joke he was supposed to tell, only to pull out a giant set list for an even bigger payoff from the audience. The set is pretty famous within the alt comedy community and was deemed to be "a master class in manipulating…tension," as well as "a convincing argument that Vatterott is a stand-up worthy of more attention" by Chicago's own John Roy in his "Great Bits" series for *Vulture*.[69]

The reason that set even existed, besides the brilliance of Nick Vatterott, was because of the artistic freedom granted by Cayne Collier at The Elevated. "The giant set list bit that I wound up doing on *Fallon* is something I wrote for The Elevated," Vatterott said. "Because [I thought], 'The Elevated is an alternative comedy place. I need to write an alternative comedy bit.'"

The reason the *Fallon* people had seen the bit was because Vatterott had done it as a New Face at the Just for Laughs Festival in Montreal. And even doing it at JFL was a bit of a risk. As Roy mentioned in his article, "Every time the festival scouts visited Vatterott's home city of Chicago, he made sure to show them his most accessible, mainstream material—to no success." Facing the prospect of even more rejection in 2010, Vatterott decided to do an audition set that would make him happy instead of one he assumed would make the entertainment industry happy.

In other words, pleasing the audience and the industry were secondary in his mind to artistic exploration and expression. It's a sentiment that seems to be consistent with other nonmainstream performers in the scene who also loved performing at The Elevated. "[The Elevated] was the antithesis of all the Hollywood things that really ruined the enjoyment of stand-up," Mike Burns said. "They rewarded the actual performance as opposed to what the audience thought. That, in our little baby comedian minds, was so important—to have someone support you as an artist, even though you bombed. To say, 'No. I see where you're going with this.'"

"[Adam Kroshus] had one of his absolutely epic meltdowns," comedian Sean Flannery said, illustrating Burns's point even further. "He used to have this bit where he would impersonate what we would now call a 'Trump Red State American'—a hillbilly. His punchline is, 'I like pussy,' and he fires a shotgun into the air. Well, it falls flat. He gets frustrated. He walks table to table pantomiming that he's shooting each customer in the face with a shotgun.…Cayne is such an understanding artist and, as Kro gets to the third table, I just hear Cayne go, 'Not sure where he's going with this.' Like, 'Cayne, he's having a psychological breakdown. This isn't part of his act.'"

"They were so loyal to people that took chances and did things that were outside the norm," Burns said. "You didn't have to worry if you did good. You just had to go up there and try something.…Because a lot of the times, when you perform at showcases or clubs, you're not performing to do what you want to do....The goal is to do the best set that gets you asked back."

When it comes to performing for industry, it's safer to make soft contact and get on base than it is to swing from your heels and wind up on your ass. In Roy's article about Vatterott's *Fallon* bit, he noted that, "Having tried and failed a dozen times to succeed with small ball, Vatterott swings for the parking lot and hits a grand slam." Conceived and developed in the absence of audience and industry, and almost as a rejection of both concepts, then met with an abundance of praise and attention once it was finally discovered by both, Vatterott's *Fallon* set is probably also a metaphor for the Chicago scene itself. Because of all of those factors, plus the fact that it was specifically written for The Elevated, Vatterott's *Fallon* set might be the best representation of our Chicago scene ever shown to a mass audience.

That tone for that experimentation and sense of play was set at the top of the show. "I don't know if I'm allowed to compare mortals to gods," Vatterott said, "but I feel like [Collier] had a Dave Chappelle style of comedy before I saw Dave Chappelle do it....He would explore ideas on stage. And I feel like a lot of Chappelle's style is exploring ideas until he finds the white hot part of it, and then it lights up from there. But Cayne's very patient, and he doesn't feel the need to be like, joke, joke, joke. And it's very improvisational, like a lot of Chappelle's stuff is. He was more seasoned than a lot of us, and I know I was uncomfortable in silence and felt the need have every second filled with something. And it took me years to understand and appreciate the value of silence and moments and improvisation. And so him sitting up there and talking and finding these things and then, once it hits, exploring it—that was a very fun, cool thing to watch. I don't really remember anyone else doing that in town at that time."

"On our T-shirts and hats," Collier said, "the tagline was 'Taking Comedy to a Higher Level.' And I questioned, 'Is that pretentious? Is that being a comedy snob?' No, it is what we're trying to do. What's the point if you're not gonna try to do a thing better than you've seen it done?...To me, if you had to say, 'What's *not* taking comedy to a higher level?' it would be anything that comes across as stale. And a way to easily be stale with any art is to stop pushing it."

Maybe the closest any of the newer comics got to seeing The Elevated at the height of its full potential was at the anniversary shows. That's when the show provided a window into why it was still held in such high regard by the scene. Those shows made all the stories about Cayne turning down Lewis Black at the Chicago Comedy Festival make slightly more sense.

They're the reason Pete Holmes still gets nervous when he thinks about the show. And they're the reason Mark Geary threw away all of his jokes and tried to produce a show as strong as Cayne's instead. And it was one of the final anniversary shows that provided one of the final great moments in the show's long run. And it might be the most fitting ending of them all.

In the middle of a hot anniversary show, in front of a packed house, in the dog days of summer, all of the power went out at Cherry Red, including the air conditioner. Collier had to use a police flashlight to give performers a spotlight on stage. "I would have had a psychotic meltdown if it was one of my shows," Geary said, "but Cayne handled it in good cheer as usual."

Nate Craig believes that he was on stage when the lights blew, and he seems to have handled it in good cheer himself. "It was one of those moments where I was like, 'Oh my God. This is incredible,'" Craig laughed. "We just invented stand-up comedy."

The Elevated was far from perfect. But in its finest moments, it was never supposed to be. There were definitely comics in the scene who felt that Cayne took the show too seriously or that he could have relinquished some control. But he had a vision, and he saw it through to the end. And as the lights went down on the show, maybe he didn't invent stand-up comedy, but Cayne Collier definitely had a big hand in its reinvention.

Chapter 21

2007

In January 2007, the THC Comedy Tour came to Chicago to do a show at the Metro concert hall in Wrigleyville. The tour, which was produced by Los Angeles–based comedy entrepreneurs Josh Spector and Ford Oelman, featured marijuana-themed entertainment from comedians Doug Benson, Al Madrigal and Jay Phillips. Shortly before the show, Spector and Oelman asked T.J. Miller to perform. And to my surprise, they also inquired about playing Mike Holmes and my Blerds video "Every Eminem Song Ever" during the show.

After everything went well at the Metro, and a few of the guys in Blerds met Spector and Oelman, we asked our manager to reach out to them to see if they'd be interested in working with us on a potential Blerds tour down the road. And I was actually taken aback by how enthusiastic of a response we got in return. "I was blown away by all you guys and how much talent there was in this one group," Spector said. "It felt like discovering treasure, and I immediately believed you guys were going to go on to a ton of success. I knew I was early in finding you, but also knew that it was highly unlikely I would be able to capitalize on what I had found. That said, I figured I'd give it a shot."

As it turned out, Spector and Oelman had a lot of ideas about what should be done with Blerds, and they sent our manager an e-mail about taking us "to the next level." That next level included integrating us into the THC Tour, as well as the Vivid Comedy Party—another project of theirs— which paired comedians with porn stars from Vivid Entertainment. And if those things panned out, they wanted to produce a Blerds-specific tour down the road. On top of all that, Spector and Oelman said they had strong relationships with the Hollywood Improv and the Upright Citizens Brigade Theatre in Los Angeles, possibly for monthly shows in both venues. Plus they had a strong relationship with MySpace, so they could get our videos featured on the site—back when that was a huge fucking deal. There was also talk of creating various pitches for web series and TV pilots, as well as comparisons to established comedy groups like Human Giant, Broken Lizard and Lonely Island.

It was simultaneously everything I'd been daydreaming about throughout the previous year and completely beyond anything I'd ever imagined when I started comedy. The only problem was that, behind the scenes, Blerds was a barely functioning logistical nightmare and organizational clusterfuck.

As individuals, most of the guys in Blerds were only competent on stage or when they were bellied up to a bar. As an entity, Blerds also had a number of glaring issues that we had yet to figure out. We had no official group leadership, so getting a consensus on even the smallest issue was either exhausting or completely impossible. Every live show booking decision was met with mistrust and scrutiny by whoever felt excluded in the given moment. Even basic tasks like getting LLC paperwork signed would get derailed because somebody would get drunk and think it was funny to have their buddy sign the official document. And since we were about to have a manager, show producers and someone doing the website, Rob Johnson's future involvement in our group, as well as his hypothetical cut of our future riches, began to be questioned openly.

Besides all the major organizational issues, there was also an increasing number of personal beefs beginning to bubble to the surface because Jordan Vogt-Roberts had basically stopped making videos for everyone in the group except for T.J. Some people in Blerds had multiple videos online. Others only had one on the site. Mike Holmes, in particular, never got his own individual Blerds video.[70] It was basically the exact scenario that T.J.'s detractors had predicted when T.J. had asked to be in the group. Except now, the stakes for the group seemed significantly higher, Jordan wanted his own representation and attachment to industry heat in Los Angeles, and T.J. happened to be one of the hottest young comics in the country.

All of those internal issues seemed to come to a head at one particularly chaotic and angry group meeting at Fizz Bar & Grill in Lake View in late January. There were screaming matches over whether or not we should sign the contract with Spector and Oelman, whether or not Jordan should be

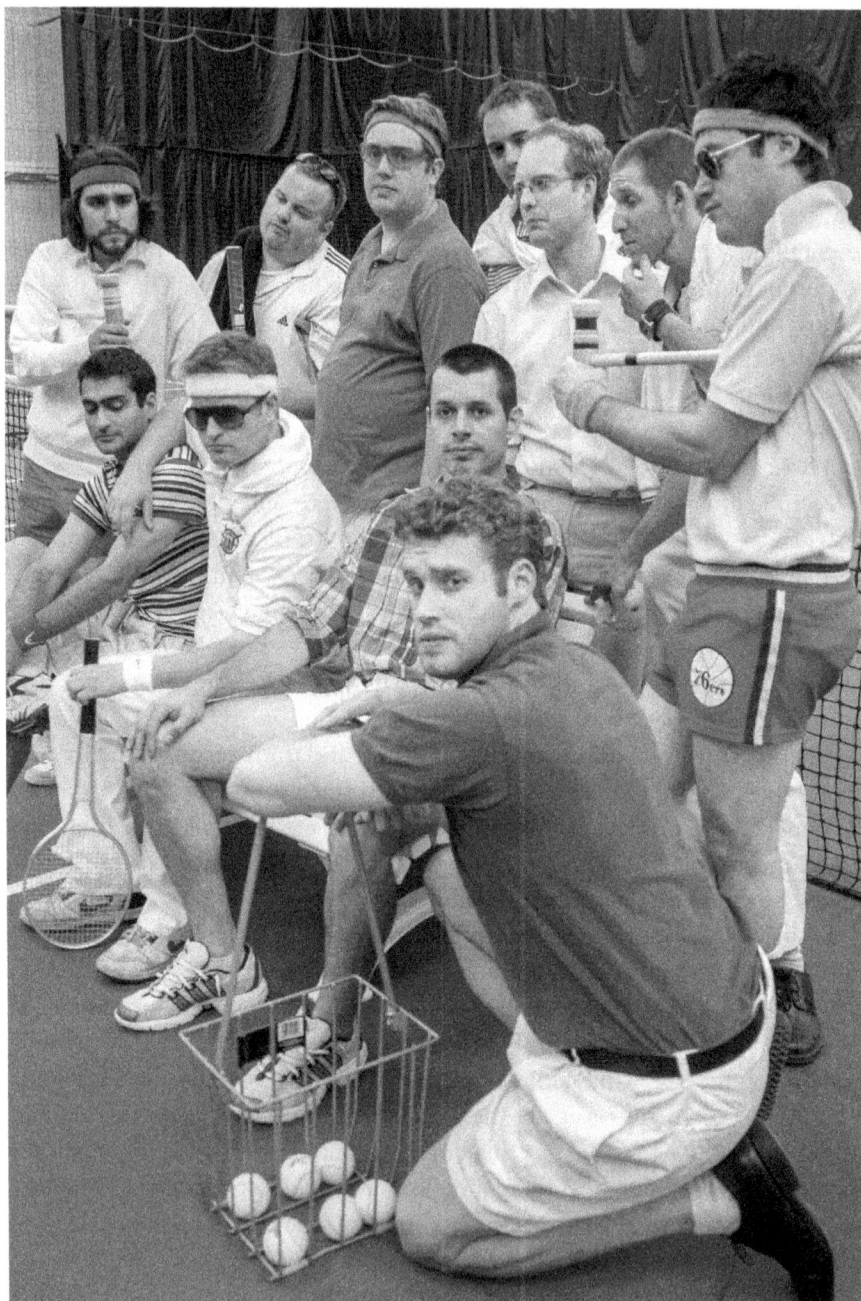

Blerds photo shoot. *Clockwise from left*: Jordan Vogt-Roberts, CJ Sullivan, Jared Logan, Mike Holmes, Sean Flannery, Prescott Tolk, Pat Brice, T.J. Miller, Nate Craig, Mike Bridenstine and Kumail Nanjiani, 2006. *Forest Casey.*

booking the live shows and even whether or not Pete Holmes should host an upcoming show at Upright Citizens Brigade Theatre in New York. "I remember it being pretty crazy," Sean Flannery said. "We were all hot-headed drunks back then. Or close to all of us." And when the dust finally settled, Rob Johnson showed up in a cheery mood only to find that he'd been kicked out of the group.

Rob's removal had been voted on before he arrived, but I was hoping nobody would have the heart to actually do it. And nobody actually did, except for Pat Brice. Without a hint of discomfort or timidity, Brice just matter-of-factly let Rob know that he was no longer wanted in the group. And just like that, the person who had come up with the initial idea only a year prior was now being kicked out of that same group while everyone else in it just stared awkwardly at their beers and nodded.

"I was a little pissed about it," Rob remembered, "because I never asked for money and was really only involved to help my friends. I was a little confused by why I was getting 'kicked out'…It's not like I was going to take you guys to the promised land, but I think it's weird that the conversation was 'go away' and not 'thanks for getting it started.'"

The whole thing was brutal for me to watch. I'd been friends with Rob longer than anyone else in the group, including Mike Holmes. I wish I could have figured out a role to keep Rob involved or at least give him a softer landing so that he wasn't blindsided like that. It's still not a fun thing for me to think about fifteen years after the fact, even though Rob seemed to take the whole thing in stride.

"I loved Blerds," Rob said. "It was fun until it wasn't. But it was a highlight of my twenties for sure."

Pat Brice, 2006. *Krystle Gemnich.*

The biggest irony, at least in my opinion, is that Pat Brice probably walked out of the meeting as the unquestioned leader of Blerds. It was as if everyone in the group had been waiting for him to take the reins, and he just hadn't wanted to until then. But going forward, he was going to be our quarterback. Because the truth is, he probably always had been.

"He was the quarterback," Kristy Mangel agreed. "He was the good-looking one. He was the one with the good job. He was the one who had his shit together, seemingly. But he was also the fucking funniest."

"He sort of epitomized Chicago," Jared Logan said. "He was a South Side boy. He talked like a Chicago guy. He was a Board of Trade guy. And on paper, he's all the things that would make up a person that I might not get along with—a handsome, sporty, tough guy—but I never detected one *iota* of judgment from him....He just threw his arm around you because you were part of the party that night. You were part of the crew."

"When I saw Brice, I remember being like, 'That's the fucking Guy,'" comedian Joe Kilgallon said. "He was doing material that was smart, but in a way that was like, 'I'm not gonna be clever. I'm just gonna hit you right in the face with this stuff.' And I remember thinking, 'Yeah, that's the type of comic I want to be.'"

"Brice was the coolest guy ever," comedian James Fritz said. "I was like, 'That's who I want to be.' He was like the cool football player who would stomp the bullies. He was amazing."

Mike Burns referred to Brice as "the ultimate alpha male." Matt Braunger has said he looked like a model but sounded like a teamster. And as cliché as it might sound, Pat Brice was our scene's version of "Women want to be with him, men want to be him."

"He was The Guy," Bill Cruz said. "People had John Roy. People had Pete Holmes. We had Pat Brice....It was an eventuality that he would make it. Everybody knew it. Same with T.J. What are you doing here? Go away. Go be famous."

T.J. was, in fact, about to go away and be famous—he booked the ABC sitcom *Carpoolers* in February, and he would be off to Los Angeles within months. But things really started moving at lightning speed for Blerds, on a much smaller scale, around the same time as well—especially when we decided to upload our videos to YouTube and MySpace. "At that time your videos were only on your website as Quicktime files," Spector said, "and one of the first things I said to you was that you needed to put them on YouTube. In fairness, YouTube was probably less than two years old at the time. It was a simpler time."

On top of our big NACA audition to potentially tour colleges for good money, we also started to get approached by different web series platforms about projects and even got offered $50,000 to make an online ad campaign for Jose Cuervo tequila. It was obviously way too much and way too fast for us to handle, and because of it, the infighting became constant and was escalating. All of which might explain why I missed the single biggest story to ever come out of that scene.

Besides the all-female SpitFire comedy collective and the *Bastion*, the other major thing Kristy "K-Rock" Mangel kicked off was a tiny community of comedy fans who would regularly attend shows together, take photos of the performers, drink together afterward and sometimes post about the shows on social media. The immediate benefit was that, as comedian Emily Dorezas put it, they documented the scene for us in a way that we hadn't to that point. I also think this played a pretty big role in the scene starting to take itself a little more seriously. K-Rock legitimized us to ourselves.

Noteworthy among the regulars in this tiny community of fans were Angel Busque, who had discovered K-Rock through the *Five Drink Minimum* blog and then become her most trusted sidekick, and Krystle "K-Roll" Gemnich, who took the torch from Mangel and became the scene's official photographer. But the comedy show regular who would go on to the most renown, actually far exceeding the fame that most comedians in the scene would attain, was Emily V. Gordon.

"I got Googled by one Ms. Emily Gordon," Mangel said. "She was like, 'You look like you're having fun. I'm going through a hard time in life. I'd like to have some fun.'"

It wasn't long after that, according to legend,[71] that Gordon attended a bar show where Kumail Nanjiani performed. According to Andrew Marantz of the *New Yorker*, "Nanjiani asked, facetiously, 'Is Karachi in the house?' Someone in the audience, also facetiously, let out a 'Whoo!' Nanjiani could see that she was a white woman, a pretty brunette with a streak of purple in her hair. 'I don't think so,' he said. 'I would have noticed you.' Two nights later, they ran into each other again, and she introduced herself."

"I think I remember the show where Kumail and Emily met," Gemnich said. "I was at that show. And I think I was at Lincoln Lodge."

"I think I was there the night they met," Jared Logan also said, in a story that could be equally true. "I remember a house party. And it might have been at CJ Sullivan's apartment."

Kumail and Emily's blossoming romance was complicated by Gordon's recent divorce, as well as the traditions and expectations of Nanjiani's Muslim parents. And it was made even more complicated when Gordon became pretty seriously ill in 2007.

According to Marantz, "[Gordon] was having trouble breathing. [Nanjiani] rushed to the hospital and spent the night. By the next morning, Gordon was heavily sedated and was drifting in and out of wakefulness. Her lung was infected, and the infection was spreading fast. In order to treat it, the doctors told Nanjiani, they needed to put her into a medically induced coma. They asked if he was her husband. He said no—he wasn't even sure that he was her boyfriend. They asked again, pressing him to sign a release form. Finally, at the doctors' insistence, he signed it. The doctors tied Gordon down and injected her with an anesthetic. She thrashed against the restraints and then fell into a coma."

"Even a decade later," Marantz continued, "after having recounted the experience dozens of times, Nanjiani still chokes up whenever he talks about it. 'I was sitting by her bed,' he said. 'She was unconscious, and she was hooked up to all these beeping machines, and I very clearly remember thinking, If she makes it out of this, I'm gonna marry her.'"

The story was retold in the Judd Apatow–produced movie *The Big Sick* (2017), which starred Kumail as himself and Zoe Kazan as Emily. It also earned both Kumail and real-life Emily Oscar nominations for the screenplay. And honestly, the whole saga barely registered with me in real time.

In a journal I found from around that time, I wrote exactly two things about the incident. The first, which I wrote on March 15, 2007, said, "Emily, Kumail's girlfriend, is in the hospital with pneumonia."[72] But not before I also mentioned that Pat Brice and CJ Sullivan had lectured me to not brag

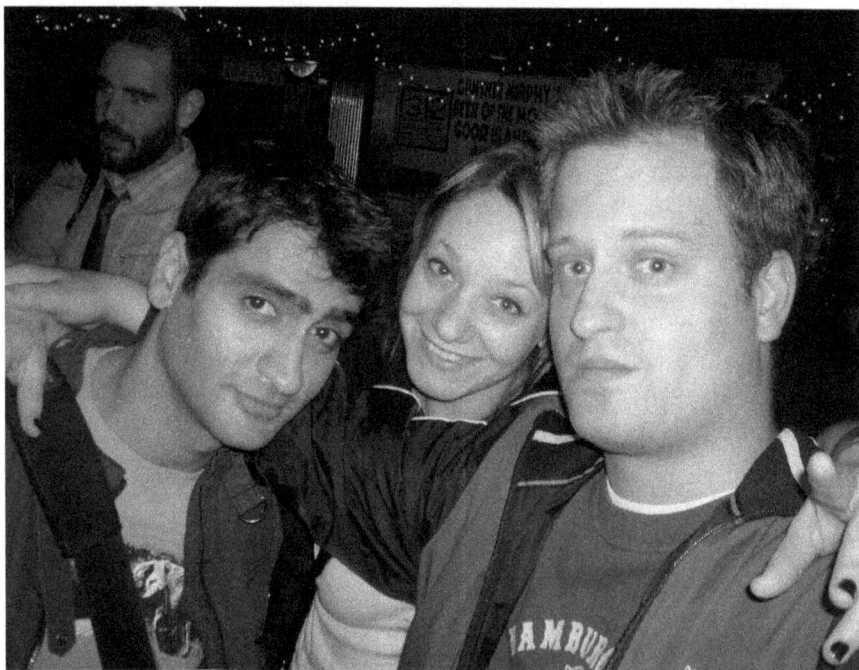

Kumail Nanjiani, Emily V. Gordon and Mike Bridenstine at the last ChUC at Gunther Murphy's, 2006. *Author's collection.*

about Blerds to comics who were not in the group. That was apparently the bigger concern to me at the time. And then on March 27, I wrote, "Jared is upset that Kumail might propose to Emily." And that's about as much as I seemed to notice about the whole thing.

"Here's my version of *The Big Sick*," Logan said, "Kumail comes back after just being gone from open mics for two weeks. [I asked] 'What happened?' [And Kumail said] 'Oh. It was crazy. My girlfriend got in a coma.' [So I said] 'Oh. But she's okay now?' [And Kumail said] 'Yeah.' [I said] 'All right. I gotta go do a set.' Like, that was my entire take on it. I didn't go, 'Oh my God, is she okay?!?!?' I was like, 'Oh. Is she okay though? All right. Great. Now let's go drink beer.' Didn't even show any empathy for my friend or his girlfriend at all. Now there's an Oscar-nominated movie about the thing I didn't care about at the time."

Later that summer, Kumail's one-man show, *Unpronounceable*, opened at the Lakeshore Theater in Lake View. The show covered Kumail's strict Muslim upbringing in Pakistan and his subsequent move to Iowa at age eighteen. In the movie version, Kumail's one-man show was depicted as a tedious slog about the country of Pakistan, mostly performed to yawning, empty houses. But in reality, it was sold-out shows, stellar reviews and standing ovations. And then he took the show to New York, performed it at the Upright Citizens Brigade Theatre and did it all over again. But hey, *The Big Sick* is a movie, and it wouldn't make as much sense if "Movie Kumail" was awesome the entire time.

While all the action in the movie was occurring, I was probably hyper-stressed about some sort of contractual document that everyone in Blerds needed to sign or was unsuccessfully trying to wrangle everyone to come up with more pitches for a digital ad campaign about tequila since we'd been told our ideas weren't "fun" enough. And the fact that I even noticed that "Kumail's girlfriend is in the hospital" might have been in response to me frantically asking, "Where the fuck is Kumail? Why hasn't he gotten back to me with fun pitches for 'Cuervo Season'?"

In June, the "Every Eminem Song Ever" video I had made with Mike Holmes and Jordan Vogt-Roberts got featured on the front page of MySpace. This was when MySpace was still by far the biggest social media site on the Internet. And I repeatedly refreshed the page just to watch the number of views climb by the hundreds or thousands. It wasn't the first time a Blerds video had gotten that type of exposure or even that type of view count. Pat Brice's "Rent or Own" video also got on the front of MySpace, as well as T.J. Miller's "Giraffe Facts." Plus Kyle Kinane's "Embarrassing Music

Kumail Nanjiai's one-man show, *Unpronounceable*, 2007. *Krystle Gemnich.*

Mike Burns, Eric Andre, Kumail Nanjiani and Mike Bridenstine, 2007. *Kristy Mangel.*

Downloads" and a "Mac vs. PC" parody video featuring Brice and adult film star Monique Alexander entitled "Filthy" were on the landing page for MySpace Comedy. But this was our last video to ever get featured on the site. It was also just about the biggest rush I'd ever felt in my life.

"I can remember the morning when 'Every Eminem Song Ever' was on the front page of MySpace," Holmes said. "You called me to tell me....It was about six o'clock in the morning....Remember when you handed me the phone when Hedberg was on the other line and how I reacted? I reacted in such a way that [my then girlfriend] knew that the video was on the front page of MySpace."

The idea for the video came from a road trip that Holmes and I had taken in the summer of 2005. During the drive, Eminem's single "Mockingbird" came on the radio. It was about his wife, Kim, and his daughter, Hailie. And Holmes had been on a rant just recently about how the only things Eminem rapped about were his mom and Kim and Hailie. So when the song came on, I began repeatedly rapping "Mom and Kim and Hailie" over the track. Holmes started laughing and then jumped in on the riff. We both thought it was hilarious. But when it got to the chorus and Holmes began singing "Mom and Hailie, Mom and Kim" over the hook, it was clear that we had something special.

Our Blerds video, which was essentially a parody of Eminem's 2002 movie *8 Mile*, was shot around Holmes and my neighborhood in Lake View and around Pat Brice's place in Bucktown. But it was also shot at the Lathrop Homes housing projects, because Jordan loved the visual of steam coming out of the sewer grates right in front of it. Jordan also thought it was hilarious how uncomfortable I was shooting a rap video in the projects while holding up a stolen 8 Mile Road street sign from Detroit. There's even a specific shot where Jordan says he can see the fear in my eyes. But hey, the video is great, so I guess it all worked.

Ever since the video was posted on social media, it had gotten mini bursts of attention, getting featured on "Big in 2007" sites like Super Deluxe, eBaum's World, Fark and Funny or Die. Each time it got featured, we'd also get a number of angry comments from Eminem fans. So Holmes and I added a supplemental routine we'd occasionally perform where we'd read our negative comments out loud, and after tracking down the commenters' MySpace pages, we'd go through the commenters' own profiles and talk about the stuff they thought was good. My favorite "negative" comments were the ones on Daily Motion that we translated from French to English, which we would then compare and contrast with the comments left by American teenagers.

From left: T.J. Miller, Jared Logan, Sean Flannery, Mike Bridenstine, Kumail Nanjiani and Mike Holmes. Blerds photo shoot, 2006. *Forest Casey*.

A typical comment from a French speaker would say something like, "To be the critic is easy. To be the artist is difficult. Which of these things are you?" And then the typical American comment would say something along the lines of, "I hope your whore mother goes to hell and sucks the dicks of Hitler *and* Satan." So, needless to say, Holmes and I got a lot of mileage out of that video. Not in pay, obviously. But in bits.

The summer of 2007 was an exciting time for me. I had signed with Spector and Oelman as my personal managers. Blerds was given a monthly show at Upright Citizens Brigade Theatre in Los Angeles. Comedian Renee Gauthier, who I was still dating long distance, had been selected to portray Victoria Beckham's personal assistant in her reality series *Victoria Beckham: Coming to America*. A ton of other comics were also talking about moving to Los Angeles. And all signs were pointing to me moving to Los Angeles as well. It truly felt like a major shift in the scene was about to take place, and everyone I knew was about to become famous. It was the logic and excitement of a naïve twentysomething. But also, a few of them did become famous, so it's not like I was wrong.

It was abundantly clear to everyone that T.J. Miller would be first. That much was obvious. But if I would have had to bet money on any of the

Sean Flannery, CJ Sullivan and Pat Brice at ChUC, 2006. *Krystle Gemnich.*

people in the scene to be the next surefire, no-brainer superstar, it still would have probably been Pat Brice. And in July, at a Chicago Underground Comedy show, upstairs at the Beat Kitchen, he might have had the single greatest set I've ever seen in my life.

It was actually Pat's "return set" to ChUC because he had been banned by the Beat Kitchen a few months prior. "We were at the Beat Kitchen late," Sean Flannery said. "It was just comics left in the bar. Pat wanted to smoke weed but didn't have a [bowl] or rolling paper so he ordered a tall boy with the intention of using it to smoke. But he was hammered and not subtle about it at all, so he gets the beer and dumps its entire contents into the trash bin right by him. The bouncer saw this from the corner and was like, 'Okay, what's this guy's plan?'"

The bouncer in question was Jim Staffel, who would go on to work at ChUC shows for fourteen more years. "It was near last call," Staffel remembered. "Pat and two of his buddies were pretty much the last people in the bar. I noticed him order a PBR tall boy. He usually drank High Lifes. Then he proceeded to share it with the other two. Minutes later, he disappeared to the men's room in the basement. Shortly after that, the bar started to smell like weed."

"I smoked weed with him in the basement bathroom out of a beer can," Mike Holmes confessed. "I was obviously drunk. So that, plus weed, triggered a classic 'I gotta get out of here right now' [response], so I bailed. I think he got busted shortly after."

"[I] went downstairs to check it out," Staffel said. "Looked into the stall and found the PBR can-bowl. I went back up to the bar and called him out for smoking in the bathroom. He denied it."

"I think what really pissed the bouncer off," Flannery said, "is that Pat was denying it and probably calling [Staffel] an asshole....[Staffel] basically bum rushed Pat out and told Pat and us he's banned for life."

"[I] told him that he can't perform here anymore," Staffel confirmed.

"They were very mad about it," ChUC producer Tony Sam said. "I mean, they were *really* mad."

Eventually, cooler heads prevailed. "I begged," Sam said. "I wore them down after a while. And I said, 'I will vouch for him. He won't ever do it again.'" And finally Tony and the venue came up with a compromise. "He was allowed to perform if he came in the side door," Sam said, "and directly onto the stage. But he couldn't stay. He'd have to perform and then go."

"There were definitely negotiations," Flannery said, "and everyone at ChUC—in particular Pat, me and CJ—were told he had to be on his best behavior. But what was so funny is [a bouncer] essentially shadowed him all night."

With his arms crossed and a scowl on his face, Staffel kept a watchful eye while Brice took the stage and addressed the elephant in the room by retelling the story of his own banishment. And here's the thing: Brice was going to have a good set no matter what. He could have talked about anything and it still would have been great. And he was obviously funny enough to kill telling the same story at a different venue, without the bouncer present. But the fact that Brice was performing at the Beat Kitchen *while on probation from the Beat Kitchen*, and the guy who busted him was standing feet from him, trying not to laugh, gave the set a particular immediacy that, once the audience figured out it was real, made the room fucking erupt. Eventually, Staffel joined in on the fun.

"To [Staffel's] credit," Flannery said, "he never held it against Pat, and I remember [him] laughing super hard at Pat's set. But then, once Pat got off, [he] began following him around again, very seriously....God, Pat was the best."

There's a big difference between "having a good set" and "killing." But that terminology doesn't really feel adequate to describe what Pat did that night. It felt like the floor was literally shaking beneath me. And I remember looking around, observing people in hysterics, listening to the volume of the response he was getting and thinking I had never seen a person make a room full of people laugh that hard before. I still don't know if I've ever seen anyone kill any harder than that. Or if it's even possible.

For that reason alone, it's probably the greatest set I've ever seen. But it's also special to me because that was the last time I ever saw Pat Brice alive.

Chapter 22

EXODUS

On July 15, 2007, I ate lunch and had drinks at Toons Bar in Lake View with Jared Logan, Mike Holmes and Prescott Tolk, then Logan came back to Holmes and my apartment to hang out. It was shaping up to be just like any other lazy Sunday in Chicago. And that's when I got the phone call from Brady Novak.

Brady sounded like he was fighting tears as he told me the news. Pat Brice was dead. He had been at a wedding in the suburbs, and they'd found his body in his hotel room. And then Brady asked if I could help spread the word.

I can still place myself in that living room, on that dusty couch by that big front window, with my flip phone pressed up against my ear. The moment seems forever burned into my memory. When I told Holmes and Logan what had happened, Logan sat motionless on the couch and stared straight ahead, while Holmes burst into tears. So did Mike Burns when I called him. After I had calmly delivered the news to the three of them, I stood up and took a few steps toward the kitchen, and that's when the weight of it hit me all at once. I collapsed onto the floor and just started sobbing. The first thing I remember saying still embarrasses me. But through my sobs I mumbled, "He was gonna be so big," and then repeated it one more time as Holmes consoled me.

That night, Brady and CJ invited the entire scene over to their shared apartment. As the gathering began, it seemed like almost everyone was still in a state of shock. A few people cried. Mostly, it felt like nobody knew what to do. I was waiting on CJ, Pat's best friend, for cues on how I should be acting, or feeling, or handling the situation.

Finally, CJ decided to address the room. "This is just like Brice," he, said smirking ironically to an apartment full of people suddenly hanging on his every word. "He had to ruin a perfectly good Sunday." The collective release of tension was palpable and immediate. We were going to be there for one another the only way we knew how. And that night became one big, sloppy drunken celebration of the life and comedy of Patrick Healy Brice, the coolest motherfucker any of us had ever known.

"Nick Vatterott is walking up our back stairs," Novak said, "and he's like, 'God, I wonder if it's gonna be serious or what it's gonna be.' And he opened the door and T.J. was pouring beer down a funnel into my crotch. And he was like, 'Oh. Okay. It's gonna be a party.'…That party helped immensely."

"We had not had a tragedy that affected all of us [before then]," Fay Canale said. "We were close before that, and it made us closer."

"As awful as that day and moment was," Sullivan posted on Facebook in 2021,[73] "it did start off an amazing week of laughter and tears that brought so many communities together [with] shared memories and stories in a way that only Pat and an Irish funeral can."

Renee Gauthier's reality show, *Victoria Beckham: Coming to America*, aired on NBC the very next night. At first glance, I thought the timing couldn't have been worse. But it did give me somewhere else to focus my energy, at least for a night. Unfortunately, my own grief, as well as the collective sense of loss in the scene, could only be postponed for so long. And as the news spread, and as the outpouring of support circulated on the Internet, reality started to sink in, and we began to understand just how much we'd lost.

"It's like knowing Led Zeppelin right as they were recording, before their first album, and they die," comedian Brian Potrafka said. "And all the music stops, and they don't make anything else. And you know they were gonna put out seven hall of fame albums. And they're just gone. And it's so fucking brutal. It's so unfair. I can't even believe it."

"It's almost like you guys were grunge and Brice was Cobain," Joe Kilgallon said. "It felt like, [for] that scene, it was the end of that chapter."

"It was so awful," Tony Sam said. "And it was really the catalyst for a lot of people to leave."

Teams tend to fall apart without their quarterback. And within months, large waves of comics from the scene, myself included, started heading to the coasts. I don't know that the mass exodus was a direct result of Brice's death per se. T.J. had obviously gone to LA and landed an ABC sitcom.

He'd also booked a role in the monster movie *Cloverfield*, which was set to be released in January 2008. But I think that knowing T.J. Miller was about to become a star, while simultaneously knowing that Pat Brice didn't get to be one, gave some people that same post-9/11 feeling that life was short, nothing was guaranteed and moving to LA or New York was a risk worth taking. Especially now that there was safety in numbers.

In terms of our own story, I think 2008 feels like the cleanest end point to our alternative or underground era. Besides the death of Pat Brice in the summer of 2007, and all the coastal moves that happened over the course of the next year, it was also harder to remain an underground scene and for comedians there to fly under the radar when the comics who had moved out of Chicago were beginning to burst onto the national scene at an alarming rate around that same time. The year 2008 is also when Matt Braunger began breaking out in LA and Pete Holmes and Kumail Nanjiani began to break out in New York, not to mention the continued success of T.J. Miller, Kyle Kinane and Hannibal Buress.

Just for Laughs would even set up its own Chicago festival in 2009, seven years after Dan Carlson's independent festival had folded. And industry showcases were getting set up at the Lincoln Lodge for Los Angeles management companies to scoop up unsigned talent. "There are more agents and managers doing showcases," comedian Cameron Esposito, told the *Chicago Reader* in 2011, "trying to find the next 'those guys.'" And to paraphrase John Roy in *The History of Standup*, the comics who left (which he referred to as "the Den comics") had built an infrastructure from which the next generation of comedians like Esposito, Drew Michael, Beth Stelling and Liza Treyger could emerge.

All that being said, I wanted to make sure I asked the comics from our scene if that 2008 end point still felt true to them all these years later. The last thing I want to do is declare an era to be over shortly after I left if it wasn't the case. And while some of them said the scene has always been changing and evolving, the overwhelming majority seemed to feel like 2008 was a definite shift. "I think the vibe of what you're looking for," Sullivan said, "when people talk about Chicago comedy, like, 'What was in the water?' People [are] talking about Pete Holmes, and Hannibal, and Kumail, and Braunger, and Kinane."

"When you guys all kind of graduated," Joe Kilgallon said, "it felt like a lot of it was '07 and coincided with Pat Brice's death. It was a weird time in Chicago comedy, where it's like, 'We gotta step up now, because all the big kids are off to New York or in LA.'"

Cameron Esposito, 2006. *Krystle Gemnich.*

The moves seemed especially to deplete the female talent in Chicago. "There were those seven or eight women [in SpitFire], and then they all moved in like, a year," James Fritz said. "7/8ths of the women who did comedy on the North Side of Chicago were gone."

"I think there were five women in the scene [in 2008]," Esposito told *The History of Standup* podcast. "It was me, and the Puterbaugh Sisters [Danielle and Tiffany] and Beth Stelling and Jena Friedman."

That's actually a pretty impressive replacement group, which is another reason why 2008 feels like an appropriate transitionary period for our story, since it also happens to coincide with the scene becoming vastly more welcoming to and subsequently producing a ton more awesome female and non-cis male comics who would go on to national prominence—the first of those being Cameron Esposito.

"When I moved back to Chicago from Boston in 2006," Esposito said, "there was a generation or more of women ahead of me still clawing their way up—folks like Renee [Gauthier], Emily [Dorezas], all the SpitFire gals, but I didn't see them get the same respect as the dudes in the scene—dudes like you and the other Blerds guys."

Nevertheless, Esposito would quickly become a cast member at both Chicago Underground Comedy and the Lincoln Lodge, where Mark Geary told me she was one of the best to ever do the show's long-running "Man on the Street" segment. "She's a person people instantly connect with," Geary said, "so she could get them talking on the street. She could improvise off what they were saying, and she just attacked it."

That's not all she was attacking. Esposito initially chalked up the male-to-female respect differential she was experiencing in the scene to the numbers being weighted so heavily toward dude comics. And while she was at the Lodge, she decided to do something about it. "I approached Mark Geary," Esposito told *The History of Standup*, "and I said, 'I want to teach a class for women. I'll come up with a curriculum. It'll be eight sessions. And at the end, the women will do a five-minute set at the Lodge for a special show.'"

Cameron Esposito at Chicago Underground Comedy. *Erin Nekervis.*

The class, which was called Feminine Comique, or Fem Com, launched in 2008. And it became a pretty big success for Esposito and the Lodge. "It sold out many times over," she said, "so we added a second level. Hundreds of women went through and it still runs."

While Fem Com was starting, Esposito also approached Coleman Brice, who was a friend of her sister's, about starting an open mic at his new bar, Cole's in Logan Square. "I asked Cole to let me experiment with throwing an open mic," Esposito said, "and invited all my Fem Com students to perform there. After that, there were just a shit-ton more women hanging around there. And because I am queer, it really felt to me like queer folks and women felt like they wouldn't be shat on and would be given an equal shot."

"When I started," River Butcher, a trans male comic, told me, "there were a bunch of women starting, so it seemed normal. And I really believe that Cameron starting that open mic was gigantic. Because not only did people in her class have a place to go, we all did."

"Before long," Esposito said, "we'd put up thirty women for every sixty spots given per week. We drew real crowds—like, two hundred people would come see the mic. And my buddy Adam Burke joining as co-host gave the whole thing a credibility that women just didn't have in the scene at the time."

At the same time all that was happening for Esposito and the women she was inspiring, another comedian in the scene, Jena Friedman, also wanted to start something of her own. Friedman would go on to work as a producer for *The Daily Show with Jon Stewart* and as a writer for *Late Show with David Letterman* and for the *Borat* sequel. But her biggest impact might have been starting a show at Town Hall Pub in Boystown.

"I started 'Entertaining Julia' in 2007," Friedman said, "because it felt like the female stand-up scene in the North Side was small...so I wanted a room that was 50/50. And I created that space."

The show, which was named for the show's bartender, Julia Pishko, got an early boost from a comedy legend. "I was on a show with Robin Williams at Lakeshore the previous night," Friedman told me, "and I just invited him and he said yes. It was kind of nuts."

"Jena texted me," Nick Vatterott said, "and was like, 'Robin Williams is at 'Entertaining Julia.' Do you want to go up? You gotta be here in fifteen minutes.' And I got on my bicycle and rode from Uptown all the way down to Boystown, and got in and it was so packed....I was like, 'There's no way he's in here.' And then he walked right by me. He was magical. He truly was the real deal. This sketch group left a prop on stage. It was one of those old time-y radios....And he improvised a radio play with that thing, with a bunch of different characters. Because he saw that thing and started playing with it. It was absolutely amazing. I was like, 'Oh. He's *Robin Williams*.'"

When Friedman left for New York in 2008, she passed "Entertaining Julia" to Danielle and Tiffany Puterbaugh, as well as to Beth Stelling, who would be the next female star to emerge from the scene after Esposito. "I moved to Chicago from Ohio in 2007," Stelling said, "and was curious about the scene, and if I had the guts or talent to do stand-up in the big city....I had to case the joint, so I went to ChUC."

What she saw there was not very encouraging. "I distinctly remember Sean Flannery...on the main stage downstairs. Just when I was getting the guts to try it, I saw him and thought, 'I can't do *that*,'" she told me. "He *killllllled*. And then I went to the SpitFire show. It was all women. How cool! And I remember Kara Buller, Allison Leber, Fay Canale, who I looked up to a lot, Joselyn Hughes, Hannah

Beth Stelling at Chicago Underground Comedy. *Erin Nekervis.*

[Gansen], Renee Gauthier—I still remember their names because they were like, local celebs....Seeing those gals perform was inspiring, and it also made me think, 'Hey, I can do that!'"

Representation matters. But when those same women split for the coasts soon after, that too served as inspiration for Stelling. "I probably had a notion that with all these women leaving town for the coasts, I might actually have a chance at making it," she said. "Or standing out. And maybe other women felt that too. There was room for us."

"Chicago and the Midwest wasn't always an easy place for women," Tiffany Puterbaugh said. "There wasn't a lot of space for women, trans, non-binary or gay comics to perform. There wasn't anywhere that would book them. [Danielle] and Beth and I always tried to book alternative people other than just the popular guys—women, gay people or marginalized groups that didn't get the stage time in other venues. Since it was in Boystown, people actually wanted to see that and felt comfortable going to see comedy."

"Even if I was avoiding other shows or had said [to a disrespectful male comedian], 'If you do that again, I'm never coming back,'" Stelling told ChicagoMag[74] in 2017, "I would always have 'Entertaining Julia.' So would all the women who came out of Cameron Esposito's class, Feminine Comique, at Lincoln Lodge. Creating your own space is a viable option now."

In 2008, Stelling told the *Tribune*[75] that "she and a group of female comics who regularly perform at the weekly 'Entertaining Julia' show...deem 2008 'The Year of the Lady.'" And I think they were absolutely correct.

The scene had always produced fantastic female comedians. There was Deb Downing, Susan Prekel, Jen Kirwin, Bridget Smith, Alyson Lyon, Liz Poirier, Rocco, Blaire Butler, Jen Slusser, Liz Stewart, Emily Dorezas, Brooke Van Poppelen, Kara Buller, Fay Canale, Hannah Gansen, Becky Garcia, Renee Gauthier, Joselyn Hughes, Allison Leber and Hattie Snider. All of them were brought up and lauded multiple times by other comedians during these interviews. But those names were spread out over twelve long years.

On top of the lack of women in the scene, there wasn't much representation for queer comics prior to 2008 either. "No one openly identified as non-binary or trans," Esposito said of that pre-Cole's era, "and there wasn't really anyone queer regularly working in the alt scene besides Bill Cruz."

"I had never *not* thought about being gay in my act," Bill Cruz said, when he described his first set ever at the Lyon's Den. "People really weren't expecting it. The only person I knew at the time that was doing [gay material] was Jen Slusser. So I go up, do my set, it goes well, I come off the stage and Jen runs from the back of the room and just gives me the biggest

Beth Stelling, Tiffany Puterbaugh and Danielle Puterbaugh at Town Hall Pub. *Kristy Mangel.*

bear hug, and she's like, 'Thank God! You were great. Oh my God, I'm so happy you're here.'"

It changed after 2008. Cameron Esposito, Jena Friedman, the Puterbaugh Sisters and Beth Stelling changed it. And thankfully, it seems they changed it for good. The following year, Liza Treyger, Lauren Vino and Renee Schultz started Riot Comedy at Chicago Joe's in North Center. Then Mo Welch, Megan Gailey, River Butcher, Lindsay Adams, Ever Mainard and a string of other fantastic women and non-cis male comics would emerge from that scene in a continuous wave for years to come. "By the time I left for LA in 2012," Esposito said, "there were a ton of creative, funny as fuck queers and women and every kind of non-cis straight dude comics. It's even more now."

At the same time the Chicago scene was becoming less of a boys club, the city's most prominent boys club was given a proper burial.

Chapter 23

BLERDS (END)

On November 17, 2007, a tribute show was held for Pat Brice at the Lakeshore Theater, just days before what would have been his thirtieth birthday. And that same weekend, I was in Las Vegas with Mike Holmes, Mike Burns and Nate Craig representing Blerds at the HBO Comedy Festival at Caesar's Palace.

We were part of a show called "Broadband Theatre," which also featured comedians Brody Stevens and Chelsea Peretti and was basically just live presentations of viral videos. But the thing I remember the most from that festival was probably the VIP lounge at Caesar's, which I overheard another comedian describe as the "We Are the World" video for comedy—as in, you could be walking to the bar and someone like Chris Rock or Carrot Top would walk right past you.

The reality was, it's pretty weird that we were still doing anything Blerds-related at all at that point, let alone at an HBO festival at Caesar's Palace. This was at the same time Jordan Vogt-Roberts and T.J. Miller were pitching the Blerds-style show that would become *Mash Up* on Comedy Central, separately from the rest of us Blerds. This probably made our little Blerds-scripted web series pilots we had written and filmed for Warner Bros Studio 2.0 and Comedy.com seem a lot less compelling to them. So I knew that when those web series went away, it would be the end of the group.

In January 2008, we lost our shows at Lakeshore Theater in Chicago and Upright Citizens Brigade Theatre in Los Angeles. And when Comedy.com passed on our web series in April, Blerds had no projects left. Even before

Blerds photo shoot. *Clockwise from left*: Jordan Vogt-Roberts, CJ Sullivan, Jared Logan, Mike Holmes, Sean Flannery, Prescott Tolk, Pat Brice, T.J. Miller, Nate Craig, Mike Bridenstine and Kumail Nanjiani, 2006. *Forest Casey*.

that, I remember Prescott Tolk telling me that our novelty had worn off and that we had milked everything we could out of a few months' worth of work two years prior.

Oddly enough, that final Blerds web pilot, "Sub Par," which was about a local celebrity golf outing, ended up being pretty good for me personally. After I had a scene with an actor named Mark Teich, he wound up recommending me to his commercial agent. She signed me pretty soon after. And I've been repped by her ever since. Which has all been extremely helpful, monetarily, over the years, especially considering I had to borrow gas money after that pilot shoot so I could make it home.

As for "Sub Par," the final product was good too, if you ask me. Everyone was awesome in it. We had some pretty great comedians in guest roles, like Rob Delaney and Al Madrigal. Marc Evan Jackson and Carrie Clifford, who we loved from their "Sky & Nancy Collins" act, basically stole the show with brilliantly improvised lines. And I really don't know why a place like Comedy.com, whose most popular series was "Make a Hot Girl Laugh," would pass on it. It's probably why it didn't last much longer either.

The unofficial end of Blerds was pretty anticlimactic. There were a few back-and-forth meetings with Comedy.com about reshoots until Jordan finally decided that he was over it, and everything just trickled away from there. During that time, I would consistently be out at shows and have Hollywood industry types tell me they heard Blerds was the next big thing, or they'd rave about the videos. And I'd just go along with whatever they were saying because Blerds heat was the only currency I had in Los Angeles at that point. But I knew it was dead, no matter how much I wished it wasn't.

"It would have been impossible for us to keep that group together," Flannery said. "We weren't at an age or place where we could handle that well in a group that large. Particularly me....But it was a blast."

Technically, there was still *Mash Up*, which I assumed I might be a part of, especially since T.J. told me that the Eminem video was killing in their pitch meetings. But Holmes and I basically just got strung along in the process with various "Every Song Ever" ideas throughout 2008 and 2009. At one point, Anthony Kiedis was supposedly interested in making an "Every Red Hot Chili Peppers Song Ever" video with us at Funny or Die. At another point, Holmes and I got a record deal with Comedy Central Records. To Funny or Die's credit, the Kiedis thing went away pretty quickly. The record contract dragged on for a while until we were eventually told that the Comedy Central lawyers got scared off. But who knows if any of it was ever real or just used to let Holmes and me down easy.

The official public death of Blerds was on January 20, 2009—the day Barack Obama, another little-known Chicagoan who made it big in 2008, was sworn into office as the forty-forth president of the United States. That night, "The Roast of Blerds" was held at the Blue Goose Lounge in East Hollywood. The Comedy Coalition, a group of young Hollywood industry types who put on comedy shows there, had asked for it. And we delivered for them, roasting one another and Blerds ruthlessly. Matt Braunger hosted a night of drunken debauchery and vicious personal insults, which included sets by me, Mike Holmes, Kyle Kinane, Mike Burns, Jordan Vogt-Roberts, Nate Craig, T.J. Miller and Brady Novak. "They just wanted a dogfight," Nate said. "I got murdered. And all I did is make fun of you guys, and I should have turned on those fucking assistants."

There were hurt feelings and bruised egos. But for a lot of us, it was also really cathartic. And it all ended with a big, sloppy cheers to Pat Brice, whose tragedy was the one thing truly still bonding us together. It was a fitting end to Blerds. And maybe it was just in the air that day, but I think we were all in the mood for some hope and a little change.

OUTRO

In just over a decade, a tiny do-it-yourself stand-up scene on the North Side of Chicago went from not existing at all to producing some of the most influential and successful stand-up comedians of their generation. They did it without industry attention, without a home club and mostly performing to drunks in the backs of bars on their off nights. The fact that it existed at all made it special. And the fact that it got the results that it did made it historic.

"I was so convinced of the specialness of the Chicago scene *while we were in it*," Pete Holmes said, "that I said, 'Isn't it crazy that they're gonna write books about this time?'" And I think it's finally time, in one of those very books, to finally pin down some of the reasons this scene had its success.

First of all, yes, Second City made Chicago a destination for funny people. It's just ingrained in the culture. And that training and those experiences, good and bad, heavily influenced the stand-up performances in the city. It was an improv city, after all, and everybody knew it.

The second factor was that Zanies, the only comedy club in the city, did not nurture the local scene. The scene existed out of necessity because of that rejection. And the response from the newly created alt scene comics was oftentimes to differentiate themselves and their style from the type of comedy happening inside Zanies.

The third factor, and the reason Zanies was the only club in the city to begin with, was a downturn in the popularity of stand-up nationwide. "If you were doing stand-up in 2002," Pete Holmes said, "in a non-industry city, you might as well have been a *Dungeons & Dragons* nerd."

"It was nothing in the pop culture until *Bring the Pain*," Roy said, referring to the Chris Rock HBO special from 1996. "There was a lull between *Jammin' in New York* from Carlin [in 1992]. It was a [four]-year lull where stand-up didn't matter…there just wasn't a big thing between Andrew Dice Clay and Sam Kinison and Chris Rock. Nobody even cared."

"All the talk was that we were at the tail end of a really, really fallow period," Robert Buscemi said. "It was going through this complete rethinking of itself. And we were seven or eight years behind the Boom of clubs, and that had all died. And now the art form was all just existing on scraps it found in the alley. And we were the only ones keeping it alive among ourselves, and we were waiting for a cultural shift."

Which all just means that the people taking part in this small alternative scene were doing it because they loved it and not because they were trying to cash in on a fad. "There was no hope of getting famous from being in Chicago," Kyle Kinane said. "People wanted to be good at comedy. Because they liked and respected comedy."

The combination of people needing to perform because they loved it and rejecting the comedy that came before them led to DIY shows, and it meant that likeminded comedians were playing to one another and off of one another at those shows. And those comedians were not impressed with what they saw on stage unless it was fresh or unique. That statement is as true for Bill O'Donnell performing at Midnight Bible School as it is for the Puterbaugh Sisters at "Entertaining Julia." Hell, nobody paid any attention to Adam Kroshus's stalker until she started performing Wiccan love rituals on stage either.

Sometimes "fresh or unique" just meant the jokes had to be really tight. Sometimes it meant the performers had to take bigger swings. All of this upped the ante and pushed the other comics in the scene to do the same. It could simultaneously be a supportive community and a weekly arms race of weaponized weirdness. The end result was that the comics got better, the shows got better and the scene got better. And that's about when social media made it all get noticed for the first time.

There were also a few lucky breaks along the way. There was the return of Dwayne Kennedy and the mentorship he gave the young comics in the scene. There was the layout of rooms like the Lyon's Den, Gunther Murphy's and the Beat Kitchen with the bar in front and the show through the back, which created a hang and fostered a community. There was the abundance of stage time offered by Dave Odd and the artistic freedom offered by Cayne Collier. But there was also someone who I would consider

Mark Geary. *Kristy Mangel.*

our fourth factor to Chicago's success: Mark Geary.

Geary had arrived from the Midlands of England in 1996 right at the birth of the scene. He'd thrown away all his jokes after seeing a show at The Elevated, started the Red Lion open mic, became involved and invested in the Chicago Comedy Festival and then put his heart and soul into the Lincoln Lodge, often thanklessly, for decades. "If there's any credit to be given for the wellspring of great comedy or talent that may have come out of there," O'Donnell said, "the credit goes to him. It's Geary. It really is. If you're looking for the common denominator in what great came out of that scene…it's Geary."

"He's the only one you need to talk to, really," CJ Sullivan said. "Unless you want it funny."

"Obviously, the show continues without me, but not without him," said Tom Lawler, who left the Lincoln Lodge in 2008. "You can't deny what he's done.…The endurance of doing this for twenty seasons is ridiculous."

"Obviously they were doing something special," Matt Dwyer said, "because it's still around."

Oh. I almost forgot, the Lincoln Lodge still exists as of 2023, except it moved out of the Lincoln Restaurant in 2013, jumped to a few other locations and now resides in its own 5,500-square-foot space in Logan Square complete with three theaters, two classrooms, a podcast studio and a front bar.

After launching a fundraiser for $30,000 in 2016, the Lodge got an unexpected response from a wealthy retiree named Ed Toolis, who wanted to help their cause. "[He] came to us and said, 'I'll give you the thirty grand, but I think your value to the Chicago comedy community is so big that I would like you to entertain grander plans, which I would also be willing to bankroll,'" Geary told the *Chicago Tribune* in 2019.[76] It's almost karmically perfect. And pretty close to actual perfect as well. The new venue is a major upgrade, but it still feels authentic to the DIY spirit of the original room.

Of course now, stand-up is exponentially more popular in American culture than it was twenty years ago. And the clubs have returned to Chicago.

And the comics often avoid "the hang" by bouncing around from show to show on a nightly basis. "Now Zanies is more inclusive," Mike Wiley told me. "They're embracing the Chicago stand-up scene. So now there isn't that anti-club comedy [mentality] anymore. And a lot of people are going more towards the club style of comedy. So I feel that really smart writing is no longer there. Nobody is doing that experimental stuff. It's very accessible to your general crowds at a club now."

"There are so many good comedy shows in the city of Chicago," Joe Kilgallon said. "Way more than when I started and definitely way more than your entire time here. Because back then, you guys were talking about, 'Oh, it was The Elevated. Then it was ChUC, then Lodge was always there.' Now, every night there's three or four shows that are just as good as The Elevated at its peak."

I wouldn't doubt it. And yet the scene isn't cranking out three to four times as many Kinanes, Kumails, Beths or Hannibals as when it was just The Elevated, ChUC and the Lodge. So I don't know if the scene being "better" is necessarily a good thing. This may sound counterintuitive, but I can probably more fully explain what I mean, in closing, by telling you a story about a comedian I loved named George Tracy.

"George Tracy was an interesting figure," Jared Logan said, "because he was an older guy who was clearly starting later in life. Maybe a 'I'm gonna finally do my dream' [type]. And he was a real person. He wasn't some kid fresh out of college who had, like me, four years of experience being in plays and performing in a sketch group. Instead, he was just some guy who really was the quintessential comedian—someone who needed to do it."

"He was the most genuine comedian," Nick Vatterott said. "There was no act. It was 100 percent who he really was. He was just being himself, telling stories the way he would tell them at whatever water cooler he was at that led him down this path to our lives."

Sometime around 2004, toward the end of the Lyon's Den and the beginning of the Crush or Mix days, George Tracy started appearing at open mics around the city and became an immediate phenomenon within the scene.

George was already unique because of his age and his blue-collar aesthetics. But he also had a speech impediment from a head injury he'd suffered when he was twenty-one. He was fully aware of what people thought about him the first time they heard him. And he seemed to use that self-awareness to his comedic advantage. And he would absolutely murder. "Do you know how many times people told me about that movie, *Forrest Gump*?!?!" he'd shout.

"They'd say, 'Hey George, I'm not saying you're stupid. I'm just saying you gotta see this movie!'"

He seemed excited to be there, almost breathlessly so. Sometimes he would literally run out breath and say something like, "I'm sorry. Sometimes I forget to breathe," once he'd regained his composure. But he looked and sounded like he was the happiest person in the world to be performing, winded or not, impaired speech or not. It was all extremely raw, but much like the Tasmanian Devil, it was his spinning, snorting, spitting imperfections that made him so watchable and endearing. "He was kind of the Mix mascot," Becky Garcia said. "We all loved him so much."

One night, I remember George standing on stage in a show that happened to have a spotlight. But instead of finding his light and standing in the center of it, he stood so just the tip of his right shoulder was in the light. It was like an extra layer of hilariousness that was completely unintentional but worked anyway.

But then the inevitable happened: George Tracy actually got good at stand-up. He went up every week, and he got the requisite amount of stage time he needed to make big improvements that made him more confident and comfortable on stage. And all of those improvements started to polish away a lot of the untamed, wild qualities that made him so special in the first place. The gold was in his imperfections. And the better George got at comedy, the less special it actually became. He became a guy who was good at stand-up, but he was no longer a phenom.

And that's no knock on George—go see him perform! You'll have a great time! I'm just using him to illustrate a point. And I guess my biggest fear is, with comedy becoming so popular and the clubs returning to Chicago again, something like what happened to George could also happen to the scene. Because up until that point, Chicago had been a lot like Greg Mills's World's Worst Ragtime Piano Player, just hammered away on the keys while it mugged to the audience. And it had been like bartender Mary's comically loud cash register at the back bar of the Lincoln Restaurant. Or like Mark Geary standing on a ladder, running cords through a drop ceiling in a pancake house. Or like the L train whooshing past Philosofur's on a Wednesday night. And yes, the Chicago scene had been like George Tracy murdering at an open mic in 2004.

In the end, Chicago was special not because because it perfected anything or even did anything right. Chicago was special because it was the perfect amount of wrong.

NOTES

1. Johnson, "Funny Thing Happened."
2. The Chicago Improv at 504 North Wells Street opened on June 7, 1988, with headliner Bobcat Goldthwait. And it went on a permanent "summer hiatus" in 1995.
3. The Funny Firm at 318 West Grand Avenue officially opened on December 16, 1987, with headliner Carol Leifer. It closed in early summer of 1994, reopened as the Fallout on January 13, 1995, with headliner Paul Provenza. And then it closed again in the fall of 1995.
4. Zanies, at 1548 North Wells Street in Old Town, was the first full-time comedy club within city limits. "Zanies opened its doors the day I was born," comedian Brooke Van Poppelen said. "November 4, 1978. You only find that out after you've been in the green room looking at all those dumb fucking framed newspaper articles."
5. Lambert, *All Jokes Aside*.
6. Strauss, Neil. "Take the New Comedy. Please."
7. Johnson, "Funny Thing Happened."
8. Johnson, "Elevated Is on a Fun-Fulled 4-Year Ride."
9. Kogan, "Jolly Good Spot Now Bloody Gone."
10. Chicago Bar Project, "Red Lion Pub."
11. Johnson, "Dwyer's Midnight Bible School Isn't 'Standup-y.'"
12. Patinkin, *Second City*.
13. Via Newspapers.com, page 112.
14. I'm guessing the move to 10:00 p.m. is the most important ingredient of that press release.
15. Green, "Midnight Bible School."
16. Helbig, "Midnight Bible School."

17. When I asked CJ Sullivan if the eulogies were sincere or a put-on, he said, "It was both. I mean, we were just weird."

18. Johnson, "Chicago Comedy Festival Full of Promise."

19. The headline from the *Hollywood Reporter* seems to have been, "NBC Gets a Kick Out of Stebbins," and the first line of the article reads, "Who needs the Montreal comedy festival to find the next sitcom star?" Later it says, "Stebbins' presence and brand of comedy have been compared with those of Michael J. Fox," but I don't see a mention of the Chicago Comedy Festival itself.

20. McKim, "UPDATE DAY FOUR."

21. Isaacs, "Stand-Up! Stand-Up! Fight! Fight! Fight!"

22. Johnson, "Strong Talent to Mark 4th Chicago Comedy Fest."

23. Johnson, "Traveling Salesman Goes Into a Bar."

24. Collo-Julin, "Dwayne Kennedy Is the Voice of Chicago."

25. Freeman, "Philosophy and Comedy."

26. Kennedy won the Emmy for W. Kamau Bell's CNN series *United Shades of America*. "He didn't go to the ceremony," Kondabolu said. "He also never picked up his Emmy. His sister had to track it down and have it sent to Chicago."

27. Metz, "Now, This Is Entertainment."

28. The road is spelled differently than the name in the program. But Lawler is a Bay Area native and a big fan of the Oakland Athletics.

29. Neil Hamburger performed at the Lincoln Lodge on June 2, 2001, and April 23, 2004.

30. I interviewed Lawler in a MySpace blog series I dubbed "Talkin' Comedy," on October 27, 2006.

31. *TimeOut Chicago*, "Lodged in Our Memories."

32. Betancourt appeared on *Late Friday* on NBC in November 2001.

33. Federman and Steven, "Lyon's Den and the Lincoln Lodge."

34. Riekki, "Stand-Up Guys."

35. I interviewed Buscemi on my "Talkin' Comedy" MySpace series on June 20, 2006.

36. Johnson, "Snubfest's Buscemi the Odds-On Favorite."

37. Johnson, "Critics' Picks."

38. Elder, "094: Kumail Nanjiani."

39. The manager of the Schaumburg Improv once said to me with a straight face, "You know how you tell people your worst jokes? I think they want to hear your *best* jokes."

40. I interviewed Dave for my MySpace blog on June 3, 2006.

41. Johnson, "Jimmy Dore Has Made It Very Good."

42. Johnson, "'Mr. Show' On the Road."

43. Johnson, "Legends, Locals Bring Laughs to Area."

44. He did wear some shiny ass shirts.

45. I once did a show with Dave in Milwaukee. And on the ride home, he stopped the car and ran out into the pouring rain because he thought he'd seen a "ghost panther."

46. Tommy Johnagin reminded me of a time we did a road gig with Dave, and when we asked him why his car smelled so bad, he told us one of his snakes had crawled into his air conditioner and died.
47. I interviewed T.J. in my "Talking Comedy" blog on June 10, 2006.
48. Johnson, "Stand and Deliver."
49. Johnson, the man who consistently referred to Odd as a "comedy impresario," died of "complications from a brain hemorrhage" on January 6, 2006, at age forty-six.
50. The exact quote was, "[T]he underground scene will never replace Chicago stand-up institution Zanies...many of the comedians playing the underground rooms can't get work there."
51. Johnson, "Stage Guide: Critics' Picks."
52. Johnson, "Hedberg Weaves Hip One-Liners."
53. Johnson called Hannibal "unexpectedly special with simple, but effective material."
54. Hedberg died of a drug overdose less than a month later, on March 30, 2005.
55. Everyone loves to point out this definitely means "Black nerds" now.
56. I did a "Talkin' Comedy" interview of Jordan for my MySpace blog on November 7, 2006.
57. Mangel, "Lookin' for Some Hoes, Hoes."
58. I guess I could have included Dane Cook backlash in that list.
59. Mangel, "I Don't Know What Y'all About to Do."
60. Mangel, "ChUC, 3.28.06."
61. *Bastion*, "Inside With: T.J. Miller, Comedian."
62. *Bastion*, "Monday Mutterings."
63. *Bastion*, "HBO Comedy Festival Industry Showcase."
64. *Apiary*, "New Talent Discovered."
65. *Bastion*, "Inside With: Mike Bridenstine."
66. Heisler, "Laugh Tracks."
67. Jeffers, "Taking Stand-Up for a Walk on Cyber Side."
68. *Bastion*, "Holiday Hilarity and Special Mentions."
69. Roy, "Examining Nick Vatterott's 2010 Stand-Up Set."
70. Mike Burns never had a Blerds video either, but he was away in New York.
71. Marantz, "Kumail Nanjiani's Culture-Clash Comedy."
72. She actually had adult-onset Still's disease, which, according to the *New Yorker*, is "a rare inflammatory syndrome that is manageable once it's identified and treated."
73. The fourteenth anniversary of Pat's death, July 15.
74. Wellen, "Beth Stelling on HBO."
75. Smith, "Make Us Laugh."
76. Freeman, "Preparing to Open for Business of Comedy."

BIBLIOGRAPHY

Apiary. "New Talent Discovered: T.J. Miller!" August 18, 2006.

Bastion. "HBO Comedy Festival Industry Showcase, Seminar at the Lincoln Lodge Thursday." October 25, 2006.

———. "Holiday Hilarity and Special Mentions." December 6, 2006.

———. "Inside With: Mike Bridenstine." November 27, 2006.

———. "Inside With: T.J. Miller, Comedian." July 10, 2006.

———. "Monday Mutterings." August 14, 2006.

Bridenstine, Mike. "Talkin' Comedy with Dave Odd." MySpace, June 3, 2006. https://myspace.com/mikebridenstine.

———. "Talkin' Comedy with Jordan Roberts." MySpace, November 7, 2006. https://myspace.com/mikebridenstine.

———. "Talkin' Comedy with Robert Buscemi." MySpace, June 20, 2006. https://myspace.com/mikebridenstine.

———. "Talkin' Comedy with T.J. Miller." MySpace, June 10, 2006. https://myspace.com/mikebridenstine.

———. "Talkin' Comedy with Tom Lawler." MySpace, October 27, 2006. https://myspace.com/mikebridenstine.

Chicago Bar Project. "Red Lion Pub." https://chibarproject.com/reviews/red-lion.

Collo-Julin, Salem. "Dwayne Kennedy Is the Voice of Chicago." *Chicago Reader*, June 15, 2020.

Elder, Mike "Box." "094: Kumail Nanjiani." *Box Angeles*, August 31, 2015.

Federman, Wayne, and Andrew Steven/The Podglomerate. "Lyon's Den and the Lincoln Lodge." *The History of Standup*, July 16, 2019.

Freeman, Zach. "Philosophy and Comedy: Dwayne Kennedy Kicks Off a Homecoming Week at Zanies." *Chicago Tribune*, August 1, 2017, Section 4, 1.

———. "Preparing to Open for Business of Comedy: Lincoln Lodge Hopes Its New Venue Will Be Ready by Late October." *Chicago Tribune*, October 16, 2019, Section 4, 2.

Green, Nick. "Midnight Bible School: An Evening of Sit-Down Comedy." *Chicago Reader*, January 6, 2000.

Heisler, Steve. "Laugh Tracks: blerds.com." *TimeOut Chicago*, no. 74 (July 27–August 3, 2006).

Helbig, Jack. "Midnight Bible School a Haven for Standup Comics in Chicago." *Chicago Daily Herald*, January 28, 2000, 45.

Isaacs, Deanna. "Stand-Up! Stand-Up! Fight! Fight! Fight!" *Chicago Reader*, May 24, 2001.

Jeffers, Glenn. "Taking Stand-Up for a Walk on Cyber Side." *Chicago Tribune*, December 6, 2006, 98.

Johnson, Allan. "Chicago Comedy Festival Full of Promise for Local Laughsters." *Chicago Tribune*, April 24, 1998, 118.

———. "Critics' Picks." *Chicago Tribune*, July 8, 2005, 7.

———. "Dwyer's Midnight Bible School Isn't 'Standup-y.'" *Chicago Tribune*, February 26, 1999, 115.

———. "Elevated Is on a Fun-Filled 4-Year Ride." *Chicago Tribune*, August 11, 2000, 284.

———. "A Funny Thing Happened: In a Business Where Timing Is Everything, Comedy Clubs Are Past Their Prime." *Chicago Tribune*, November 17, 1998, 49, 55.

———. "Hedberg Weaves Hip One-Liners, Layered Jokes." *Chicago Tribune*, March 9, 2005, Section 5, 3.

———. "Jimmy Dore Has Made It Very Good in Hollywood." *Chicago Tribune*, November 30, 2001, 137.

———. "Legends, Locals Bring Laughs to Area." *Chicago Tribune*, September 7, 2003, Section 7, 22.

———. "'Mr. Show' On the Road." *Chicago Tribune*, September 27, 2002, Section 7, 19.

———. "Snubfest's Buscemi the Odds-On Favorite." *Chicago Tribune*, January 24, 2005, 2.

———. "Stage Guide: Critics' Picks." *Chicago Tribune*, June 10, 2005, Section 7, 14.

———. "Stand and Deliver: Thriving Underground Scene Puts the Edge Back in Comedy." *Chicago Tribune*, April 8, 2005, Section 7, 1.

———. "Strong Talent to Mark 4th Chicago Comedy Fest." *Chicago Tribune*, May 25, 2001, 120.

———. "This Year, Chicago Comedy Festival Is Getting the Word Out." *Chicago Tribune*, May 7, 1999, 114.

———. "A Traveling Salesman Goes Into a Bar." *Chicago Tribune*, June 1, 2001, 117.

———. "Where's the Punchline? In Alternative Comedy, What's Not Funny Is Funny. But Its Proponents May Have the Last Laugh." *Chicago Tribune*, April 4, 1999, 112.

Kogan, Rick. "Jolly Good Spot Now Bloody Gone." *Chicago Tribune*, October 27, 2013, 124.

Lambert, Raymond. *All Jokes Aside*. Chicago, IL: Bolden, 2016.

Mangel, Kristy. "ChUC, 3.28.06." *Five Drink Minimum*, March 29, 2006.

———. "I Don't Know What Y'all About to Do, but I'm About to Hit the Street." *Five Drink Minimum*, May 31, 2006.

———. "Lookin' for Some Hoes, Hoes." *Five Drink Minimum*, April 30, 2006.

Marantz, Andrew. "Kumail Nanjiani's Culture-Clash Comedy." *New Yorker*, May 1, 2017.

McKim, Brian. "UPDATE DAY FOUR." *SHECKY!* (June 2000). http://web.archive.org/web/20020224122811/sheckymagazine.com/dayfour.htm.

Metz, Nina. "Now, This Is Entertainment." *Chicago Tribune*, April 25, 2003.

Patinkin, Sheldon. *The Second City*. Naperville, IL: Sourcebooks, 2000.

Riekki, Ron. "Stand-Up Guys." *The Tap*, April 2004, 1.

Roy, John. "Examining Nick Vatterott's 2010 Stand-Up Set on Jimmy Fallon." *Vulture*, February 2, 2021.

Smith, Ryan. "Make Us Laugh: Small, Feisty Band of Women Battle Stereotypes for Respect in Chicago's Shrinking Stand-Up Scene." *Chicago Tribune*, September 6, 2008.

Strauss, Neil. "Take the New Comedy. Please." *New York Times*, May 31, 1996, Section C, 1.

TimeOut Chicago. "Lodged in Our Memories: A Local Mecca for Alt Comedy Turns Ten" (September 22, 2009).

Wellen, Brianna. "Beth Stelling on HBO, Harassment, and the Weirdest Comedy She's Ever Seen: Ahead of the Comic's Return to the City that Launched Her Career, We Ask the Entertaining Julia Cohost About How the Industry's Changed Since She First Went Public About Her Own Abuser." *ChicagoMag* (December 5, 2017).

INDEX

U

Upright Citizens Brigade Theatre 46,
171, 179, 181, 185, 188, 200
Upright Citizens Brigade (troupe) 46,
63
US Comedy Arts Festival 83, 103, 111,
146, 166, 171, 172

V

Van Poppelen, Brooke 107, 119, 120,
123, 131, 145, 148, 149, 150, 153,
154, 164, 169, 171, 173, 198
Vatterott, Nick 15, 20, 84, 96, 107,
113, 115, 116, 117, 118, 119, 120,
121, 122, 123, 126, 136, 153, 164,
174, 175, 176, 193, 197, 206
Victoria Beckham: Coming to America 188,
193
Vogt-Roberts, Jordan 103, 157, 158,
159, 179, 185, 187, 200, 201, 202

W

Welch, Mo 199
Wheelan, Brooks 18
Wiley, Mike 96, 116, 117, 126, 128,
152, 163, 206
Williams, Robin 112, 197

Y

Y2K 43, 44, 58
Yahoo! message boards 139
YouTube 57, 154, 156, 157, 182

Z

Zanies 15, 21, 22, 24, 28, 32, 35, 36,
43, 44, 58, 61, 66, 68, 77, 87, 107,
135, 148, 152, 162, 166, 170, 203,
206
Zulevic, Jim 47

ABOUT THE AUTHOR

Mike Bridenstine is a product of the Chicago stand-up scene. He has performed at festivals all around the United States, Canada and the UK, including New Faces at the Just for Laughs Festival in Montreal. Some of his TV credits include *Last Call with Carson Daly* on NBC, *Adam DeVine's House Party* on Comedy Central and *The Eric Andre Show* on Adult Swim. You can listen to his podcast, *Hunk with Mike Bridenstine*, or listen to his comedy albums, *The Hungry Wolf Hunts Best* and *Hustle* from AST Records on Apple and Spotify. This is his first book.

Visit us at
www.historypress.com